T0278348

GAZING EASTWARDS

Romila Thapar at the entrance to a cave at the site of Maijishan.
[Photograph by Dominique Darbois, presented to the author as a memento
of the visit. From the author's archives.]

GAZING EASTWARDS

Of Buddhist Monks and Revolutionaries in China, 1957

ROMILA THAPAR

LONDON NEW YORK CALCUTTA

Seagull Books, 2021

Printed in arrangement with Aleph Book Company.
Text and photographs (except the frontispiece) © Romila Thapar, 2020
First published in India by Aleph Book Company, 2020

ISBN   978 0 8574 2 816 5

British Library Cataloguing-in-Publication Data
A catalogue record for this book is available from the British Library.

Typeset by Seagull Books, Calcutta, India
Printed and bound by WordsWorth India, New Delhi, India

CONTENTS

Author's Note

Our visit in 1957 into China's past, the subject of this account, was made possible by an invitation from the Society for Cultural Relations with Foreign Countries, of the People's Republic of China. I would like to thank the Society not only for its hospitality during the period we were there, but also for its helpful assistance in our research at both the sites where we worked. We arrived in China taking flights from Paris to Prague to Moscow to Beijing. We travelled in China from Beijing to Xi'an where initially the route went through Hebei province with its loess plateau to the west and cultivated land to the east. The journey was largely north-south and at one point we turned west and entered the valley of the Huang He just before the river turns north. This took us into Shaanxi province and to Xi'an. We then moved up to Lanzhou after which we went into the Wei Valley that took us to Maijishan. At the end of our stay in Maijishan, we resumed our itinerary to the north-west. The onward journey from there took us again along the plateau at the southern end of the Gansu corridor. We travelled in the shadow of the Qilianshan on one side and the edge of the Gobi Desert on the other. We flew from Lanzhou to Su Zhou and then travelled by jeep to Dunhuang. On our return from Dunhuang we took a slightly different route and drove through Yumen. We took the train to Nanjing, Shanghai, and Hangzhou before returning to Beijing. Our final departure from Beijing was a flight to Canton from where we went to Hong Kong.

My special thanks go to Xinru Liu for her meticulous reading of the text, and the occasional correction where necessary, especially of transliterations from the Chinese. For those who read the manuscript and made comments and suggestions, and urged me to publish it, my grateful thanks. These included Shiv Shankar Menon, Deepak Nayyar, Romi Khosla, Naveen Kishore, and Valmik Thapar. Deborah Klimburg-Slater's comments on the Introduction were very helpful. Sreedeep Bhattacharya spent much time and effort in digitizing the photographs and helping me sort them out, as did Valmik Thapar and Sunandini Banerjee. The photographs are my amateurish attempts to capture something of our journey in visual form. Naina Dayal and Kanad Sinha gallantly carried two hefty volumes on Dunhuang to Delhi from Dunhuang. These recently published volumes were very useful in providing coverage of the sites in Central Asia. Burzine Waghmar was as always unfailingly helpful with getting me copies of the articles which I did not have access to in Delhi.

I was delighted when David Davidar and Aienla Ozukum agreed to publish the book. My hesitation was that as a travelogue its appeal would be limited—but with their editing it should be in hopeful shape.

Both Xinru Liu and Mingo Wong, in their different ways, made me aware of a contemporary China as well as a Chinese past that was new to me. This book is for them.

Romila Thapar
January 2020
New Delhi

Preface

On rummaging through a box full of old papers I came across a diary that I had kept largely for my own entertainment, and that of close friends, when I visited China in 1957. I had virtually forgotten about it. But on rereading it, I wondered whether it was worth publishing as these were observations on being in China sixty-two years ago. I would like to emphasize that this narrative and description refer to a time period of more than half a century ago—a fact that the reader must keep in mind. It was a visit that enabled me to understand some aspects of another civilization comparable to mine and not unconnected, and about which I knew so little. It was also to experience the early stages of the revolution in China. Reading the diary was a way of recalling a historical moment as I experienced it. I thought it might be of interest as a memoir of a time and condition that no longer exist. Let me emphasize that this is neither an analytical study of, nor a commentary on, the China of 1957. Its publication is an attempt to recall a viewing of a few historical events as witnessed in a moment of time. And for me it is an entirely new way of looking at the past, quite different from my usual historical studies. The perspective, however, was not unconnected with my general interest in early periods of history.

This text therefore is a brief account of a period spent in China in 1957, from July to October, working mainly at two Buddhist cave sites and monasteries, working on their murals and sculpture; and spending a little further time at the major museums in Beijing, Xi'an, Nanjing, Shanghai, and a few other places, focusing on objects of the same period as the murals in the cave sites. I went as a research assistant to Anil de Silva—an art historian from Sri Lanka. The two sites were Maijishan (earlier known as Maichisan), and Dunhuang (earlier known as Tun Huang). The transliteration of Chinese words into the Roman script has changed from when we were there. The words now use a system called Pinyin. I have tried as far as possible to initially give the old spelling and then keep to the new spelling.

The diary was largely about people and places. I have left it substantially unchanged from what was written barring a few instances where explanation was required. The account as it emerges is not about the studies that we made—except marginally—but largely other observations about the visit to China. It is limited to being a personal account of our travels, framed by the two sites where we worked, and essentially just my reaction to being where I was and when I was there recording what interested me. This is important. I would like to reiterate that it attempts to describe my experiences of six decades ago. I have deliberately not updated it, partly because to do so would take a lifetime since it was written almost a lifetime ago, but more because I think there is a hint of a flavour of China sixty years ago that may be worth recalling—for instance, in something as significant as the relations between China and India. My stray remarks about the future with reference to India and China, may today seem ironic!

At a personal level, rereading it has been a recall of a brief stay in China, narrated in what can only be called an entirely non-academic rendering. The academic studies we made are quite different and naturally so. These were written and published soon after we returned. The focus was on the murals and sculpture at the two sites—the work we were doing there. We wrote on the range of murals and sculpture at Maijishan, the first time such coverage had been given in an English-language publication. At Dunhuang the focus was on landscape paintings to show how their concept and style evolved over a long period and the extent to which they can be compared to contemporary free-standing paintings. These studies have been published separately. They are available in Michael Sullivan, *The Cave Temples of Maichisan* (with photographs by Dominique Darbois; Berkeley: University of California Press, 1969); and in Anil de Silva, *Chinese Landscape Painting in the Caves at Tun-Huang* (London: Methuen, 1967). The first study was eventually taken over by Michael Sullivan who had greater experience with the study of the Maijishan material. The author of the second book was Anil de Silva. The present book, therefore, is of an entirely different genre.

Since our purpose was a partially historical study of the sites, some historical thoughts do enter this narrative as well, largely to give it a clearer context. The only addition that I have made to the original text is that I have provided a brief historical background to the sites in the introduction. I realized that few would know of their importance other than specialists in Chinese Buddhist art or in the history of Central Asia. The more general readership for which this book is intended might find it helpful to read such a chapter and place the sites I refer to in context. And yet they also represent much else as I was to learn on visiting them. The two sites are part of the history of what is often referred to as the Silk Route, or Silk Road—now more correctly Silk Routes—namely the trade, initially dominated by the exchanges in silk, that linked China, Central Asia, India, and the eastern Mediterranean mainly during the first millennium AD, but continuing to a few centuries later. I thought a sketch of the context might be useful to the reader unfamiliar with this history.

For me this particular visit to China was initially the anticipation of acquainting myself with historical cultures I was not familiar with, but which were of immense significance to my understanding of the Asian past. This was my formal justification for wanting to get to know something about China, past and present. My observations were, in a way, a response to the two perspectives on China that were uppermost in my mind at the time.

One was the possibility of seeing the visual representation that registered the transmission of Buddhism from India to China, as articulated at many sites including the two that we worked at, pointing up in both places important intervening connections with Central Asia. This was especially so of Dunhuang. It is an aspect of the ancient past to which we in India have given little attention. There is a limited academic interest but virtually no popular interest. Yet it is of fundamental importance in understanding so much of the Asian past and inevitably therefore much of the Asian present. The histories of these regions are a continuum of entangled interfaces. We are now aware of the evolution of Buddhism in those parts and some of its links with the northern part of the Indian subcontinent, links that moved between being close to becoming distant. It is almost as if having banished Buddhism from India we have also banished the histories that accompanied it. Yet the proximity of these regions impinged on the history of each. I was interested in what prompted the closeness and how it was expressed.

The second interest came from the many discussions that I heard initially, and later participated in, during my late teens and early twenties. These discussions in the early and mid-fifties focused on contemporary China, an Asian society and civilization that had undergone a revolution with the promise of establishing a socialist society. Many were interested to see what would be the shape of this new society and how this would differ from the earlier attempts in the USSR. This became a crucial discussion in the light of the Twentieth Congress of the Communist Party of the USSR, held in 1956, having revealed aspects of bureaucratic and political functioning in the USSR that had not been spoken of so far, and that were troubling those that had endorsed the revolution. Questions were raised as to whether the Soviet model, being so proximate to the Chinese, would become the earlier pattern to be repeated in the latter case. There was at the same time much romanticism about Maoist China building an entirely new model of society that would bring about the many changes that had captured the imagination, especially of the young. So I was eager to see the reality.

Much had been written by journalists visiting China, some returning with a positive view of the change, and others presenting negative observations. In many ways it was, as the Chinese would say, a period of 'interesting times', in other words problematic times that had no easy solutions. Being China, the dimension of change was impressive, as for instance, in the collectivization of agriculture. The question being asked was what would this lead to and would it solve China's agrarian problems.

Then came other changes—liberalization towards intellectuals followed by a reversal and a rectification campaign. Mao Zedong's words resounded in his much-quoted sentence of 1957, 'Let a hundred flowers bloom, let a hundred schools of thought contend.' We arrived in China eager to witness the efflorescence, if there was one. It is perhaps worth keeping in mind with hindsight that a few flowers might have bloomed but many would wilt or would be ploughed in by the end of that year. The Great Leap Forward, initiated by Mao Zedong and the Communist Party, was intended to accelerate the economy and give a new impetus to social change and the transformation of China into a Communist state. But the agrarian crisis resulted in the disastrous event of the long famine and put paid to many earlier explorations, with the final closure to the blooming of flowers being the taking over by the Cultural Revolution. This was called the Great Proletarian Cultural Revolution, a movement that dominated Chinese politics and society during the 1960s and early 70s. It was a movement intended to purge China of 'bourgeois' elements plotting to bring back capitalism, but in fact it was a way of also bolstering the power of Mao. In the process both people and cultural items were silenced or physically removed. The *Little Red Book* with fragments of Mao's writing was made essential reading—young people were organized into Red Guards who frequently used violence to intimidate people at large. In later times, the Cultural Revolution was viewed as a major disaster by the Chinese Communist Party. Nevertheless, what is worth taking into account is the impact of these events on political and social thinking in other parts of the world. It led to some rethinking about flexibility and openness in concepts and institutions emanating from socialist thinking, drawing legitimacy from more than one event. It also prodded the social sciences in academic programmes into investigating more expansively the many theories of knowledge and explanation that were being written about. These not only required the asking of questions but asking more pointed questions from what had been asked before. It was indeed in an inverse kind of way a creative period in many branches of thinking in the wider world, especially in the arts and humanities, some nudged by Maoism and some by other theories.

But these are not the central themes of this book since the period when we were in China was prior to the radical changes. I am mentioning them as ideas that were being discussed elsewhere, and that may have been germinating whilst we were in China but of which we were seldom made aware. We did try on occasion to politely ferret them out, but were not overly successful. This narrative of a journey therefore has limited relevance. It is only an attempt to try and capture a moment in modern history. However, by extension, it was a moment that was to have ramifications and continues to have them, reaching into the wider world—perhaps more so later in terms of recognizing the pre-modern contacts between various regions of Asia. This becomes all the more important given that the areas under discussion are now independent nations focusing on their own histories. The project that took us to China touched on these histories, and being at the required locations we experienced the emergence of China. It no longer saw itself as 'the Middle Kingdom', the civilization surrounded by barbarians, as it called itself in history, and isolated from the rest of the world. It now saw itself as entering the collective of Asian nations which in time was to expand in various ways to a wider collective.

There was an intricate network of contacts in pre-modern times of which we today need to be aware. The past does not always fade away, it occasionally persists but in new guises. The extent to which we recognize this can go into the making of the present. My interest was more in the Asia-wide networks of early times and how these were expressed through the spread of Buddhism as evident in the texts, shrines and monasteries that it inspired.

From the Indian perspective, at the time of our visit, the Asian world was just starting to open up to some of the connections that it had had in precolonial times. Overland there had been in the past, both confrontations between peoples, as well as peaceful exchanges of material goods and ideas, across the expanse of the continent and beyond. Maritime connections and exchanges, occasionally conflicting, were generally peaceful. Both kinds of connections led to migrations, settlements in new locations, and intermingling of ideas. Weaving their way through these connections were the institutions that evolved from a variety of religions. Confucianism and Hinduism tended to be rather stay-at-home religions, although the latter did venture out into some new areas. The two religions that travelled through and settled in many parts of Asia were Buddhism and, later, Islam.

There was a bewildering multiplicity of objects and ideas available to us from pre-modern Asia. Colonialism divided Asia into disparate compartments as each European power established its control over a different region and these were artificially cut off from each other. From the 1950s, some of the past experience was being rediscovered and subjected to explanations different from those of colonial scholarship, and some who remained loyal to colonial readings of their past created new divisions among themselves in accordance with the colonial readings of their past. One example of this was the early connection between India and China. In terms of our visit in 1957 to the two Buddhist cave sites, I saw both of these as historical links of earlier times evolving in the milieu of Chinese cultures but they also reflected, although more faintly, possible explorations of contemporary times. Looking back on our visit from the current perspective, one realizes that the explanations of the past, made half a century ago, had their own anxieties and aspirations.

Having reread the diary I now feel that it does perhaps carry a faint aroma of what China was like, but seen through my eyes, and seen in a very different moment sixty-two years ago. Being there in the early years of a revolutionary change and observing some of the elements of what were to evolve into powerful dictatorial ideologies and practices, such as those that took form as the Cultural Revolution, one can't help but feel that the experience of that historical juncture may attune one to recognizing other dictatorial changes that overwhelm societies of our times—even if the changes emanate not from a socialist revolution but from its reverse, namely, ideologies drawn from exclusive majoritarian nationalisms deriving from a single identity and set in the economy of neoliberalism. Of course, at the same time, one also has to think of these elements in their relation to the other more simple and direct changes, particularly of improvements in standards of living for the many. These may not have been a universal achievement but held out hope for the many, and it was a hope that was not altogether belied, as in some other cases.

My own perceptions of China naturally changed over the years. As a child I grew up, as I have often said, in the cantonment culture of the British Raj that inevitably influenced to some degree our ways of looking at people and cultures that were dissimilar to our own. Hence the view both limited and stilted of things Chinese. We had little access to things Chinese. Through my teenage years China took on the contours of yet another Asian country struggling to disentangle itself from European bindings of various kinds. The awareness of the struggle found its echoes in events in India and brought about in us a less unfamiliar attitude towards China, and a lessening of the strangeness that had existed previously. There developed a sense of seeing them as a part of Asian nationalism even if we barely knew them. The revolution revealed yet another aspect that led to a variety of attempts to understand the reasons for it. For me the revelation of the more traditional Chinese cultures and the earlier pre-modern past came initially with the course that I studied at London University. The visit to China answered some of my questions that had surfaced in these early readings, and at the same time raised many more.

Historical patterns are sometimes repeated but the form differs. One has to be wary of the undesirable ones and learn of their causation from past experience. This is when history can provide some insights, provided it remains history and is not converted into mythology.

INTRODUCTION

The reader who is new to Buddhist cave sites of Central Asia, linked to what has come to be called the Silk Route/ Silk Road (and more recently referred to in the plural as Routes since there were many) may find a brief history helpful as background. Here, I would like to give a short summary of the relevant historical context to the Central Asian trade, so crucial to the existence of Dunhuang and Maijishan. The reader, therefore, has a choice: she may go directly to the journey and keep the reading of the historical background to later, after having read about the journey; or, alternatively, she may first read the brief historical background and then proceed to read about the journey. The introduction was written recently unlike the text of the travels.

A BRIEF HISTORICAL BACKGROUND TO DUNHUANG AND MAIJISHAN— IN THE CONTEXT OF THE 'SILK ROUTES'

The Setting

The two sites where we worked, Dunhuang and Maijishan, were towards the Chinese end of a long and complex set of routes cutting across Central Asia and continuing as far as the eastern Mediterranean. It is somewhat misleading to call it the Silk Road, for, as pointed out by many scholars, it is not a single road across Eurasia but interconnected nests of routes. Nor was silk the only item exchanged along these routes although it was in a sense what initiated the trading networks. The making of this and other similar exchanges were moulded by a number of activities that shaped many concepts and actions and allowed the construction of an interconnected history. Sites such as these are welcomed by archaeologists and historians since the reconstruction of the ethos that inspired them, when studied in depth, provides information about the history of this complex interconnected region. What was a great help, as it usually is, was that the dead were buried together with grave goods, or grave furniture as it is sometimes called, which is tangible evidence of material culture, complementing what one gathers from the murals and manuscripts found in the region.

What the Silk Routes in all their complexities did do, was to cut a swathe of exchange relations across Eurasia establishing innumerable links through which silk produced in China found its way to markets of the eastern Roman Empire. In the course of doing so, other items of various kinds were also conveyed from place to place. Many exchanges of varying kinds took place along the way. The process was slow and hinged on a variety of factors such as ecology and geomorphology, forms of exchange and trade, the evolution of religions, and the meeting points of multiple languages. What emerged as the many cultures of this region became as thought-provoking as the nature of commerce that accompanied them.

The region is perhaps best viewed as a series of segments. Moving from China in a westerly direction, the first segment was the area from Central China to North-west China. From the imperial capital first at Luoyang and then at Xi'an, a route takes off for the Buddhist caves at Maijishan that lie at a distance but not excessively far from Xi'an. This was our first port of call. It grew to be a big market town. From here there was a connection through the area of Gansu and the hexi corridor, and through Xinjiang to the site of Dunhuang. This is located at the edge of the Takla Makan and the Tarim Basin and with the Gobi Desert in partial proximity. This was the borderland between China and Central Asia, and the site of Dunhuang was a hub in this borderland. Just a little beyond Dunhuang, going west is a point that was called the Jade Gate, viewed as the entrance to Central Asia from the Chinese side.

The second segment takes the form of two routes from Dunhuang westwards: one going north to the oasis of Turfan, and beyond to Kyzyl, Kucha to Kashgar; and the other taking a southerly direction through Miran, Yarkand, and Khotan to Kashgar. The point where the northern and southern routes met was the city of Kashgar. The routes skirt the desert of Takla Makan since this was a virtually impossible desert to cross, with an unwelcoming landscape.

The third segment lies west of Kashgar—the Oxus plain and the Pamirs coming down to Afghanistan and North-west India. The Pamirs are a wedge. Another major hub on the western side was the region of Gandhara, south of the Oxus plain and extending towards the upper Indus Valley; the latter route coming to the Karakorum area and Ladakh. It incorporated the Kabul and Swat valleys and the regions that included Purushapura and Takshashila. That Chinese silk was a familiar commodity in India is evident from the terms used for a variety of silk which are 'cinansuka' and 'cinapatta', suggesting a link to China. This segment had a history of being the area to which many peoples and objects gravitated and had done so since proto-historic times, attracted by its fertility. The Swat Valley north of the upper Indus and the Jhelum Valley in Kashmir hosted a range of cultures. The Swat Valley was a significant node of trade and a meeting point of cultures. This is evident from the descriptions in the travel account of the Buddhist monk Xuan Zang, of whom more later. Routes were opened across the Hindu Kush to Bamiyan in Afghanistan. The area becomes important again in later times when ruled by the Shahis and subsequently the Ghurids.

The fourth segment is the area south of the Caspian Sea and across Iran up to the coast of the eastern Mediterranean with its major centres at places such as Palmyra, Aleppo, and Petra. To its north lay Constantinople and the Byzantine centres all greatly interested in acquiring silk, which became central to its use in church and courtly ritual.

Our project was essentially concerned with the first segment where the two sites are located, but the historical fallout of the links with the second and third segments could not be neglected. Seen together, the three segments constitute the area through which India was in varying degrees linked to China. My references to Central Asia in the text are mainly to the second and third segments. These are the segments that hosted the major Buddhist sites of cave shrines and monasteries in almost every large oasis on the two

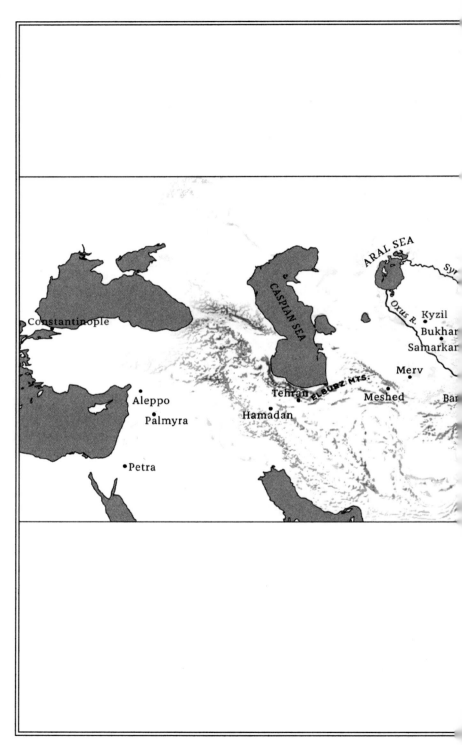

LOCATIONS LINKED TO THE CENTRAL ASIAN TRADE

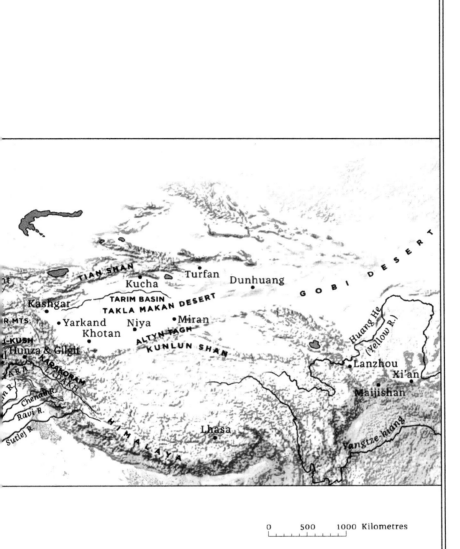

0   500   1000 Kilometres

routes around the Takla Makan and continuing into the Oxus plain, the Pamirs, Afghanistan, the Indus Valley and its distributaries, and North-west India. There was another route that skirted the Tian Shan to the north but it was less used. The contemporary states of today involved in this area are Kazakhstan, Kyrgyzstan, Tajikistan, Turkmenistan, and Uzbekistan, each carrying the name of its dominant set of clans, more frequently referred to in the past as tribes.

The history of the area was also conditioned to some extent by its geomorphology. In northern China, the routes go through the loess plateau to the edge of the Gobi Desert with the desert of Takla Makan and the Tarim Basin to the west. This area is encircled by mountains—the Altyn-Tagh, Kunlun Shan, Tian Shan, and such like. The third segment begins with the plains of the Syr and Amu Darya (Oxus), that were a part of Bactria and Sogdiana, a different landscape from the deserts to the east. To the south of the plains there is a divergence caused in part by the Pamir mountains. Some routes go to Afghanistan and others to the northern Himalaya and Karakorum. These routes generally involved travelling across mountains as in the Gilgit and Karakorum areas. Khotan on the southern route from Dunhuang was connected to Gilgit and Ladakh. The northern end of North-west India and across the Indus was part of Gandhara in early times, its location making it the meeting point of many routes and also linking it to the fourth segment. The fourth segment involved the much travelled routes through the Iranian plateau, across the northern edge of the Mesopotamian plains to the eastern Mediterranean.

Generalizations are often made about the grasslands of Central Asia— the steppes—and the nomads who herded their animals in these areas. From time to time, they raided the cities in the vicinity thus intervening in their histories. The people of the steppes provided an essential link in the complex trans-regional economy. Needless to say, Central Asia is far more complex both in itself and in its role in the making of these cities. Ecologically, distinct zones are demarcated: the icebound tundra remained isolated but for the lucrative trade in furs—ermine, mink, fox, sable, beaver; the extensive steppes, that were home to many communities of largely nomadic and semi-nomadic herders of cattle, sheep and goats, yaks, camels, and above all the commercially valuable and militarily effective, horses; the many deserts of the latitudes further south—especially the Gobi and the Takla Makan—were unfriendly to human settlement except in the scatter of oases. These were fertile areas along tree-lined rivers that supported marginal agriculture, as also some splendid towns, dependent on an intricate trade and exchange of goods. In their vicinity cave shrines were often cut into the cliffs. The steppes with their agro-pastoral societies were significant in the early contours of Central Asian history as also along the borders of kingdoms to the south.

The horse in Central Asia can be described as a pivotal animal. It eased the herding of large numbers of sheep and goats, it was a crucial source of extra power when saddled and used by archers, it provided transportation when drawing carts or chariots, it provided milk and meat, and inevitably became an animal symbolic of ritual and social status in all the cultures that were touched by migrants from Central Asia—the speakers of Indo-Aryan and Old Iranian, the Mitannis, waves of Turkish migrations, and others. Central Asia, and valleys such as that of Ferghana, became the prime breeding ground for quality horses and these in turn were a prized item in trade, on par with the silk that came from China. Horses were supplied to the cavalries of the major kingdoms along the routes.

The agro-pastoral societies of the steppes played a role in the early contours of Central Asian history, as indeed also along the borders of the larger kingdoms to the south. We have to recognize that these societies were more than incidental to the histories of large states in Iran, northern India, and China. Their interventions took two forms: one was the lightning raid on wealthy towns and the acquisition of much booty that left the cities gasping for a while; the other came about from the conflicts among themselves that resulted in massive migrations from one area to another in Central Asia, disturbing local economies but helping create mixtures of cultural idioms. We, today, may marginalize pastoralist cultures but they are often of greater importance than we are willing to admit.

Among those significant to the history of Central Asia were the Xiongnu, a confederation of nomadic clans for whom the eastern Eurasian steppes were their homeland. They were for long regarded as the barbarians at the gates of north-western China, constantly raiding the wealthy cities of the Han Chinese. The building of the Great Wall was an extravagant attempt to keep them out. Some of the clans such as the Yuezhi broke away and gave rise to the Kushans who ruled in Bactria and North-west India. The Xiongnu seem to have faded out by the mid-first millennium AD. Among the speculations of what happened next is the theory that they took form as the Huns. Subsequently to the Xiongnu, the Sogdians were powerful in the western part of Central Asia with affinities to Iranian culture, and the Uyghurs with Turkic affinities in the more easterly regions.

The nuclei of the kingdoms were the oases and the scattered fertile valleys and these, for the people of the grasslands, were profitable sources of loot and other luxury goods. They were sometimes kept at bay with gifts of the goods that were being traded, pre-eminently bolts of silk and other luxury goods. These could be carried west and traded in the third and fourth segments. This did lead to the pastoralists sporadically taking on the role of traders. Where they did so their role differed as there were sometimes clan connections or their control over local ecologies enabled them to protect the trading caravans, or to collect dues from them when they entered the market centres, and to defend these centres if need be. The Sogdian and Uyghur merchant communities maintained friendly relations with them where possible.

The western side of Central Asia saw the passage of merchants and religions that travelled to the eastern side, the most significant being Buddhism in the first millennium and later Islam in the second. A large number of other religions were also making their presence felt. Not unconnected was the emergence of Manichaeism, claiming Zoroastrianism, Christianity, and Buddhism as sources. Scholarly astronomers (and doubtless astrologers as well) and mathematicians, and those with medical knowledge, travelled with the Buddhist bhikkhus and Muslim mullahs and merchants, to exchange knowledge in China and in later times to centres in Central Asia.

Such diverse ecological zones had to be balanced and more particularly between those zones supporting a large population of herders and the urban centres that acted as a support system in the trade. Transhumance and some degree of pastoralism were important in the equation. But the situation changed with the rise of trade and exchange centres that grew into major commercial towns. Pastoralism and agriculture often have a symbiotic relationship with herds feeding on harvested stubble and thereby fertilizing the fields. This symbiosis may have prevailed in some limited areas where pastoralism and agriculture were juxtaposed, but it does not accommodate urbanization. The frequency of migrations among the nomads of the steppes, sometimes leading to confrontation with the oasis towns, required more than an occasional reconciliation. The migrations could be in search of new pastures and these could sometimes lead to conflicts if these lands were already occupied. Or, they resulted from breakaways within the nomadic group that required one of them to migrate. The result was a range of categories of relationships that were initially often conflicting but eventually could enrich the ways of life of the groups involved.

The crow's nest of routes stretched across Eurasia. It is as well to keep in mind that the first millennium AD was also the period when maritime trade was picking up, linking similar segments of the coastal areas of the Indian Ocean. Arab traders were active across the Arabian Sea, Indian merchants took the initiative from the Bay of Bengal to the mainland and islands of South-east Asia, and the Chinese initially confined themselves to the area just to their south. In both areas, Buddhism and Hinduism followed by Islam had missions propagating new and effective religions. Buddhism had a monopoly in Central Asia, where Hinduism tended to fade away. This was not the simple process that it has sometimes been made out to be. There were existing religions in these areas and what emerged were new forms rather different from the original forms and associated institutions. Religious teachers travelled and taught in areas unknown to them and through languages equally unfamiliar.

Mahayana Buddhism, in its many versions, for example, evolved distinctive features that were different from the earlier Hinayana school and the pristine Buddhism as taught by the Buddha and his disciples. This is inevitable in the history of every religion. The foundational teaching would be similar but some concepts and forms of worship would be adaptations to local requirements. One could argue that in some ways Mahayana Buddhism was a response to the cultures, social norms, and ideologies of the regions in which it spread, starting with its evolution in North-west India. This is particularly true of religions that migrate from their place of origin. The eminence of Mahayana Buddhism lasted for more than a millennium before Islam slowly took over. Buddhism was by then settled in China and the lands to its east. The evolution of schools of Sufi Islam, that differed recognizably from the original Islam of the Arabs, brought their teachings successfully from Iranian and Central Asian centres to the Indian subcontinent, making a substantial contribution to the varieties of Islam as they took form in Central Asia, Iran, and India.

A question perhaps worth investigating is the degree to which those Sufi schools that emanated from Central Asia were imprinted with strands of the earlier Shamanism prevalent in Central Asia as well as Mahayana Buddhism, both being religions that preceded them in the region. In travelling out from Central Asia to India, such Sufi teachers were entering the homeland of one of the religions that had preceded them in their own homeland—Buddhism. One could ask whether there is any reflection of this in their teachings and their arts.

The Trade

'Seidenstrassen' or 'Silk Road' was coined by German geologist Ferdinand von Richthofen, in 1877. It was seen as a well-defined route that began at one point in China and continued until it terminated at a designated point in the Levant, suggesting that Chinese and eastern Mediterranean traders carried goods from one end to the other. On the contrary, it was an intricate network of routes, active in segments and meeting at specific points. The segments were under the control of the local communities. Thus the Chinese traded with the Uyghurs as immediate neighbours and the Sogdians further away and these in turn traded with the Indians and Iranians in the Oxus region, Afghanistan, Gandhara, and further west, who then traded with the merchants of the eastern Mediterranean. For example, silk travelled through this network and passed through the hands of various communities until some of it arrived in the Roman Empire and in Byzantine centres. Similarly, horses from Bactria and Central Asia were brought to the plains of northern India and to China.

The notion of a route may have given a geographical frame to the trade and migrations of varying communities that were linked to the segments of this route. Similar to a chain-stitch pattern, the stitch was a small fragment of the route and provided a point of exchange for goods coming from different directions. The items of trade would be substantially the same, for example, silk moving from east to west and horses going in the reverse direction, but commodities would change to local traders in each segment. Neither the same group or guild of traders nor those of a particular community transhipped the same item along the entire route from Central China to the eastern Mediterranean. The advantage of this pattern of trade is that profits tend to be more widely distributed.

The processes involved in the exchange need not have been uniform and would have changed by degree. They ranged from simple barter to gift exchange to exchange using a single object as an item of evaluation, such as a bolt of silk, to money transactions in a market. It has been argued that initially the bolts of silk were the units in a system of gift-exchange, which later extended to other objects. This would have involved Chinese centres of power negotiating with local Central Asian societies that protected the exchange until such time as they themselves became traders. Technically, objects with material value were donated to a monastery in exchange for which the monastic establishment bestowed blessings and status on the donor. Monasteries played a complex but essential role in this long-distance trade. Parallel to this was the system evolving out of barter, such as an object being gifted to a person of authority, not necessarily a religious institution, in return for status or concessions to the person gifting the object. It has been suggested that bolts of silk were given by the Chinese frontier authorities to the nomads to buy them off from raiding the frontier towns. This might have then led to the nomads exchanging the silk for objects from areas further west that were attractive to or required by the Chinese. Gradually this would get converted into a regular trade involving markets, merchants, and middlemen, and presumably the nomads were as quick as others to get a foothold in this exchange. The luxury items acquired by monasteries could either be used in further trade exchanges or could be used to decorate the monastic shrines used for worship.

The items traded were also dependent on demand and there would have been a rise or decline in some items. The segmentation of the Silk Routes is also reflected in periods when trade in high value items was not at its height. Political and economic changes in the various segments affected the trade. For example, when the Parthians obstructed the route from the Oxus to Palmyra in the eastern Mediterranean, the availability of Chinese silk declined. The threat of raids by the Xiongnu or the Huns brought about a similar result. It is said that the Great Wall in China was built by Qin Shi Huang to keep out nomadic raiders. An oft-repeated statement, its actual effectiveness is debatable. Nor can one overlook the complex diplomatic relations between those on either side of the Wall. Perhaps it was also built to discourage the nomads from looting the items. If bolts of silk were looted before they reached the exchange centres there would be nothing left to trade. The attempt to keep out the people of the grasslands was also to ensure that their search for fresh pastures would not bring them into lands that were a part of the Chinese kingdom. And we should not forget that walls are also built to keep people in. These many networks touched on diverse cultures. This led to the introduction of new customs and beliefs and acted as catalysts in the making of what we now call civilizations.

What I have described elsewhere as a chain-stitch route was fairly common in precolonial times. The traders of area A would exchange goods with those of area B and the latter then exchanged goods—some of the same, some subtracted and some added—with traders of area C, and so on for a considerable distance. So the goods could move long distances but through local traders who were also beneficiaries. On them depended the ultimate movement of the trade. The Chinese produced the silk but its trade was often in non-Chinese hands as indeed the trade in horses was in non-Sogdian hands after the initial exchange. The chain-stitch was a stretch of interlocking circuits which would go in directions determined by produce and demand. The circuits were broken with the rise of the Mongol peoples and subsequently the arrival of the Russians and other European powers in the area.

Dunhuang was a particularly important point linking central China via the Hexi and Gansu corridor with the eastern end of Central Asia. The corridor was important as a place of exit and entry. At the western end Khotan, Yarkand, and Gandhara served a similar function. The location of Ashoka's Edicts at Mansehra and Shahbazgarhi is an indication of this. From the mid-sixth century, the route included the Karakorum and the Hindu Kush, with Bamiyan becoming the hub. Both merchants and Buddhist monks were the most evident users of these routes, not to mention others with a lesser presence, propagating various other religions or carrying other items of trade.

The list of religions is large. With an initial practice of Shamanism, the religion of magic and trances, there grew further mixtures to some degree with religions coming from China such as Daoism and Confucianism. The earlier Shamanism and Bon religions were known to northern India and the Himalaya region. Subsequently, Buddhism as well as a few strands of Shaivism came from India, the latter not having a lasting effect. There was also the presence of Manichaeism, Zoroastrianism, and Nestorian Christianity but with smaller followings. All these were present before the coming of Islam.

Chinese interest in Central Asia was known by the second century BC from which time there are references to preventing the steppe nomads from raiding the cities of North-west China. The north-western borders of the Qin empire were close to the pastures of the Xiongnu pastoralists with their huge herds of animals. To contain the nomads, apart from building the Great Wall, a garrison was settled in the oasis of Dunhuang in 111 BC, and a line of forts built to control the Gansu corridor. Garrisons were also settled in the oasis towns to the west and some of these grew to be trade centres. Exchange probably emerged from the earlier system of giving bolts of silk to the Xiongnu to keep them from looting the oasis towns and later discovering that these bolts could be exchanged further west with those interested in trading the silk. At this point, it was an unsettled area surrounded by nomads sometimes in conflict among themselves.

The Xiongnu, nomad herdsmen and horse-breeders, had a confrontation with the Yuezhi so the latter migrated away from the Dunhuang area and settled westwards. They began to play a role in the trade and some among them were obviously successful. The Kushans were a branch of the Yuezhi, controlling the Oxus plain and North-west India. The latter area was familiar with migrants from Central India who settled in the upper Indus area. The Aryan speakers were the earliest followed by the Shakas/ Scythians and then the Kushans/Turushkas—according to Kalhana, the author of *Rajatarangini* (River of Kings). The post-Mauryan Kushan administration opened up the area. The trade was inching its way to places such as Khotan, Kucha, Turfan, and possibly Dunhuang.

Kushan politics were rooted in Central Asian events. As has been said, the Kushans were significant in encouraging Buddhism as a dialogue between India and China. The Kushan kingdom stretched from Transoxiana to northern India, symbolized by the location of two royal shrines, one at Surkh Kotal and the other at Mathura. Was this what gave Buddhism a status in China prior to its importance as a Chinese religion? Were the Kushans a Central Asian dynasty that viewed northern India beyond Gandhara as a southern extension at the edge of their kingdom or was it a southern focus of their kingdom?

A familiar administration stretching across the area meant expanding contacts, extensive patterns of exchange, and inevitably, more mixed belief systems. Buddhism as it evolved in Afghanistan, Gandhara, and Swat was in part a response to the local mixed population and in part to its role in Central Asia and, of course, to adjust to the changes within the religion and its new practitioners. It became a closely connecting link in the region. It claimed to be incorporating the original teachings of the Buddha although it did register some departures. The Fourth Buddhist Council called by Kanishka, about which there is some uncertainty, may have ratified these deviations. Such departures and consequent changes are common in religions that have a wide reach.

The mountains that we regard as barriers were obviously not so. The valleys and the passes provided a natural route which when need be was taken up. (A striking example of this is that when in recent times the Karakoram Highway was planned, a visit to the sites revealed that it had already been used as a major link route via Gilgit and its vicinity to Central Asia in the first millennium AD.) The kingdom of Khotan, for instance, seems very distant but it had a close connection with Iranians who controlled it for a while and then with Indians. The legend in Khotan was that Ashoka Maurya visited the area and founded the kingdom. This is most unlikely. Clearly an association with a respected ruler of the past raised the status of the kingdom. One of the rulers took the rather fancy popular title, Khotana-maharaya-rayatiraya, familiar to North Indian kingdoms.

Among the manuscripts from the cave at Dunhuang were two that had versions of the story of Rama, which in this case ended happily ever after. It was not only material objects that passed through their hands. Myths, narratives, scrolls, and paintings, sculpture from Gandhara, were all items that came to them from both Xinjiang and Sogdia. Khotan was not the terminus because some people from Gandhara went on further east to Niya and are known from their use of the Kharoshthi script.

The melange of peoples, goods, scripts, religions, and ways of trade continued from the late first into the second millennium AD. Dynastic controls were interwoven with the rise and decline of small kingdoms. The next great sweep as it were was when the Mongols, who by the thirteenth century held parts of Eurasia, swept down to raid the richer towns and were generally politically feared. Genghis Khan was regarded as the epitome of the Mongol ruler. The political hegemony of the Mongols lasted a couple of centuries but the heritage of cultural forms, as in architecture, held great potential and became one of its hallmarks. The ghastly plague in Europe in the four-teenth century, called the Black Death, is thought to have come from these contacts that brought particular types of fleas and microbes to Europe, quite at variance from those already inhabiting those parts. By the fifteenth cen-tury, Mongol power was gradually disintegrating as also the gains that came to it through the Central Asian trade. This came to a virtual closure with the Ottoman empire discontinuing the routes.

Dunhuang

The Mogao caves or grottoes, or Qianfodong, also known as 'the Caves of a Thousand Buddhas' because of the many small paintings of the Buddha repeated by the hundred on the walls and ceiling of some caves, form a complex and lie at a short distance from the oasis town of Dunhuang on the edge of the Gobi Desert. The area is described as the land of the singing sands, as indeed they sing when the wind blows them in all directions! The Chinese emperor threatened by nomads in the north-west sent a diplomatic mission to the rulers further west, but all that resulted was a couple of Buddhist monks being persuaded to come to China in 68 AD. It was at around this time that Sogdian traders began to participate in a small but effective exchange. Their documents mention a threat from the Xiongnu, identified by some with what later came to be called the Huns or the Hunas. This precipitated the westward migrations of others. The Huns were, of course, to play a bigger role when they attacked northern India, and another branch attacked Eastern Europe. Had the Central Asians contained the Huns, these histories would have been different.

The earliest caves were cut at the initiative of a monk in about 366 AD, and surviving many invasions the place flourished, continuing into the sec-ond millennium AD. By this time Chinese contacts had taken shape and goods were being regularly exchanged. The requirement of horses was becoming a prime necessity now that their usefulness in warfare had been established. Horses bred by pastoral nomads were exchanged for bolts of Chinese silk. The demand for this silk in the western regions and all the way to Rome was such that the nomads became suppliers and entered the trade. Pliny, the Roman historian, had earlier complained bitterly about 'ex oriente luxe', the buying of oriental luxuries at exorbitant prices for the Roman market, draining the Roman exchequer. This complaint was prior to the flourishing of the silk trade, so one can gauge the impact of this trade on an existing market.

Silk was becoming the unit of exchange. Even the soldiers in the garrisons were paid in grain, silk, and a few coins. This form of exchange did not initially involve a long-distance market since it was more frequently in the nature of a gift—exchange or a system of sophisticated barter, in a series of local markets. The item passed through many hands before it covered the route. Narratives of the trade and the accounts of traders are written on fine strips of bamboo, birchbark, wood, and later, paper. These are available, forming part of the discovery of manuscripts from some of these cave sites and oasis towns.

Buddhism is also dramatically presented in rock engravings and inscriptions on the mountain rocks through which a road was cut, as in one of the many routes that linked northern India to Central Asia through Gilgit, Chitral, and Hunza. The worship of the Buddha included donation of money and objects at the shrine or to the monastery, and rituals were not confined to meditation nor the practice only to social ethics.

This was also the period when there was some competition from Nestorian Christianity that met with opposition as Sassanid rule moved into the erstwhile Kushan territories. Confrontation was also evident in China between Confucianism and Buddhism both vying for patronage and authority. That Confucianism did not spread to Central Asia may have been in part because its followers were tied to ancestor worship and this may have kept them confined to relatively permanent settlements. Nomad societies do not carry the remains of their ancestors with them but those that slowly ceased being nomads and settled in the oases could have built ancestral shrines. As has been said, the existence of a very few pre-Buddhist caves at places such as Dunhuang may indicate their being used in some Shamanic ritual.

It is equally interesting that Brahmanism or even Puranic Hinduism, as expressed in the worship of Shiva and Vishnu, did not go far into Central Asia nor become a major religion in this area. Brahmanas migrated great distances but within the subcontinent and seldom outside except in small numbers or as traders and generally at the invitation of those in authority.

Kingdoms in South-east Asia invited Brahmana ritual specialists for coronations. The linking of rituals to caste may have acted as a restriction. Tantric worship had some popularity at places in Central Asia but more often linked to Buddhism.

Why Buddhism lost its premium status in Central Asia in the second millennium AD, although it did not altogether decline, has still to be explained. Its patronage came from local authorities all along the route and from wealthy merchants. Doubtless artisans also contributed with their work as they did elsewhere as well. Trade declined to some extent in the early second millennium and, possibly by the time it picked up, Islam had already entered the scene. Was Islam more attractive to herder communities than Buddhism? Were they still largely herder communities or were they now partially traders?

The caves at Dunhuang began to be excavated in the fourth century AD. There may have been some familiarity with the cave monasteries in Central India and there would certainly have been knowledge of the same in the oases of Central Asia, some of which date to the same period. Dunhuang was to become China's largest Buddhist site with almost 500 caves. Some were simple and small, but others were enormous and complex. One went as deep as 23 metres into the cliff, and another set of caves was seven storeys high. A few also had colossal Buddha images on the cliff face. As elsewhere, the early sacred sites were rock-cut caves such as the ones we visited at Maijishan, Dunhuang, Longmen, and Yungang. Would it have been easier to build free-standing structures or to cut caves in the loess or the softer rock at these places? Perhaps caves were initially associated with meditation, and they were easier to protect—from nomads, herdsmen, and raiders. Using caves in mountains was a tradition going back to early times.

Buddhist scholars travelled from Indian centres to Central Asian towns, often invited by patrons among the well-to-do, both the local rulers and the wealthy notables. Kumarajiva was based in Kucha but travelled extensively and eventually taught in China in the fourth century AD. In the same period, Dharmaraksha arrived in Xi'an. Initially Buddhist monks had to be near settlements from where they collected their daily alms in the form of food. Later, when donations of land were made to the monasteries and they employed labour and cultivators to work the land, monasteries began to include refectories where the monks ate their meals. Monasteries were commonly located in the oasis towns or partially in caves in the neighbouring cliffs. Pagodas were often in the vicinity of the monastery.

The walls of the caves were painted with murals and had sculpture either cut from the rock or made from stone or clay and placed in the hall or shrine. Reliquaries placed in beautifully adorned caskets were revered objects. The earlier art carried traces of the Gandhara aesthetic with its mix of the Indian and the Hellenistic. Some caves have yielded manuscripts—documents providing evidence on traders, items traded, accounts, and such like, that indicate the nature of the exchange at various places. They are written in Gandhari Prakrit, Khotanese, Tocharian, Sogdian, Uyghur, Tibetan, and Mongolian, in short, all the languages used in Central Asia, and in Sanskrit and Chinese. The latter two were generally original Buddhist texts, some with their translation into Chinese.

The texts translated were the canonical Buddhist texts such as the *Saddharmapundarika-sutra* commonly known as the Lotus Sutra and a foundational text of Buddhism, some fragments from the *Tripitaka* that formed the Buddhist Canon, the *Jatakas* (e.g., *Vessantara, Shibi, Mahasattva, Ruru*, etc.) that were stories of the earlier births of various persons, and stories from the *Avadanas*. In later times, they included Vajrayana Buddhist texts and the commentaries on them. Pictorial storytelling was an effective way of conveying a message especially to a new audience. This technique had also been used earlier in the sculpture decorating Buddhist stupas in India. A comparison of a *Jataka* narrative depicted in stone sculpture at Bharhut and Sanchi can be interestingly made with the same story depicted in a mural at Dunhuang, and there are a few such examples. The narratives tend to be similar focusing on the familiar landmarks of the Buddha's biography: renunciation, temptations of Mara, first teachings, and the mahaparinirvana, the scene of death. These are all recognizable at Dunhuang in various styles that gradually show less diversity and more conformity to a Chinese style. The narratives painted in the murals are neither casual nor casually located since there is a meaning and purpose to each and a reason for the juxtaposition. Bodhisattvas were added with their own mythology. Later the *Sukhavativyuha* was also translated and illustrated in the murals.

Another important text was the *Vajracchedika Prajnaparamita Sutra*, the Diamond Sutra, as it has been called, that is a dialogue between the Buddha and his disciple on how one should, like a diamond, cut through illusions when in pursuit of enlightenment. Kumarajiva, when in Xi'an, translated it into Chinese. The earliest printed version of the text was found at Dunhuang dating to 868 AD, gifted to the shrine by a local patron, in memory of his parents.

There were paintings of events that are described as referring to the ancient past, the distinction between legend and history being somewhat fuzzy. Most are familiar stories that visitors in earlier times would have known. I was interested to see that the Mauryan emperor Ashoka turns up in more than one mural. The obvious source is Buddhist texts that hold him up as an exemplar, the ruler who was a man of compassion, who propagated the dhamma and who performed pious deeds. The *Ashokavadana*, a source of such legends, had been translated into Chinese in 306 AD. Sometimes Ashoka is shown as constructing a multitude of stupas, 84,000 in the text, while the Elder Upagupta hides the sun so that the construction can be completed in one night! In other cases, it is recorded that a Chinese ruler built many stupas to enclose relics and claimed that he was doing so in imitation of Ashoka. To these were added stories of Ashoka placing images close to the stupas. But there seems to have been some confusion about a clear identity between Buddhist and Daoist images. Associated with the images were the usual stories of how the images themselves indicated where they wished to be placed. It would seem that Ashoka was indeed, as he has been described, a paradigmatic ruler.

Where the Buddha figure is larger than the others, the focus is often on him meditating or preaching. Narratives are sometimes illustrated like the reel of a film, each frame linked to the previous one. Landscape scenes gradually come to be like those in other Chinese painting or on scrolls. The illustrations are set in gardens, palaces, mountains, with rivers and trees or occasionally, have urban settings. They reflect the lives of the elite or of monks. Was this the aspiration of Buddhist and other teachers or does it reflect the elite that patronized the religion? There is little doubt that even where there is a scene referring back to the Buddha's life, the incident would have to be located in India, but the portrayal is set in the China of that time. Some of this would, of course, depend on where the craftsmen-artists came from although it is likely that they would conform to the wishes of the patron.

Transforming the conventional architectural complex of Buddhist places of worship into a rock-cut structure would have posed problems. The three structures that are associated with worship are the stupa that contains the relics of a venerated person, the chaitya hall where worship is conducted, and the vihara, the monastery where the monks lived. There is usually a free-standing pillar as well. The stupa took the form of the pagoda in China and was generally not as large as the ones in Central India or further south in Sri Lanka or in Java. The stupas of Gandhara were generally much smaller and these would have been the models, although the shape was not the same. The monasteries could be just caves to live in or constructed as a cloister at the base of the cliff or hill. The chaitya hall was more complicated. Traditionally it was apsidal but this may have posed problems in the local cliffs. So it tends to be rectangular with the votive stupa at one end often connected with the rock both at the top and the bottom, presumably to make it more secure. The larger caves have a vestibule entrance leading into a small corridor that may lead into the main hall of worship or else into an antechamber with yet another corridor that leads into the main hall. There was therefore more than ample wall space for the murals and this was entirely covered.

Chinese interest in Buddhism advanced during this period with Chinese monks and pilgrims travelling to India to read the Buddhist texts and bring back manuscripts. The period up to the seventh century saw a gradual increase in the goods exchanged, through trade and migrations, and in the spread of religious ideas and observances. This was when Chinese Buddhist monks trekked across the deserts of Central Asia to visit 'the western heaven', the sacred land where the Buddha had lived. Faxian was an early one who travelled out in the fourth century and wrote a short account of his visit.

The seventh century saw more monks and pilgrims coming to India. The best-known of Buddhist monks was Xuan Zang whose travels were more ambitious. He was based in Xi'an and was brought up in a family of scholars learned in Confucian thought. He undertook a long journey through the oases towns of Central Asia, spending time in some. Since the Mahayana form of Buddhism was not universally observed, this too would have been of interest to him. He travelled through the Hindu Kush to Bamiyan, the painted cave shrines of which he describes, and which resembled their central Asian counterparts. He went on to the western heaven and travelled across northern India visiting various important Buddhist sites and places of pilgrimage.

Finally, he spent some years at the monastery of Nalanda in eastern India, studying a range of Buddhist texts. He kept a careful itinerary of his travels in the *Si-yu-ki* or *Xiyu-Ji*, of where he went and its exact location, of what he saw, and of what he surmised. His descriptions and comments are a remarkable historical source. He returned to China eventually after sixteen years, and brought back an enormous number of texts to the monastery at Xi'an. He and others translated these texts into Chinese. In one painting at Dunhuang, he is depicted as literally leading an elephant-load of texts. If the spread of Buddhist teaching in the east can be attributed to the labours of Buddhist monks, then Xuan Zang has to be placed at the forefront. There were, of course, many Indian Buddhist monks invited by the Chinese who spent a lifetime in teaching and preaching and it is impressive that the Chinese took this aspect of the new religion so earnestly.

Xuan Zang made a deep impression on intellectual life in the capital and among Chinese Buddhists and his travels came to be associated with the Silk Routes. He was clearly a man of considerable intellectual acumen. Chinese authorities made intelligent use of his experiences in Central Asia, particularly to formulate their own interests. The same account was used many centuries later by Aurel Stein to locate sites in the Takla Makan and by Alexander Cunningham to track Buddhist sites in the Gangetic plain.

Interest in Central Asia increased during the Tang period. A landscape cartography of a kind was made with a Tang official locating places and routes based on the information provided by those who had travelled across Central Asia to India. The same curiosity is reflected in a couple of Arabic texts that discuss routes and kingdoms. In one, there is a reference to eastern routes linking Kamarupa in Assam to Yunan. The link is associated with trade in rhinoceros horn and this makes the statement more authentic, the rhinoceros being the major animal of the jungles in Assam and the Himalayan foothills, and the horn being a component of Chinese medicine.

Not only was Buddhism being introduced into new areas but many aspects of current knowledge from India and West Asia were also finding their way into China, such as Sanskrit texts on astronomy, mathematics, and medicine. The ideas of Jivaka and Nagarjuna were better known in these areas than those of Charaka and Sushruta. The inevitable search for the drug that bestows immortality was a big draw. This interest doubtless encouraged the reading of Tantric texts.

In the Tang period, the depiction of architecture, dress, and landscape in the murals was more in keeping with the paintings on paper and cloth. The context of the Buddhist themes had taken on a distinctive Chinese form. The new arrivals shown in the murals were the occasional Sassanian traders from Iran. Another change was the more extensive use of paper rather than strips of bamboo or wood. This in turn would lead to woodblock printing used imaginatively by teachers of various religions. Moveable type that facilitated printing goes back to the ninth century in China. The invention of gunpowder was to change political equations. Thus trade began to include new items. Khotan produced the best jade so this remained high on the list of items traded, as also did porcelain and lacquer vessels from China.

The texts brought back by Chinese Buddhists were translated into Chinese with much of this work being done at the famous White Horse Monastery. The insistence on translating the original texts is a remarkable assertion of a rational way of approaching new information: of importing the agent! The translation of texts is always problematic as the meanings of concepts in the original language cannot always be rendered with exactitude into the language of translation. It was during these centuries in the late first millennium that Vajrayana Buddhism, with its Tantric links, entered China using both the Central Asian and the Tibetan route. The last was made feasible with the increase in the Tibetan intervention in North-east China. Mention is made of prolific translators such as Vajrabodhi and Amoghavajra being active. The routes from Afghanistan and Kashmir via Ladakh to Khotan were also used. Connections with India were slowly reinforced by the more frequent use of the maritime route as well, going through the Bay of Bengal, Strait of Malacca, South China Sea to the ports on the south coast of China.

In the late first millennium, the western area of Central Asia came under the Iranian Sassanian control. Further east, the nomadic clans were coming together to form what in later centuries were referred to as the Turkish khanates—principalities that grew into substantial kingdoms along the northern edge of the routes and further, and into Bactria. The profits from the trade no doubt whet their appetite for the wealth of the commercial cities in the kingdoms along the southern Silk Routes.

The themes painted in the murals at Dunhuang remained broadly Buddhist but adapted to Chinese locations and persons. The representation of deities gradually began to include the occasional Daoist and Tantric deities. Some of the major figures of the earlier pantheon such as the Buddha Maitreya became less important in the later period. Physical features gradually become more distinctly Chinese. The multi-armed figures reflect familiarity with Indian iconography. The presence of dragons and other Chinese mythological figures are predominant in the backdrop to the figure, where such a backdrop was required.

Donors are given due prominence. Royal persons are depicted in all their regalia, together with their entourage. These presumably were also some of the patrons and additional donors in many instances. The nobility and the senior bureaucracy appear in their robes of office or associated with their insignia. Wealthy merchants were also donors as were guilds of craftsmen and artisans. This parallels the mention of guilds as donors at some stupas in India. At Longmen, the statues of donors are more frequent. The identity of person and place is often clarified by a small inscription, located at a convenient place that not only registers the donation, but also kinship links where they exist and other relevant information, to give the donor due status and identity.

Items of great variety continued to be traded apart from silk and horses, and much of the trade was in luxury goods. Indian traders supplied coral, pearls, glass beads and vessels, incense and perfume, and mention is also made of exotic animals. The supply of bolts of silk from China seemed to be never ending. It is said that in one season of trade, 90,000 bolts were exchanged. Payment for a woman of status was forty-one bolts and for a female slave was only three to four bolts. Further afield the nomads brought rugs, furs, and blankets as items of trade. But the trade was not restricted to barter and gift exchange. Coins were used in the markets and these were currencies of various kingdoms and dynasties involved in the commerce, and were of various metals such as gold, silver, and copper.

The painting of murals over such an extensive space and over so many centuries leads to the question of who were the artists, artisans, and craftsmen responsible for the paintings. Were they individual artists or did they belong to guilds? Were they employed by the patrons or were they employees of the monasteries as were the cultivators who cultivated monastic lands? Were they paid a wage or did the monastery give them food and accommodation? Were they permanently in residence and sedentary or were they mustered when required and migratory? Given the number of caves and donors they could well have been in permanent residence. Some of the documents provide a list of expenses such as land, labour, and irrigation contracts, a register of corveé or forced labour, and the taxes paid by the people of the oasis, but there are few details about the employment of artists.

Narratives from the Buddhist texts set in a Chinese context would in itself indicate this context as being different from the Indian. The difference is clear from the treatment of the landscape that is not the same as in Indian mural painting. Painting the landscape had importance since it carried its own symbolic message. Considerable attention is given to the deployment of space and the way the eye is meant to move in and across spaces. There is also a concern for the placement of buildings, humans, and animals in relation to space. Murals depict forts, palaces, towns, hunting scenes (despite the Buddhist negation of violence), social gatherings, and the lifestyle of the elite and more, especially the royal court. Dragons, of course, are frequent but the pheasants and cranes are not left out.

The technique of painting murals was first to plaster the wall with a mixture of clay, dung, straw, and hair; this was then covered over with a layer of white kaolin. Pigments were made from vegetables and rocks. Where the layer was damaged it was removed or plastered over for fresh painting. Was there a link between painting and calligraphy since the medium of the brush is used in both?

Buddhism faced persecution in China from time to time, and quite substantially in the ninth century, from which it recovered a century later under Song rule. Tibet had made a bid to control the eastern end of the trade and invaded Dunhuang and its neighbourhood. Apart from hostility to Tibetan Buddhists caused by this invasion, it has been suggested that anti-Buddhist sentiment in China also arose from the fact that the monasteries had received large donations of property in land that were exempt from tax. This made them something of an economic liability, apart from making them rivals of the non-Buddhist landowners and nobility. Forced labour employed on monastic lands put them in a category apart. Another rivalry could have been with those who followed the teachings of Confucius, who may have been a near contemporary of the Buddha—although completely unknown to each other. Persecution meant that monastic lands were confiscated, monasteries disallowed to function, and monks had to take up secular occupations.

Coincidentally, this was the period when Buddhism, which had also faced persecution earlier, was suffering a decline in India prior to its being ousted altogether. Persecutions tend to be ostensibly on religious grounds but are often also linked to other causes, such as ownership of land. In India the making of large grants of land was shifting to such grants being made to individual Brahmanas and groups of Brahmanas rather than to Buddhist monasteries. There is an appreciable decline in Buddhist monasteries in India as compared to the increased building of temples to Hindu deities and grants to Brahmanas. Monasteries of religions that had celibate monks holding substantial property, whether they are Buddhists, Jainas, Sufis, or Christians, often suggest a contradiction in belief. This could be one among the many reasons for their ceasing to be the dominant force in a society.

Nevertheless, the monasteries in China survived and surfaced even more effectively than before in the next century. They were able to face further but lesser persecution and hold their ground. This was doubtless helped by the fact that monasteries had become involved once again in commercial ventures—as happened with monasteries in India and other parts of Central Asia, with mutual benefit. This was a source of wealth in addition to landholding. The accumulation and investment of wealth is partially indicated from the excavation at Mes Aynak near Kabul in Afghanistan that revealed a huge hoard of coins and silver and gold objects. Xuan Zang is among those who mention the wealth of the monastery at Bamiyan. This explains how monasteries could not only invest in trade but could also play the role of bankers. The rejuvenation of the monasteries in China may well have been one source to help firm up the economy in Song times. That monks and nuns also made donations, and sometimes quite sizeable ones, as in India, points to their investing in trade as well, perhaps to have a private income that could be further invested. The acceptance of donations in money was, of course, controversial in the early years of the sangha and was one of the issues among others, on which there was a sectarian split.

Towards the latter part of the first millennium there was a gradual shift in the pattern of patronage. Families involved in governing Dunhuang commissioned the excavation of caves together with murals not only of a religious nature but also depicting the patron and his family. This was both an extension of an earlier system and also a departure from the cave being only a place of meditation for monks and for worship. It was now associated with the bestowal of social and political status on the patron in a much more direct way than before. This may have been occasioned by some of them being from societies that had been earlier regarded as alien, or that they had kinship links with such societies. Patrons belonged to important families. One family could be the patron of one or more caves or else a group of families could jointly be patrons of one large cave. Such patronage stemmed from religious concerns but can be seen as social and political statements.

The Zhang family had some problems linked to their political loyalties to the Tang dynasty when faced in the eighth century with the An Lushan Rebellion against the emperor and the invading Tibetans. Loyalty to the Tang dynasty depicted in the portrait of the emperor had to be covered up for the period when the Tibetans controlled the area. The ninth century saw the Tang back in power and the murals were restored or repainted. The Uyghur presence was noticeable when Cao Yijin was governor. He commissioned some caves for his wives who were Uyghur, Chinese, and Khotanese. Influences from these areas in the styles of painting, especially from Khotan, are also noticeable as is the fact of the political alliances through marriage. The patronage of the Zhang and Zhai families was considerable. The Cheng family was among those with a fairly extended kinship reach. The Yin family seems to have been more deeply involved in politics, despite Dunhuang being at quite a distance from the centre of power. The style of painting again is a mix of Chinese and Central Asian. The former was in keeping with changes of style in other parts of China. The murals also carry brief inscriptions that explain the event and who is being depicted.

Towards the later first millennium AD, there was a political change in Gandhara and the borderlands beyond the Indus in north-western India. This was triggered by the Turks in the Oxus region and the competition between the Turki Shahis and the Hindu Shahis in Gandhara and its vicinity.

The religion was largely Buddhism but of a kind that was to undergo some change. The encroaching importance of the Tantric religion and practice was being recognized in neighbouring Kashmir where some aspects were associated with Shaivism, but were also entering Buddhism. There finally emerged another variety of Buddhism—Vajrayana—that endorsed some aspects of the Tantric religion as well. The spread of this variety of Buddhism into Tibet is attributed to Padmasambhava, a somewhat mysterious figure who was said to have come from Uddiyana, a later name for a northern part of the Gandhara area. The emergent Vajrayana Buddhism is also associated with eastern India from where it entered southern Tibet. Much discussion on Tantric teachings of various kinds took place in Kashmir and Tibet. Tantric themes can be recognized in the late murals in Dunhuang and the Yulin caves. This marks its arrival in Central Asia.

Yet another and different variety of Buddhism was now popular in China and this was Chan Buddhism, the term Chan derived from the Sanskrit dhyana, the Buddhism that focused on meditation. The birth of Chan Buddhism is associated with the earlier arrival of scholars such as Bodhidharma, but its evolution incorporated a few aspects of Daoism and other belief systems then prevalent in China. This school critiqued some of the dependence on scholarship and texts and gave greater attention to other sources of knowledge. There would have been active disputations or agreements in the discussions at centres such as Dunhuang. An unsurprising change is that persons from India or of Indian origin gradually begin to be depicted with Chinese features. This 'localization' as it were in representing significant persons is common to all religions. The Gandharan Buddha, for example, has a different physiognomy when compared to the Buddha from Mathura or Amaravati.

The early centuries of the second millennium AD saw the spread of the Mongols over a significant part of Eurasia in the form of the Mongol empire. It was a period of frequent raids in various directions associated with Genghis Khan, and perhaps the gentler image of Kublai Khan in the thirteenth century. The next century saw similar raids by Timurlane. In some ways, the empire was too large to survive as a unit nevertheless its stamp continued, although there were many Khanates. This was the time of the Great Horde, the Great Khans such as the Chagatais who spread to various regions. Interestingly, the latter part of the second millennium witnessed the major empires of Asia as being of Mongol and Timurid ancestry: Safavid, Ottoman, Mughal, Yuan.

The parts of Central Asia that were involved in the trade routes discussed above present complex pictures of many layers of patterns of living and intriguing juxtapositions of cultures. The nomads long seen as barbarians by some emerge as role players in a complicated series of relationships. Among the nomadic groups there were some that roamed the wide, open spaces searching for pastures to feed their vast herds, and others that had reasonably complex cultures which included seasonal interdependence between sedentary, nomadic, and semi-nomadic groups. Sometimes they would be intruding into the lives of settled populations. Major migratory movements and the occasional raids on the oases seem to coincide with new recognizable patterns of exchange and trade along the oases routes. A differentiation has to be made between migratory movements and raids or invasions. Migrations among the nomads initially led to a shift in peoples and settlements, but when they were transmuted into raids and even invasions, their arrival however temporary was traumatic, as their looting was disastrous.

The sedentary populations seem to come alive with an initial gift-exchange and an eventual evolution of a market-exchange with the nomads and regional militia safeguarding the trade. With merchants travelling along the routes and the volume and value of goods increasing there was an obvious need for change. Cultural patterns have to change but they can best change if there is a pivot. Does Buddhism in its many manifestations provide that pivot? Buddhism extended its reach from Central Asia and the oases settlements into China itself and the cultural patterns mutated, especially in the negotiations with existing belief systems and patterns of living. In the process a range of Buddhist sects emerged as they did earlier in the homeland of the religion, and as they inevitably do in all successful religions. However, the balance seems to have changed from the first to the second millennium AD. Buddhism declined in Central Asia in the second millennium but became powerful further east and in South-east Asia.

At the end of the first millennium AD, the lands and peoples that had been drawn into the Silk Routes trade were now open to other trading networks as well, including more intensive trading within each segment. Identities in frontier regions are never stable and static, as they change frequently. Xinjiang, for example, would identify with changes in Central Asia when looking westwards and with changes in Xi'an and central China when looking eastwards. Populations would be mixed in areas bordering Tibet or in the oases along the routes. The maritime route that linked Eurasia was becoming more and more widely used with trade less segmented since some ships traversed the Indian Ocean. New economic outlets and demands were coming into force turning commercial interests to other directions. Almost repeating the pattern of the early first millennium AD, was the entry of Islam into the areas that had hosted the earlier trade and been prominent in the arrival of Buddhism. In the second millennium AD, Buddhism slowly lost its patronage and the sites of its worship gradually declined or were replaced by the presence of other religions.

The discovery of Dunhuang by European scholars and others in the nineteenth century brought home with greater force what had earlier been a faint recognition of the importance of Central Asia to the history of Eurasia, thus changing the perception of what Europe had earlier regarded as the back of beyond and unimportant. It now moved into focus with the revelation of its pivotal role in history in the trade between Asia and Europe in the first two millennia AD. The nagging insistence of some scholars was that there was now a difference in the perception of the history of the region, that highlighted the contacts between India and China and the changing histories of the many states that constituted what came to be called Central Asia.

This coincided with what has come to be called 'the Great Game'. The expansion of Czarist Russia into Central Asia, which was to become its colonized 'Orient' brought Russian power threateningly close to India. This disturbed the British who were anxious to keep the Russian expansion at bay in Central Asia. Reconnaissance and diplomatic moves began in the. territories that lay between the two dominating powers. British frontier policy was an attempt to keep the tribal peoples in these areas in a perpetual state of political uncertainty with rumours and counter-rumours and occasional skirmishes keeping them occupied and allowing for convoluted diplomacy on the part of all. Spies and double agents criss-crossed the region. Inevitably there developed a growing interest in the histories of these territories and a search for historical sites, a search that sometimes could provide a political foothold. Central Asia with its vast grasslands and its nodal urban centres was unfamiliar terrain to the many explorer-diplomats who traversed the region, nevertheless it was felt that it had to be 'opened up'.

The major thrust of European interest dates to the early years of the twentieth century. The Swedish explorer Sven Hedin travelled in the area and wrote about it. Scholarly interest, however, increased with the visit of archaeologist Marc Aurel Stein. The dramatic story of 1907 came with the discovery of manuscripts and paintings secreted away in a cave dating to the eleventh century. A Daoist priest, Wang Yuanlu, had taken it upon himself to maintain the caves that were still accessible. Whilst cleaning Cave 17, one of the walls collapsed and revealed another hidden cave that was stuffed with scrolls and manuscripts. Stein persuaded the priest to sell a vast number to him for a pittance and took these back to India and Britain. The scrolls and manuscripts had been well-preserved owing to the dry climate of the region and this nurtured the possibility of more being discovered. The manuscripts were written in the languages of the original texts as well as those used in the region. So some were written in Chinese, Sanskrit, and Gandhari Prakrit; and others in Khotanese, Tocharian, Sogdian, Uyghur, Mongolian, Tibetan, and even a few in Hebrew. They were either transla-tions of the Buddhist texts or else were letters, accounts, contracts, admin-istrative orders, and matters pertaining to the monasteries. These many languages involved many scripts, and this might suggest that those working in these towns would have been multilingual both in speaking and writing. The manuscripts and paintings were stored, and the cave bricked up in the eleventh century presumably because of some threat. It was truly an exten-sive library of more than 40,000 manuscripts—an impressive comment on monastic activities, religious, and secular, at Dunhuang. Stein recognized the imprint of both India and China in this region and named it Serindia (Seres/China + India).

Once the news got around, there was a scramble, not just to study the site but to also tear away some of the murals and bring them to museums in the West. The photographs taken by the team of Paul Pelliot (the French Sinologist and Orientalist) in 1908–09 were useful and are sometimes the only source today of knowing what was on a particular wall. But there were others also interested in the site such as Albert von Le Coq, Albert Grünwedel, and Kozmi Otani. The American archaeologist and art historian Langdon Warner destroyed some of the murals and sculptures in trying to tear them off the walls and transport them to a museum in the West. The search for antiques also introduced the Western art market to Central Asia. It was, therefore, important to have access to strategic places. The Russians and the British were playing chess with the area and the Chinese, Indians, and Iranians were softly nudging their moves.

Efforts were made by successive Chinese governments to preserve and study the site, but this had to wait until later in the twentieth century. A small research institute came up in 1944 but the more serious one was the Dunhuang Institute for Cultural Research established in 1951. The Research Academy was set up in 1987. The International Dunhuang Project was founded in 1994 and a bigger Research Academy in 2007. The former was concerned with locating and correlating the manuscripts, scrolls, and paintings found in the caves, which had got dispersed over three continents. With the collecting of the documentation and the research on the art, the study of these sites of Buddhist cave monasteries and shrines, such as those at Maijishan and Dunhuang and other connected sites, came into its own.

References Cited

FELTHAM H. 'Encounter with a Tiger Traveling West'. *Sino-Platonic Papers,* 2012, p. 231, pp. 1–29.

FRANKOPAN, P. *The Silk Roads: A New History of the World.* New York: Vintage Books, 2016.

HANSEN, V. *The Silk Road: A New History.* New York: Oxford University Press, 2012.

KLIMBURG-SALTER, D., et. al. *The Silk Route and the Diamond Path: Esoteric Buddhist Art on the Trans-Himalayan Trade Routes.* Los Angeles: UCLA Art Council, 1982.

———. *The Kingdom of Bamiyan: The Buddhist Art and Culture of the Hindu Kush.* Naples: Instituto Universitario Orientale,1989.

LIU XINRU. *Ancient India and Ancient China: Trade and Religious Exchanges, AD 1–660,* New Delhi: Oxford University Press,1988.

———. *Silk and Religion: An Exploration of Material Life and the Thought of People, AD 600-1200,* New York: Oxford University Press, 1998.

———. *The Silk Road in World History.* New York: Oxford University Press, 2010.

MILLWARD, J. A. *The Silk Road: A Very Short Introduction.* New York: Oxford University Press, 2013.

NEELIS, J. *Early Buddhist Transmission and Trade Networks: Mortality and Exchange within and beyond the Northwestern Borderlands of South Asia.* Leiden and Boston: Brill, 2011.

NING QIANG. *Art, Religion and Politics in Medieval China: The Dunhuang Cave of the Zhai Family.* Honolulu: Unversity of Hawai'i Press, 2004.

QI XIAOSHAN and Wang Bo. *The Ancient Culture in Xinjiang along the Silk Road.* Urumqi: Xinjiang People's Publishing House, 2008.

RASCHKE, M. G. 'New Studies in Roman Commerce with the East'. *Aufsteig und Neiderganag der Romanischer Welt.* Berlin, 1978.

RUSSELL-SMITH, L. *Uyghur Patronage in Dunhuang: Regional Art Centres on the Northern Silk Road in the Tenth and Eleventh Centuries.* Inner Asian Library Series, Leiden and Boston: Brill, 2005.

SEN. T. *India, China, and the World: A Connected History.* New Delhi: Oxford University Press, 2018.

STEIN, M. A. *Ruins of Desert Cathay: Personal Narrative of Explorations in Central Asia and Westernmost China.* Cambridge: Cambridge University Press, 1912.

TUCKER J. *The Silk Road: Central Asia, Afghanistan and Iran: A Travel Companion.* London and New York: I. B. Tauris and Co. Ltd., 2015.

UTZ, D. A. *A Survey of Buddhist Sogdian Studies.* Tokyo: The Reiyukai Library, 1978.

WHITFIELD, R. et. al. *Cave Temples of Mogao: Art and History on the Silk Road.* New York: Oxford University Press, 2000.

WHITFIELD, S. *Life Along the Silk Road.* Berkeley: University of California Press, 2015.

——— and U. Sims-Williams (eds). *The Silk Road: Trade, Travel, War and Faith.* London: British Library, 2004.

YANG XIN et. al. *Three Thousand Years of Chinese Painting.* New Haven: Yale University Press, 1997.

ZURCHER, E. *The Buddhist Conquest of China: The Spread and Adaptation of Buddhism in Early Medieval China.* Sinica Leidensia, No. 2, 1959.

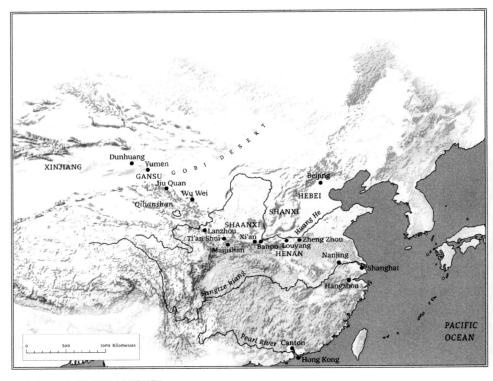

THE ROUTE OF THE JOURNEY

PRELUDE TO THE JOURNEY

The story of my visit to China begins in London in April 1957.

The phone rang in the late evening. Anil de Silva, whom I knew but slightly, was ringing from Paris. She was Sri Lankan, an art historian, and a friend of my brother and sister-in-law—Romesh and Raj Thapar—as well as a number of people active in the world of writers and artists in Bombay, such as Mulk Raj Anand, and with some of whom I had a passing acquaintance through my brother. Her field of study was Buddhist art history. That was in the 1940s when I was still in my teens and anxious to get a taste of the big, wide world, so different from the cossetted cantonment culture in which I had been brought up. Anil had subsequently moved to Paris, where she was now settled, and was focusing on studying Buddhist art. I was then a student at London University working on my PhD, and had occasionally helped her with minor research on the Buddha image for her book on the Buddha, and through this became acquainted with her.

Anil spoke excitedly on the phone about how she had received an invitation from an organization in China in response to her application to do a study for a month or so each at two Buddhist cave sites in China. She had suggested Maijishan and Dunhuang. Her proposal, addressed to the Chinese authorities, had the support of K. M. Panikkar, then ambassador of India to France. Panikkar's recent book, *Asia and Western Dominance*, had been much discussed and acclaimed in Asian countries. Anil's proposal was accepted and she received an invitation to spend three months or a little more in China accompanied by a photographer and a research assistant. The invitation was from the Society for Cultural Relations with Foreign Countries of the People's Republic of China. The society was to host the entire visit. Anil had already spoken to the photographer she wanted, Dominique

Darbois, who had agreed to come. She was now ringing me to find out if I would join them on the project as a research assistant.

The proposition was not just a surprise but was also such a windfall in some ways that I became silent for a moment, unable to reply. I was then on a research fellowship from London University, working on my PhD thesis on Ashoka, the Mauryan emperor, and was halfway through it. I explained to Anil that much as I would like to join the project, I was involved in my own research, and that since it was not connected to Buddhist cave sites in China, I would have to confer with my research supervisor, Professor A. L. Basham, as to whether I could take so much time off. So I told her that I would call her the next evening.

Needless to say, I was awake the whole night trying to decide on what to do. I was nowhere near being a specialist in Chinese Buddhist art, but nor was I a complete novice. I had come to London in late 1953 to do a BA Hons. in history, specializing in ancient Indian history at the School of Oriental and African Studies of the University of London (SOAS). SOAS had specializations in all the branches of Asian history and in the course of the first few months, the wider world of Asian history slowly unfolded in my consciousness. I was quite unfamiliar with the East Asian world. I had come from the curriculum of the Raj, and we had been exposed only to Indian and British history. We knew little about Asian history or, for that matter, the history of other continents, and more so their pre-modern history, a situation that remains largely uncorrected to this day. Only a few universities taught brief courses in the modern history of other countries. Discovering the history of China and Japan for the first time was almost a startling experience.

I had heard about a one-year course in Chinese art and archaeology that was being given at the Courtauld Institute of Art. In order to remedy my ignorance, I decided to take it, as it seemed a comfortable way of getting acquainted with an area of Asia comparable to the subcontinent and about which I knew so little. It meant one evening lecture a week and some reading to go with it. I decided I would just sit in on the lectures, do the reading and aim at merely scraping through the exam at the end, since my purpose was limited to being generally informed about the subject without being a specialist. The thought that I might actually go to China and be able to use this little bit of knowledge never occurred to me as it was the most unlikely event to happen at that point. And now it was possibly happening.

The next morning, I rushed off to discuss the invitation with Professor Basham. I approached the subject rather tremulously as I had been scolding myself for not concentrating on the thesis, leave alone considering the possibility of setting it aside for some months. Professor Basham heard me out and then asked why I was hesitating in taking a decision. It was, he said, the chance of a lifetime and I should not let it pass. The thesis, he thought, could be set aside for a short while and then I could return to it when I got back. So without another thought I decided to accept Anil's invitation and rang her soon after, so as to be sure that I did not have time to change my mind. I asked her if she wanted any preparatory work to be done and she said this would not be necessary beyond some limited reading. She essentially wanted me to be there to record what we saw and whatever discussions took place with others at these sites. I did, however, take time off from my own research to read up on the sites preparatory to the visit.

The two sites we would be working on, as I've mentioned earlier, were Maijishan and Dunhuang. Maijishan, at the time, was virtually unknown to the world, apart from the couple of monks who lived there, and the Chinese archaeological department. Over the last fifty years, it has attracted much attention and has now become a popular tourist site. Dunhuang was better known being a far more important site and having been visited by a few Sinologists and art historians from Europe and the US, who first came to know of it at the end of the nineteenth century. The site had been written about and there were a few publications. The next three months were spent in high anticipation and intensive reading. We set off in July when I joined Anil and Dominique in Paris, from where we flew to Moscow via Prague, and from there to Beijing (or Peking as it was then called). So the 'diary' of the trip begins with setting out on the journey. The entries were sometimes written on the same day and sometimes a few days later. The text that follows is essentially a transcription of the diary, barring a few sentences added to clarify a statement.

1
The Journey Begins

I should begin now to write my impressions and thoughts, as I am at Les Invalides, the international airport in Paris and with half an hour to go, before Anil and Dominique arrive and the air-travel formalities start. I feel exhausted at the mere thought of the weight I shall have to carry in my hands, on my shoulders, and in my coat pockets. Obviously, it was wise of me to have brought a reversible coat, as that gives me extra pockets into which I can stuff more things, such as a sari or two. Since I mainly wear saris it might be a bit of a nightmare to be working in cave sites enveloped in billowing yards of silk. Did I ever say that the sari was an impractical garment? Undoubtedly it is the best piece of clothing to pack—it breaks my heart though to have to stuff a sari into my coat pocket when I'm taking two half-empty suitcases, simply because the photographic equipment is so heavy. We decided that we would have to make this adjustment since it was virtually impossible to get rolls of good quality film and such like in China.

Airports have become amazingly like railway stations, people walk about with such a casual air. Maybe this is what I think because I am still used to India where to travel by air is as yet something unusual and exciting. But here in the waiting areas at the air terminal everything we associated with railway platforms—benches scattered all over, stalls selling magazines and useless knick-knacks—has been transferred to the airport, bar the ice-cream stall, but I'm sure even that will soon be here.

They are continually making announcements about passengers to Zurich, Stockholm, Rome, etc., but nothing for those going to Moscow via Prague. I wonder if I am really going. And then onto Beijing, and from there deep into the interior. I should just be able to sit back and say—it's just one of those things. But it isn't because it seems so implausible.

PRAGUE—AT THE AIRPORT EN ROUTE TO MOSCOW

The announcement for Prague and Moscow was finally made.

Here I am now, sitting at the Prague Air Terminal, cooling my heels—beginning to feel somewhat frayed. The new, much-advertised and marvellous Soviet plane that is to take us to Moscow is already an hour-and-a-half late. They say it has got stuck in the mud and they are trying to extricate it—some job that. We've been going from place to place in the airport like three pack-asses, absolutely laden with things, cameras, cameras and more cameras, overnight bags, large bundles of books and papers, strapped together with bits of string—not to speak of our overcoat pockets which are bulging with saris, underwear, and what-not. I feel this is perhaps a bit blasphemous. In places where the sari is comparatively unknown it should be presented with great elegance, as the garment of the exotic, the indolent, the unobvious, the newly awakening East. Instead, we look like over-burdened mules wrapped in folds of cloth, since Anil is also in a sari.

But I forgot that the sari is an indicator as well. Sitting in the far corner are two other Indian women. We were told on enquiry that they are part of the entourage of the famous Indian theatre actor and film star Prithviraj Kapoor and his equally famous and glamorous son, the actor Raj Kapoor. They seem to be quiet, subdued women, dressed in beautiful white silk, seemingly feeling a little out of place, perhaps because they have been neglected and are unused to airports.

More announcements, while we strain to catch the one single word of hope—Moscow. But people shuffle out to catch planes to Paris, Zurich, Athens, and heaven knows where, yet our plane remains unmoved. There is a Japanese woman sitting by me at the table. We spent ten minutes smiling at each other and eventually decided to talk. Alas, she knows only Japanese and I know no Japanese. We tried everything, signs, sketches, sounds—my pièce de résistance was when I managed to kind of sketch something resembling a collection of women, a hint of a sort of Women's Congress, on a piece of paper and she threw up her hands in joy and nodded violently—yes, yes, that was the purpose of her visit to Moscow. That was too much for me, so we relapsed into silence after that.

Half an hour later—they announced that the delay was due to bad weather at Moscow airport, so we would have to wait another two-and-a-half hours. We are going to be served dinner. I suppose dinner will consist of salami, more salami, and more salami with plum jam. I've just been downing salami rolls with apple juice, so I'm not sure I could take any more.

It's pelting with rain outside. I suppose three hours later we will be told we have to stay here overnight. Not that I would mind very much, but if we are going to Prague I would rather go now and see something of it. They have a lovely little cinema for passengers in transit. I went in hoping to relax, but it was a tourist publicity film, all about Czechoslovakia. I saw some lovely animals and pretty girls and manly youths and came out. We're going to have nightlife in this place soon. A French family going to Moscow have opened their bag and produced a portable radio, which they have tuned to Radio Luxembourg, and a young African who has produced his radio in another part of the room has tuned to the BBC news. It sounds quite incongruous and very distant.

Everyone has become friendly. Until half an hour ago we were all sitting at separate tables, looking sourly across at each other. Now people are smiling and moving about, speaking in a complete mixture of languages. I suppose the situation is analogous to the desert island. I shall soon be settling down to the book I am reading, James Joyce's *Ulysses,* unless of course, the bar makes everything even more informal and we start dancing after dinner! Or start singing community songs and folk songs. It would be interesting to find out the backgrounds of all these various people, in fact it would be such good material for a novel—or a film. The Indian film-star family just arrived from India. Fancy bumping into them here, and fancy spending a whole evening at the airport, stranded, together with them. The son is very much the matinee idol. He is a disappointment in 'real life', not nearly enough glamour, but the father is a real old-timer. Couldn't mistake him anywhere. He has real nobility of movement, très distingué, an actor of quality even if he occasionally hams it a bit, and that he is large in build no doubt gives him the right to assert at least a hint of superiority.

There is also the little Burman who has been very helpful in carrying some of our bits and ends. He's going to the Festival at Moscow. He's training to be an aircraft engineer at London and speaks broken English. This afternoon, sitting behind me on the plane from Paris to Prague, I had a detailed commentary, droned into my ears from the seat behind me, about the pitching, rolling and yawing of planes, and all the technical information of pressurized cabins and pressurized wheels. A couple of Englishmen, also off to the festival, have been appropriately aloof all evening, smoking pipes and looking bored by the whole proceedings. Suddenly there are sounds of the 'Volga Boatmen' on the radio. That's all that remained to provide an atmosphere. I wonder if it is coming from Moscow, perhaps being broadcast specially to console us. A tall, pale-looking, dark-haired Brazilian and his wife have been particularly cheerful about the travel. He's going on a 'Chemin-de-fer' delegation and his only concern is that his friends will come to meet him at Moscow airport and not find him there. His Spanish is flat and voluble—alas, hardly any one of us can understand it. A group of obviously sardonic-looking characters at the far end are some that remain untapped. They can wait till after dinner.

I have just heard a couple of people in the entourage of the film stars arguing over the merits and demerits of what they referred to as Eisenstein's *Storm over Asia*. This is agonizing. Would they think it rude if I gently pointed out to them that the film was not by Sergei Eisenstein, but by Vsevolod Pudovkin, and that the two techniques are so different that one can't confuse them. But then those in the profession have the liberty perhaps to be what we outsiders might think of as rather confused.

I could go on and on, but I must stop. I see now why it can be so profitable to sit in a French café for an entire day and just write. There's so much to write about. Another person, who looks Latin American, is beginning to warm up to the African. They look earnest, without being missionaries. I suppose some of the others must be looking at me, equally amused, and must be wondering who I am, sitting at a table with a white tablecloth spread across it, surrounded by cameras and bags of various shapes and sizes, and writing away. Surely, is that all she can find to do? What is she writing about so furiously?

Anil has been consoling me (as if I need consolation) and saying that such delays often happen. Now I feel the adventure has really started, I really am going. Strangely, the Voice of America is coming through on the loudspeaker in this area! This is no doubt the right background against which to hear it! The Voice of America beamed to the countries behind the iron curtain. Poor miserable propagandists. Can such things ever be excused by claiming that the Voice is spreading the Truth? It sounds so crude, so apparently an untruth. Unfortunately, one can't even be puritanical about these things; the moulding of public opinion seems to have become entirely unethical.

We've just finished a curious meal of unrecognizable cold cuts served with a variety of pickled fruit and vegetables. It was such a business trying to explain the menu to the Japanese lady and helping her select what she might eat. Since doing this, I have been debating with myself as to whether it is foolish, to travel in countries without an inkling of their languages, or whether it is bravery. There is often only a thin line that separates courage from being foolhardy. The latter can be instant whereas the former requires thinking through. The coffee was wonderful and I am now back at the table with the white tablecloth, in the company of another young Burman and a Madame Albe, both of whom have little conversation. But I am enjoying smoking my black Sobranie. A black Sobranie can give immense pleasure, apart from the aesthetic pleasure of smoking a faintly scented black cigarette. I shall keep the box carefully.

It is now 9 p.m. or 11 p.m., Moscow time. We shall soon know if we are ready to depart. Fancy arriving in Moscow at 1 a.m. Here I was looking forward to sleep—and a good night's sleep at that. I should have listened to my mother's advice and slept endlessly last week in London.

And China? What about China? Waiting for the flight to take off, I've been thinking about my exposure to things Chinese in my earlier years and the impressions formed by these. The worrying thing is that I didn't have any strong impressions about these. It was all a bit vague. As a child I imbibed the ridiculous stories about the Chinese that were fostered in India, no doubt by the Raj. It was the land where the sly, slit-eyed, Mongoloid-featured people lived, the land of mystery and strangeness, typifying the unknown, where people were said to disappear, kidnapped by suspicious-looking others. All because we read fiction written for European children and adolescents.

We in India knew nothing better about our eastern neighbours and had no other fiction about them to counter the image created in popular school-girls' magazines, or films such as *The Keys of the Kingdom*. The European missionaries and the converts to Christianity were always the goodies trying to bring clarity to the minds of those Chinese who performed weird rites and had barbarian values because they were Daoists or Buddhists. Or else, at a later age, one read the more grown-up fiction of adventurers travelling across the vast miles and into the interior, of treasure-seekers, geographers, engineers building bridges and railways, of revolutionaries organizing partisans or escaping from the Japanese, of art historians anxious to bring back objects and manuscripts for museums in Europe and America, etc., and it was always the same story—travelling in overcrowded trains, arriving at villages terrorized by local bandits, and fighting the hardship of being frequently caught in dust storms—this apart from the usual clichés that are used with careless abandon about the inefficient organization of administration in Oriental countries, the overriding powers of their bureaucracy, and all the subtle means that have to be used to try and obtain some degree of efficiency.

As a child, I was terrified by the dragon, to me the most frightening of all decorative art-design, the dragon with large, open jaws belching fire, its fearful fangs, its large claws with nails that seem to come alive. It was the same everywhere, on rugs and carpets, on vases, in embroidery, in lacquer work, in fact on anything even remotely Chinese; even on the silk brocades which the Chinese of the 1930s took around to sell, from house to house.

Things Chinese were familiar only to a limited extent in our lives. As far as I remember, there were three associations—the pedlar doing the rounds selling fine silks and embroidered clothes, always on a bicycle with a neat bundle at the back. The bundle had small bundles within, all of carefully folded material and clothing. Housewives with a free half-hour would ask him to open the bundles and then after seeing them all would buy a small length of cloth, for which the man gratefully accepted the money and pedalled off. Where did all the Chinese silk come from? Hong Kong? Many an upper middle-class Indian young woman had her undergarments for her trousseau made from Chinese silk bought from the man on the bicycle.

Then there were the Chinese shoemakers. Every large city had a couple of these, who made excellent shoes with good leather and charged a good price. Nevertheless, it was considered fashionable by the middle class to have custom-made shoes made by the Chinese man. There were also the

Chinese restaurants—there was a Nanking in every city, with dishes of sweet and sour meats, noodles, corn and chicken soup, fried rice, and American chop suey. This was not really authentic Chinese food as much of it was made to suit the Indian palate. But once in a while families would eat out at a Chinese restaurant and this was thought of as a special outing.

One or two cities that were centres of trade often had a small Chinatown—an area where the Chinese lived in a style that was characteristically their own, reproducing to some extent the ambience of their homeland, fuelled by the initial dream of some among the migrants of returning to their homeland in a blaze of wealth and status. Those that ventured into such places always raved about the quality of the food that was served in the special eating places in such ghettoes, and it being more authentic than what one ate in the Chinese restaurants.

And then the picture changed somewhat. I remember Poona (as Pune was then known) in the war years in my early teens. I was just becoming aware of the Sino-Japanese war, and then World War II. The story that enthralled us all and was made into a film—*Dr Kotnis ki Amar Kahani*—was the story of the Indian doctor who went to China to work among the wounded. The name of Sun Yat-sen and Chiang Kai-shek became familiar to us. Then shortly thereafter there was talk about the existence of a Communist party in China with the two names that were constantly mentioned—Mao Zedong and Zhou Enlai. Like others, I too was suspicious of American interventions in Asia, and by extension Chiang Kai-Shek's nationalism was thought of as tempered by too great a personal ambition. Those who argued in support of him, of which they were many, maintained that this was present among many of the most ardent nationalists.

This was my contact with China. Later, a few years after 1949, the New China became the subject of conversation that always began with the question as to why the second socialist revolution occurred in China, given its Confucian and Buddhist background. That was when I read Edgar Snow's *Red Star Over China*, the classic on the early guerrilla movement in China that evolved into a revolution, and I became familiar with a few names and events. It was a slow process. One met little that had anything to do with what was called Chinese civilization as described in the histories of premodern China. This I became conscious of, and of the Chinese as a set of cultures essential to the definition of Asia, and to be taken as seriously as the Islamic and Indic cultures, after coming to London and being at SOAS.

The course on Chinese art and archaeology made me realize the immensity of the cultures of Asia different from the Indo-Islamic world. The impressive imprint of Buddhism on Chinese art and thought took me completely by surprise. I had seen plenty of ghastly little statues of 'the laughing Buddha' in the homes of friends of my parents but had never asked about them. Even the objects of pre-Buddhist times in China, such as the bronze ritual vessels, had some forms that appealed to me aesthetically although I never grasped in any detail what their ritual use may have been. There were other objects that left me totally perplexed.

But what was an absolute magnet and drew me unhesitatingly to the Chinese aesthetic was the ideographic script. I was fascinated by the way the forms were drawn with specific brushstrokes and the associated ideas that determined the forms. This was not only an experience of a completely new system of writing but I saw each ideograph as a painting. Needless to say, I was encouraged in this interest by friends who taught Chinese at SOAS and I attempted reading Chinese. I did not get too far as I was diverted by trying to understand the form and shape of each ideograph rather than its meaning. It is a curious thing about calligraphy. Why do some cultures nurture it to the point of writing in virtually abstract forms whereas others keep it elementary with just a few deviations in the forms? Some scripts, of course, do not lend themselves to complex designs.

But China remains at this moment, somewhat distant, something I want to be better acquainted with, but which I fight shy of because I'm not sure that I can get to know it better. Is it perhaps too different?

2
Moscow

The plane was finally released from the mud and arrived at Prague. We boarded it and left for Moscow. I don't think I have ever been in such incongruous surroundings. It takes away from the pleasure of all the romantic ideas that sprang to my mind this morning. Driving into Moscow at 3 a.m. can be such a wonderful illusion—it's like the backdrop to an opera or ballet, of *Petrushka* or *Firebird*. The avenue of trees, the hint of a blue-green sky just prior to sunrise with an occasional spangle of stars and the soft suffused light of a partial moon—so ethereal that I almost resented each bus or truck on the road and wanted it to be a reindeer-driven troika. The Kremlin was glowing with its red-brick wall. Then the hotel, and that startled me. The outside is typical of a certain phase of Soviet architecture. The dull, square concrete variety—tier upon tier and long lines with little baubles—like the Palace of Culture in Warsaw which was the location of the Youth Festival in 1955, and the Ministry of Communications here—all forbidding structures. The lines don't even have the elegance of a perpendicular.

The heavy wooden front door was opened by a smiling and aged man who greeted us with an air of 'another lot coming at a ridiculous hour'. The night air had been cool and fresh but as we entered, I felt the stuffiness of closed rooms hitting us. It was a large room like the hall of audience in palaces with pale marble floors and columns—thick massive columns in dark grey marble. After a moment, I began to feel as if I had entered a mosque, but quickly saw it as a Greek Orthodox church. There it was, of course, the diluted Byzantine all over. We were conducted through thickly carpeted corridors bursting with ornamentation and arrived at last at a room, a small room with two beds. Another thick carpet of Persian design, large windows that were almost impossible to open, draped with tree-green linen curtains, heavy and clumsy. A large upright sofa upholstered in floral velvet of deep red, a large carved wooden table and a cupboard with doors of framed mirrors. A writing table with a marbletop and marble accessories in the way of inkstand, penholders, etc. Chairs all over. The beds were draped in Chinese brocade bedcovers and so were the pillows (which were half the size of the bed, literally). In addition, there were two bedside tables. We were too exhausted to think of anything except an initial misgiving, that all Moscow may be at this level and that our fairy-tale drive through the city at that hour was just a dream.

I am coming to Moscow in a state of much anticipation. It is my first visit to the Soviet Union. I am seeing it through a haze of contending images— some based on my reading of Tolstoy and Chekhov, both of whom I much admire, interfaced with my reading on the Russian revolution that initially I endorsed and then began to be uncertain about. I realize that this interface does not make it easy to understand where I am and what I am observing.

Breakfast arrived next morning, brought in by a well-proportioned Slavonic-looking maid all in black with a frilly white apron. I opened my eyes and seeing her beamed at her, in fact flashed one of my most brilliant smiles—her face had a deadpan expression and she looked straight through me as if I had been a stuffed pig. Fortunately, the other maids in the Leningradskaya Hotel were different and smiled cheerfully—the lift girls were a particularly happy brood. Looking out of the window the first thing I saw was a knife-grinder—a real one with a large wheel busily grinding knives. I hadn't seen one such since I left India. I sat on the windowsill in a yellow sari, observing a Muscovite and his wife going by. I wondered whether there would be any curiosity about the hotel and its resident. But no one looked up. They just went on walking past, up and down the street.

During the day, the city makes a distinct impression of wideness and open space. The roads are very broad and are flanked by tall imposing buildings. Some of the post-revolution architecture I found too cloying. It goes up in long lines with fancy bits at the top. Always the same frame-work—the central portion rising higher than the side wings. It becomes monotonous—some of the simpler buildings are pleasanter though plain. It is not an elegant city except for certain sections such as those with late eighteenth and early nineteenth-century buildings often associated with literary figures. For the rest, it is an immense city, strong and powerful but with much of the self-consciousness of a new capital, a city suddenly coming into importance—in short, very much like New Delhi in spirit. The lifeblood of cities like Paris and London is not noticeable all over Moscow, but then we were restricted to being within a certain area. But perhaps it is unfair to judge it on so short an acquaintance and especially to compare it with West European capitals. Their counterparts in Russia would more likely be Leningrad (as St Petersburg was then known) rather than Moscow. New buildings going up and rapid construction in every area is quite apparent—large blocks of tenements and apartments, again following the same design occur at every other corner—more so, of course, outside the city centre.

If only there was a little more imagination in the planning. But we are told that quick construction ensures the early availability of homes for Muscovites, so that matters. We heard later that the architect who had designed the hotel was the subject of great controversy, and that he was finally sacked. But we never could discover what the controversy was about. Fortunately, all the hotels are not the same—the others were more palatable and some quite pleasant.

There are no espresso café in Moscow—a sad lack. I have grown particularly fond of the ones in London and missed them. Two of the restaurants I went to were decorated with window boxes of bright flowers and were quite elegant inside. The few open-air café are pleasant in the sun, fairly cheap and always full to overflowing with all sorts and kinds of people—a good institution.

In the streets people were curious to know who I was and where I was from and whether I liked their city. The sari, of course, intrigued them and whenever I stopped, a small crowd of people would gather around, sometimes to the embarrassment of the friend who was accompanying me—a colonel of the Red Army who was occasionally congratulated on acquiring such an unusual wife! He had actually been officially allotted to us as a chaperone. At the Kremlin, this interest in the sari became a positive nuisance. It was full of tourists from all over Russia and other places and each person with a camera wanted to photograph me—which, of course, tickled my vanity greatly—I felt like a known personality and smiled sweetly at every lens. What bliss—and how satisfied my ego was at the end of two hours. Yes, I have beautiful memories of the Kremlin, and not just of the buildings and their contents. The other two in the party showed infinite patience with this activity.

The women of Moscow can hardly be called elegant. In fact, they display all the characteristics of women who work and do so in a determined way. They are large, well-built with round faces, not much of a smile, and casually dressed. I had the feeling, probably not at all correct, that their attitude to dress is that it is something functional that covers the naked body—as indeed it is. In fact, I have the impression that they are quite conservative about their appearance. The men are similarly conservatively dressed, though on the whole, I would say they are better dressed. We looked in at a fashion parade in one of the large shops. There was to begin with only one model that was good by European standards. The others were very ordinary. Two-thirds of the dresses were again very average in taste and cut. But here too, these dresses were not for the well-to-do who could afford expensive clothing. They were intended for people with small incomes as was also obvious from the audience—and further these dress-shows are held every day so that women can drop in for half an hour just to see what's going on in the fashion world. Some of this contradicts the image that was given of the Bolshevik Revolution. A social and political revolution such as this is supposed to change social attitudes and something like a fashion show would be viewed as far too bourgeois and not presenting the image of a strong working woman.

The Kremlin and its surroundings are one of the more stunning areas in Moscow. Apart from its association with the romance of the revolution and Lenin and Stalin, and the fact that it is the seat of the Russian government, and what I imagine is or could be—it captures the finest spirit of the Byzantine. Of the more prosaic buildings one is a museum where one walks past huge glass cages full of astonishingly impressive objects. The jewelled icons, incredibly rich and decorative, the gold covers of large Bibles, the high coat and boots of Peter the Great (actually his!), the silver-tissue wedding dress of Catherine, pinched at the waist and flowing below, jackets covered with the imperial eagle crest of the Czars, each eye with an imperial glint—beautiful embossed saddles and saddlecloths of the finest woven and embroidered silks, Russian glass, porcelain, and the coronation coaches of the Czars.

It sounds trite when described like this, as I can't describe how luxurious the whole assemblage was—sometimes it is a richness for the sake of richness, again an undercurrent of self-consciousness—a desire to outdo everything by a sheer display of gold and jewels and the finest stuffs that money could buy. I wondered if this was not in some way the embryo of the Leningradskaya Hotel, and that to the eye acquainted with the Byzantine it may not be such a monstrosity after all. And is this what is referred to when it is said that the Byzantine has the thread of 'the Oriental', the luxury linked to Oriental courts, as viewed through European eyes?

We moved on to the Basilica with gold and silver covered domes that really did shine like mirrors in the sun. The walls inside were covered with frescoes—the walls, the ceilings, and even around the columns—not an inch to spare. Those that have not as yet been restored are, by contrast, pale in colour. The agonized look on the faces of the saints made one realize the sorrow of being in the world of martyrs. Did someone say that the Orient accepts suffering more readily than does the Occident? Would one say that this is one among the chief differences between Byzantine Christianity and European Christianity? Christianity and Islam have made martyrdom almost a tenet of their propagation. He who is killed in the cause of the religion becomes a martyr but he who dies in defence of the realm remains just a hero.

The restored frescoes are rich in colour and fit in more easily with the exhibits in the museum and with what I am beginning to think is the Byzantine tradition. However, I don't know how much of all this can be attributed to the Byzantine. I may be completely wrong. The colours are rich but not garish—rather, sadly rich and mellow. Wooden panels cover the walls at a lower level and are completely painted over. Most of them have become so dark owing to the accumulation of dust and lack of cleaning that the outlines of the paintings are hardly visible. Some patches have recently been cleaned and show an intriguing potential. The altars are in every case highly ornamented. In one church the floor was constructed of stones with variegated streaks (like pebbles at the bottom of a river) all polished and worn down to one level by the rubbing of feet walking constantly over them. I could not help thinking all the time that the caves we were going to visit at Dunhuang and the frescoes in the caves of Ajanta were after all not so alien in spirit to the interiors of these chapels. Perhaps a Buddhist of the

Tang Dynasty of China or an Indian of Gupta times would have felt quite at ease in these places.

One of the questions of which I have little knowledge is the cultural composition of the Russian or should one now say, the Slavonic people. They are not uniform, of course. Is the European tradition a little alien to them? To treat them as European, assuming that European is equated with Western Europe, cannot but lead to some misunderstandings. I presume there is much of the Central Asian in them and this tends not to be acknowledged in the West European understanding of that which is Russian. The existence of the Soviet Union complicates this image. Am I stating something that is quite apparent and of which only I was and am unaware? Or am I thinking of Europe only in terms of the Anglo-Saxon and the Teutonic cultures? These would also be different from what are referred to as the Latins? Are the variations in the Soviet Union difficult to perceive because of the imprint of the Soviet system?

To explain the taste in architecture over the last couple of decades as a kind of political nouveau-riche-ism is, I feel, not accurate. Could it be an attempt to imitate the European without internalizing the process that went into the finished product that can be seen in Europe and further west? Is it not so much a different idiom as a somewhat alien one? There was also the need to exaggerate in a sense the achievements of the Revolution through the architectural style of buildings as also in art through Socialist Realism. Not unexpectedly there was some amount of self-conscious declaration of what the Revolution stood for in various forms of life and culture. It gets to be quite complicated.

Moscow was putting on a face as the World Youth Festival was to start in four days, so flags were going up and streamers and buntings. Large posters with peace doves and peace signs—banners with words of welcome, mir and druzba (peace and friendship). Some of the delegations had arrived already, and young girls from Uzbekistan and Azerbaijan flashed around in bright plumage with a touch of the exotic. It reminded me of Warsaw and the Youth Festival there two years ago. It is being said that the 1959 festival will be held in Peking (as Beijing was then known), and the 1961 festival in New Delhi! I doubt it. We stood in a queue for an hour outside the Kremlin in the Red Square amongst various foreign visitors waiting to visit the mausoleum where the embalmed bodies of Lenin and Stalin lie in state. So, this was the famous Red Square—a high turret by the wall of the Kremlin flying the Soviet Flag from where Stalin used to take the salute. Finally, all leaders do so love to stand at historic buildings and take salutes, even those who make revolutions. I wonder what people now feel about Stalin. The Communist Party of the Soviet Union held its twentieth Congress in February 1956. Nikita Khrushchev made a speech in which he denounced the personality cult of Stalin and the resulting tyranny. This unexpected revelation opened up widespread discussion on, and some criticism of, Soviet governance. Were the issues raised discussed in the Soviet Union as widely as they were, for instance, in London? The purpose would be different inside and outside the Soviet Union. Some saw it as sounding the death knell of the Bolshevik Revolution. It will be different here when more information surfaces, as inevitably happens in such situations. That is probably why parades and salutes are so essential to the ego of nations even when they are well-established.

Facing us was the St Basil's Cathedral with its many colourful domes, each a different size and shape, and variously ornamented. Not at all displeasing though, and there was obviously a harmony among the various onion-shaped domes. Opposite the turret and stretching the whole length of the square was the GUM, the state shop of Moscow. A huge building rather Victorian in style, with a grey biscuit-coloured exterior, in sharp contrast to the red of the Kremlin walls opposite, selling practically everything in the market from tins of caviar to bicycles. The windows were surprisingly imaginatively dressed, but then as the colonel explained to me, the Russians are not fond of advertisements, the lack of which, even on city walls and on large hoardings, is quite striking. The GUM is always crowded with an endless stream of shoppers.

Behind us, on the fourth side of the square, was another red-brick building of the last century that now houses a history museum. Indeed, a spot more impregnated with history could hardly have been chosen for such a museum. The queue waited patiently till 12.45 when the mausoleum is opened to the public, everyone standing in an orderly manner in pairs. Some of the faces I recognized as those of people staying at the same hotel.

Apart from the forthcoming festival, Moscow has become quite a cosmopolitan city. Chinese and Indians are easy to spot. In fact, we met people from Bombay and Delhi who are either working in Moscow (in the foreign languages press or radio) or else are briefly visiting. People of multiple kinds float in and out of the hotel lobby, Nepalese youths in flat cotton caps and flapping pyjamas, a Persian dastoor with a pointed beard and high-hat walking with his Russian counterpart, a priest of the Greek Orthodox Church. Going to Moscow will, I fear, soon become as tame in the Eastern world as spending a weekend in Paris.

At 12.45, the procession began to move and twenty minutes later I was in the vault of the simple red-and-black-marble structure which houses the two bodies: architecturally the most convincing monument in modern Moscow. The bodies lie draped within glass containers looking pale and waxen, but not quite corpse-like. Technically they seem to be well preserved and displayed. As for the principle of it, I was undecided before I saw them and came away convinced that it was not conducive to any good. Not because I was repulsed by it—it did not move me violently either way, but it seemed futile to me. Why preserve the dead? The inculcation of the cult of the body of a dead man is surely somewhat dishonest and, more so if it is for political purposes. It is not dignified to try and elevate a man by preserving his corpse. As I left the place, I thought that if there was to be a movement against Lenin and Stalin in the future and that such a movement came to control the city, what would happen to the two bodies. Would they be reburied with due respect or would they meet with a gruesome end? Why embalm them now?

Talking about the personality cult of Stalin, there was not much of 'Comrade Stalin' visible—only pictures of him in offices and that too quiet pictures in not too prominent a position. The cult had already taken a downturn. No one mentioned him unless specially asked. The attitude towards Khrushchev was definitely 'healthy'. In fact, the colonel laughed uproariously when we showed him the Vicky and Abu cartoons on Khrushchev. Not knowing Russian made us complete strangers and we hardly got around to 'talking to the people'.

Further on there were other cult heroes. In the Bolshoi Theatre there is a gallery upstairs which has a small exhibition of oddments connected with the history of ballet in Russia—pictures, portraits, letters, manuscripts, etc. I noticed that there was nothing about Anna Pavlova or Sergei Diaghilev. This disapproval, I think, is being petty-minded. The most impressive thing about the Bolshoi, apart from the red plush and gilt decoration and the vastness of the auditorium and stage, is the complete assortment of people who go there—an assortment, and by this I mean a cross-section of Russian life, such as one would never see at Covent Garden, because the latter excludes anything below the middle class. Here there is no fuss and bother about going to the theatre. There are no décolleté gowns and furs when promenading in the upper galleries on the arm of a dashing officer under the large beautifully cut chandeliers or by the fine lines of classical décor. On the other hand, the flowers flung at the ballerina at the end of the performance and the earthy shouts of 'bravo' make up for the lack of dazzle and finery in dress and ritualistic manners.

Olga Lepeshinskaya as Cinderella gave a very fine performance—well worth a visit to Moscow in itself. The male dancers are better than any I have seen anywhere else, because for the first time I saw them establish the fact that ballet can be as much an expression for a male dancer as for a female. The stage is deep and this depth is utilized in spectacular décor and production—real fountains outside a ballroom, for instance, and actual fireworks—not that these are necessary. The décor is extremely realistic in the sense that every detail is shown, even in the most lavish scenes. The imagination of the spectator can safely be tucked away as far as background and settings go.

After the ballet, we drove to the Sovietsky Hotel for supper: it is thought to be one of the better places in Moscow for wining and dining. The modern building is built over the old gypsy inn of Yar, made famous by Russian drinking songs and gypsy ballads. In the old days, I was told, it was located just outside Moscow, where respectable women of high society, escorted by 'gentlemen', could let their hair down and dine and dance to the wild, throbbing Romany rhythms, or as the song goes:

> Nights of gladness
> Nights of madness
> When the wine was flowing free...
> Coachman, drive to Yar—

There is a Feodor Chaliapin recording of it which a friend of mine had and which I must confess I loved. I wonder if it would be available here.

Now only the emaciated spirit of Yar haunts the walls of the Sovietsky Hotel. In a large hall all in plush and marble with an ornamental dome and ceiling, people dine while an orchestra plays dance music and a few brave couples dance quietly in between the tables. The colonel surrounded by the three of us felt shy and refused to dance. We sat there eating caviar and jellied sturgeon on rye bread and drinking vodka, the latter taken in the traditional style of a gulp. I wondered if this would project me back to the time of Yar—and perhaps I might even hear the gypsy music!

I travelled eagerly in the metro the next day, having heard so much about it. It is grand and spacious and temperature-controlled—and strikingly clean, like all of Moscow, and the trains are comfortable and quick—but there is so much marble in the metro, the floors, the walls, the ceiling, and so much in stucco. It doesn't feel like an underground station any more, but that is probably because I have come to feel one with the grime and cement of the London and Paris metros.

But enough about buildings. We lunched at the Indian embassy on our second day in Moscow. The ambassador is a friend of my father's, so I was introduced to all the guests as General T.'s daughter—so I had to re-introduce myself properly, giving my name to each one in turn when I started talking. But I didn't object. I'm used to it and besides I was too exhausted with visiting the Kremlin and Lenin and Stalin to really care about such trivialities. It was a typical diplomatic occasion. The ambassador spent a few minutes with each guest and said the sort of things he'd said a thousand times before to other guests. The ambassador's wife was charming in asking whether we had had a pleasant stay and been properly looked after.

The long table for lunch was laid out for the twenty-five guests and I sat between an Indian actress, and a professor of philosophy from India. She was in Moscow for a joint Indo-Soviet film currently being shot in Moscow on the adventures of a Russian merchant turned horse-trader, Afanasy Nikitin. He came to India in the fifteenth century, spent a few years mainly in the Bahmani Sultanate, and left quite an interesting account of where he went and what he saw.

When we arrived at Moscow airport to leave for Beijing, we were told that the plane would not leave till 12.30 a.m., as it was two hours late. So I sat crossly on a sofa surrounded by a planeload of bouncing middle-aged Ukrainians who had just arrived, and read a magazine on 'Culture and Life'. I was in a difficult mood, so the other two wisely decided to leave me alone. I didn't particularly like Moscow. I know one can't judge a city by a stay of three crowded days, but my first impression was not very congenial. Perhaps, I was expecting too much. After all, one of the ideas that had floated around us in our teenage years was that the Soviet experience was the setting up of a new kind of society. I recalled the play that we had staged in Poona, J. B. Priestley's *They Came to a City* with its famous lines about the new society: 'Where men and women don't work for machines and money but machines and money work for men and women.' Was this the new world? I wouldn't want to live there for any length of time, though I would not object to visiting the USSR again for a longer period to experience their version of the socialist experiment and observe life at closer range. But I would also want to know more about the Byzantine mind. Maybe I am just obsessive about this.

At last the plane was refuelled and ready. The three of us, loaded with cameras, film, books, bags etc., finally got to our seats. It was the famous fast service from Moscow to Beijing. Very luxurious—the cabin was padded and openings lined with felt, the doors had brocade curtains, and the upholstery was in a soothing grey. The seats were of ample proportions—no doubt to suit Russian sizes—which I found very comfortable. And then the comic opera started. The flight was ten hours in all with two one-hour stops—at Omsk, a drab industrial town, that some of us first heard of through a Tom Lehrer song about the man from Omsk; and then at Irkutsk, a colourful town, slightly hilly, with very friendly people. That left us with gaps of two and two-and-a-half hours. I was collapsing with lack of sleep, so I thought I'd sleep on the plane. But alas, we were flooded with food and drink and every half an hour the hostess, a lively Russian girl would wake me up, smile sweetly and produce an orange, or a glass of wine or dejeuner or a meal— and no amount of explaining on my part in the most painfully thought-out French (the only West European language she understood) made any difference. So eventually I gave up and, smiling sweetly at her, sat and looked out of the window at what was described to me as the aurora borealis—an amazingly impressive sight. I forgave them for waking me up!

The service is said to be comparable to the best anywhere in the world. The pressure on the ears is a bit much each time the plane lands and takes off, but one gets used to that. The plane was beautifully fitted, and the three hostesses were most efficient. The passengers were partly Chinese, the others were big burly men and well-built women, all of whom started smiling at us five minutes after the plane had taken off, and we all smiled back at frequent intervals. The man in front of me was very concerned about my comfort and when the hostess wasn't pestering me with food, he was pressing bars of bitter chocolate on me. The state of my stomach that day was something quite pathetic. At Irkutsk he played chess with one of the Chinese passengers and soon defeated him. Neither knew the other's language so they gaily grunted at each other right through the game. Then he joined us in a walk round the airport, conversing frantically in broken French. I gathered, eventually, what I might have guessed earlier, that he was Polish; in fact, he was a judge of the Polish Supreme Court on his way to Korea to chair the Neutrality Commission.

And so it all dragged on. My anxiety to get to Beijing made the wait far worse.

3

Arrival at Last in Beijing

At last, the plane circled over Beijing. We couldn't see much as it was cloudy. The plane taxied down the runway at Beijing airport amidst a haze of yellow dust. Prior to that I had been straining for half an hour to catch sight of the Great Wall, but I didn't realize that perhaps we were flying too high for us to see it. The airport is unimpressive. Just an ordinary set of large rooms where everybody is bundled in. We never got to the customs area because the representatives of the Society for Cultural Relations received us. We sat down comfortably in a lounge, fanning ourselves and drinking mugs of green tea. The loveliest touch was the presentation of large bouquets of gladioli that, we were later told, is traditional in a Chinese welcome. It does make one feel quite special and particularly welcome.

We were introduced to our interpreter, Mingo Wong, a young woman in her late twenties. She was to travel with us throughout our stay. She was initially shy but soon revealed herself as being forthright, very helpful, and friendly, and all three of us soon became closely attached to her and she became one of our gang. We were to hear jokes about the four women going out on an expedition, and Mingo would enjoy translating the more outrageously funny ones for us. She obviously had her orders to keep us within limits, but in just a few hours we were raring to go here, there, and everywhere, and frequently beyond these limits. What was so impressive was that in her quiet way she often managed to arrange that we could do so.

There is an air of casualness all around which seems quite strange to me—I am too used to the briskness and quick efficiency of European airports—where no one seems to loiter or just sit and stare. There is more movement and bustle even at Indian airports. This may just be a case of too many hands for a job that could be done with less. Nevertheless, we were cleared in a short time . . . I wonder how long it would take an ordinary tourist. Another thing that was quite startling was that the officers all looked so young. Most of them seemed to be barely in their early twenties. Now that I have been here for three days, I find that this is another Chinese character- istic: the average Chinese never looks as old as his or her age, or so it would seem. The casualness of the dress, a shirt or bush-shirt in white and trousers in various shades of blue, adds to the unhurried effect of the general picture.

We drove from the airport passing under a wooden gate newly decorated in red—representing a typical Chinese gateway, rather in the same way as we in India have the Ajanta arch or the Sanchi gateway at the entrance to modern state buildings—and we were on the road to Beijing, a journey of twenty minutes. The gate was simple with turned up ends and had the characters for welcome written across it. I fancy it was put up primarily for the vast number of delegations that seem constantly to be visiting China.

Once on the road I felt I was back in northern India. There was little that was strikingly new and strange in what I saw to begin with. Vast stretches of fields lay on either side of the road, covered with what appeared to be a half-grown crop of maize, interwoven with vegetable patches. The fields stretch all the way to the edge of the city. The road was somewhat dusty. There was no pavement and only the central part was tarred for the use of vehicular traffic. Low hedges walled off the fields from the road. The traffic consisted of cars, but not too many, and many more carts and pedicabs. In India, the cart is drawn by a pair of bullocks and ambles along on the side or the middle of the tarred road. Here the cart is horse-drawn and often a donkey is also harnessed to it, the donkey being slightly in front of the horse. This amused me. There must be some good reason for it that I shall enquire into.

I didn't much like the pedicab, what we called a cycle rickshaw. I sat in one later, but I didn't take to it. To be pulled by a man sweating and puffing on a cycle in front was not so pleasant, apart from my feeling sorry for him having to pull so much weight all the time. But it seems to be very popular in Beijing. I see many women at noon going in them with bags of all shapes, probably returning from the morning's shopping, or in other cases, work. The pedicab might come in quite useful for housewives in Europe. They are, however, not very cheap and the price seems to be calculated not on the distance but the time that it takes. Perhaps we were charged more because we were obviously foreigners and knew no better.

Cyclists are very common, going all over the place and often obstructing other traffic. This again is so similar to Delhi where there are no silence zones for motor horns in the city, because a cyclist can only be warned by the sound of a motor horn, and where there are too many cyclists the horn has to be used. The swarm of cyclists is a pointer to a shortage of public transport. As in Delhi, they seem to move in formation from one traffic light to the next.

It is the melon season so driving into the city we saw large heaps of melons on either side of the road. The watermelons, pyramids of dark green with circles of red in some places where one had been cut, and smaller melons, green or yellow, with a strong fragrance, and also the large Xinjiang melon, which we also get in North India and which we call the sarda. The Chinese variety is green on the outside and white inside whereas the sarda is often yellow on the outside. I was quite delighted at seeing the melons and the baskets of corncobs that the Chinese steam in the sheath. (We roast them over live coals.) Steamed corn has a bland taste. And in between the visions of melons and maize were more clouds of dust. I don't know about sandstorms in the desert, but the outskirts of Beijing certainly have an ample fill of dust. It will take many years of tree planting to eliminate this although a beginning seems to have been made.

The road all along was lined with shops and little huts where people crowded around the door smoking or sat in small groups talking. This was exactly like the outskirts of a large town in India in summer when the evening air is still hot and makes one lethargic. A few young energetic people whizz past on cycles or shout across the road at each other, and for the rest everyone just relaxes. At the end of the day this becomes a part of the evening. Children wander away from the threshold or play in shaded corners or by the drain that runs along the road, their mothers either hastily buying oddments for the evening meal or idly gossiping. The initial shock was that China is so much like India—it is very much an Asian country. I had pretty well no preconceived ideas about China, partly because I was never overly enthused to enquire into Chinese life, and partly because I was mentally too lazy to think beyond a vague 'feeling' about what China may be like. The impact of the physical forms of these simple activities and their similarity with India has been strong. It is an impression that has continued to grow during the week I have already spent here.

In the city the buses look new and efficient. They appear to come frequently but are invariably overcrowded. The Chinese must be a very patient people. I have never yet seen a stampede for a bus, no matter how big the crowd. Trams, much like those in Europe, are dull red and yellow in colour, running through the main thoroughfares and the wider streets. The roads present a great variety of moving forms. Cars are fewer on the roads with many more buses and of course the more occasional horse-cum-donkey cart. I have also seen just a couple of motor scooters. I wish the Chinese had more colourful vehicles. Most of the cars, even if few, are black, dark blue or khaki. A canary yellow or a crimson automobile would light up Beijing's streets. The only flashy cars seem to be those belonging to the embassies, Cadillacs and such like, for most others the cars they use seem to be Russian made or Czech Škodas.

The main streets are generally broad and leave ample space for cyclists to meander along, cyclists being both men and women. There are a far greater number of women cyclists here than in Delhi. Do the 'road Romeos' of Delhi keep women away or are we more conservative when it comes to the mobility of women? The other streets leading off the main streets into the various quarters and sectors are fearfully narrow and as their name implies—hutongs—are really only lanes. They are seldom wide enough for two cars and at the best of times require expert driving, particularly at the right-angled corners.

We drove through the famous legation quarter, once the residential area of foreign legations and to which the Chinese were forbidden entry. After this we arrived at our hotel, the Tsin Chao (or Xin Qiao as it was then known), a six-storeyed building designed in a European office-block style, but not displeasing to look at from the outside. The front entrance had simple gauze doors—to keep the flies and mosquitoes out, as is also done in India. I paused on the doorstep for a moment and wondered if I was going to have an experience similar to that of the Leningradskaya in Moscow. Were we going to live in a museum of pseudo-Ming and Qing interiors? Surely the Chinese had better taste? I entered cautiously and found myself in a spacious hall painted cream and grey with a simple terrazzo floor. On either side of the entrance were counters used by the reception. The further side had the lifts and cloakrooms and there was a central staircase going up. The only distasteful thing was a large clay panel by the staircase, depicting, I assume, 'heroes of labour' being received by Chairman Mao and Co., all done in the style of contemporary Russian Socialist Realism—what some call the Stalin period of Chinese art, which I think is a very appropriate name. I sighed with relief—so far so good.

We were taken up to our rooms: a fair-sized room with two beds, a built-in cupboard, and a bathroom apportioned off. The furniture was of plain brown wood with clean straight lines. I was quite happy with that. The decoration was again cream, grey, and pale shades of natural wood with a single reproduction, a Chinese ink landscape. There was no attempt at being luxurious—just comfortable good taste. There were embroidered bedcovers on the beds, brown embroidery on a cream background—and good Cantonese embroidery too. I discovered afterwards that this hotel was financed by the overseas Chinese and is used mainly for Chinese and foreign visitors. Most delegations are accommodated here. The hotel with a history is the Peking Hotel which looks more ornate on the outside and which I must get around to seeing. Nevertheless, I feel reassured that the Chinese can't go very wrong on this. I am eager now to see the new Asoka Hotel in Delhi that is our equivalent to the Leningradskaya and the Xin Qiao.

In the evening, we dined with Dr and Mrs Cheng Han Sen, who more or less between them edit *China Reconstructs,* a puff for what is going on in China, a publicity magazine for the activities of the government. I was therefore not surprised that being the editor of this magazine, his references to what was happening in China in answer to our questions were all positive. He is an intellectual of the older generation who maintains an implicit faith in the new system, or at least that is how it would seem. He made some intelligent and piercing comments on the Five-Year Plan of India that I was interested to hear—I felt he regarded it more as a healthy rival to the Chinese plan, as we both silently wondered which would win. I questioned him on the recent floods in north-east China that according to press reports in Moscow had damaged the new crop, but he dismissed it as almost a minor occurrence that the government could well handle without the slightest anxiety. This attitude made me suspicious that his optimism was more likely government propaganda.

I find the Chinese intellectuals that I have met so far, reticent. Is it out of politeness that they keep the conversation going along the gentle path of small talk, which I did not expect from those familiar with Marxism when speaking about society in general? Perhaps it also has to do with their being officials and therefore taking acceptable positions, as expected of bureaucrats, I suppose, although there are exceptions. Or did they assume that we, not being sufficiently acquainted with the background, might misunderstand what they say? Or is it preferable for them to keep to small talk since it might be safer than getting into discussions about more significant changes in society and the economy? Perhaps my unending questions are too direct and I am missing the wood for the trees in such encounters.

I have to constantly remind myself that strong states controlled by single parties demand an intellectual no man's land where belief supersedes reality as it were, and I for one have not arrived at that point with regard to any belief. Dr Sen's wife was quiet all evening—not saying much but giving the impression of noticing a great deal. We dined at the International Club, well known in the old days as the meeting place of the foreign community in Beijing. I was again struck by the fact that this was an aspect of contemporary Eurasia, commonly found in larger Indian cities as well—the place where Europeans having to live as Europeans, made an attempt at living the artificial life of European gentry in an alien soil—where eventually the compromise consisted in certain Asian usages creeping into 'the club', usages which the Europeans couldn't eliminate. They accepted them and from this evolved the typical 'colonial club' life as a social pattern.

The atmosphere seems to have been the same all over Asia—the International Club could well have been the Delhi Gymkhana Club or the Poona Club or the Pindi Club or any similar club anywhere in Anglo-India. A post-Victorian building, pompous and domineering, large wooden doors with semi-circular skylights, tennis courts, space for Sunday morning gatherings, a billiard room with draped tables hardly used and looking a trifle mournful; a lounge with large ungainly furniture, upholstered in leather or thick coarse material for durability; circular tables with respectable newspapers and social magazines; a bar, originally designed in poor imitation of an English pub, later getting mixed up with a cheap snack bar in Europe, and where elderly bachelors clustered together talking shop and sharing smutty jokes. This atmosphere has been cleaned out of the International Club at Beijing, though they still play tennis on Sunday mornings and have dances on Saturday nights, and bachelors from the large diplomatic community still eat there: but the new atmosphere, whatever the new atmosphere of a European Club in a free Asia will be, hasn't yet been allowed entry. It looks somewhat lost and lonely.

The evening made me nostalgic for summer evenings in Delhi—the hot silent air, made me a little drowsy as did the sip of rice wine, the sky cluttered with bright stars, the strong perfume of the evening blossoms, and the stark whiteness of the oleander in the dark shrubbery, to add to the noise of crickets and the infrequent croaking of frogs. Opposite the club was the tall many-storeyed building of the office of the Peking Communist Party. The fourth floor was brightly lit and we were told that there was an important meeting going on. It was 11 p.m.

The hotel is full of individuals and delegations from all over China. Walking down the passage to our bedrooms we saw an old Chinese gentleman, thin and grey-haired, with a length of wispy beard, smoking a long thin pipe with a small cup and a jade mouthpiece. It surely wasn't an opium pipe? I couldn't help but stand and stare as it was such a standard image.

I saw my first fly in China this morning when having a shower. I announced it to Anil with great excitement. More seriously, I am amazed at the way in which flies have been cleared. There are fly swatters everywhere and a regular campaign in posters and pictures encourages the anti-fly movement. Again, this is something we could do without much effort in India, and the result, even if only half as good would be a distinct improvement. In some ways, I find myself thinking that it is a shame coming to an unfamiliar country and having to live in a familiar new hotel. Not that I have anything against this hotel. It couldn't have been more comfortable—but it is like any other hotel in any other country (save the Leningradskaya, of course). It has the atmosphere of an international hotel, of delegations and journalists—the same features, the same questions, the same attitudes. I should have preferred to stay in a Chinese inn or in a Chinese household, to have lived for a week with a Chinese family, and then I could survive any number of hotels.

Hotel living is, I think, particularly unfortunate in a town like Beijing where everything faces inwards, and unless one goes into the house, its exterior reveals nothing. There are a few streets through which one can wander, but by and large the side streets have little life to offer. Street after street has the same high grey bare walls all the way down, with openings that are the entrances to the houses. These are the outer walls of one side of each house, since the houses are built around a square courtyard. The life, the goings-on of the city do not tumble out into the streets as in other cities elsewhere. Everything happens behind and within these large walls.

This possibly also accounts for the impression that Beijing gives of being quiet and small. I was surprised at its almost small-town look. Other than the monuments that carry a different sentiment, I expected something magnificent and spectacular in an exotic architecture, forgetting that on the whole the Chinese tend to underplay, indulging in subtleties that only the trained mind can fully appreciate. So also in architecture—it looks a little barren at first—too simple till the eye becomes accustomed to it and then every curve and corner has a fullness that was not initially apparent. The walls of the hutongs certainly don't give it the dash and splendour of an erstwhile imperial capital. But the quietness is not submissive—it is full of dignity—and the more I look around the more I wish that a few more capital cities could be like it.

There was a small dinner for us at the famous Peking Duck Restaurant hosted by the Director of the Institute of Archaeology and the Director of Museums and Antiquities. The former was the well-known archaeologist Dr Hsia Nai (now spelt as Xia Nai), whom I had greatly looked forward to meeting. I tried every now and again to bring the conversation around to what was being done in archaeological work in China, but he was not too forthcoming. I was hoping that he would speak about his work on China and the Central Asian trade since our work at Dunhuang would link up with that, but he remained quiet. We did talk about the recently found Neolithic sites and the excavation at Pan Po (as Banpo was then known) near Xi'an, but not at any great length. I was disappointed with not being able to talk about this aspect of my interest but couldn't say much as he was quite civilized about his silence on those topics. However, his office sent me some reports the next day on the excavations. Those in English I read with interest.

The other person at the dinner with whom I had a lively conversation that had little to do directly with present times, was Professor Ji Xianlin who specializes in Buddhist studies and has worked on Buddhist texts. In my research on Ashoka, I had studied the chronicle from Sri Lanka, *Mahavamsa*, so we had much to talk about. The conversation became more animated when we began comparing the *Mahavamsa* with the early Chinese chronicle, the *Han Shu*.

The restaurant itself was an unimpressive place. We walked across half-built tramlines and pavements to get there, and from the outside it was like a tea shop in Beijing—brick built, though with doors and windows which gave it a slightly more 'posh' look. We walked down a long central hall on each side of which were small rooms, presumably for private dinners, as each appeared to be occupied by one big gathering, either a family or just adults. Some of the kitchens seemed to lead off this hall, as steaming trays with bowls and dishes were moving back and forth. At the further end we were received by our hosts, each dressed in a cotton shirt (or bush shirt) and trousers and each one with an elegant fan. The usual formalities were exchanged—on our part how we could hardly believe that we were in China and how wonderful it was to be here—on their part how glad they were to be able to show us China, especially the cultural past.

It was a fearfully hot evening and I sat there pouring sweat, all togged up in silk, wishing that I had worn a cotton sari instead. We then proceeded to have two-and-a-half hours of the politest of polite conversations. One just kept saying nice things all the time—and through an interpreter which made it even more comic. I played a little game on my own and tried to decide what they were actually thinking about us. It began to be vastly amusing but the food intervened. The meal was fabulous—one of those gastronomic dreams come true. I don't think I shall ever eat such a meal again. The sort of meal that convinces me that the culinary art is actually the greatest test of a civilization. The Chinese far surpass the rest of the world, not because the food tastes good and one goes on eating as if in a fit of intoxication, but because to the outsider it is unknowable. To sit there, eating delicious little pieces of something white and semi-solid, cooked in a sauce that is just sufficiently spiced as to enable a stranger to guess some of the spices but not all—one starts with the basic question, is it meat or vegetable?—and then to be told after frantic guessing that it is kidney, leaves me quite astounded. As far as we were concerned, the meal was a chorus of oohs and aahs.

And the other delightful thing about a Chinese meal is that the dishes never stop. Every few minutes something new appears, until there comes a stage when one is almost relieved to see the appearance of a large bowl of soup, signifying the end of the meal. At the Peking Duck Restaurant, the pièce de résistance is the duck itself. It appears at a most dramatic moment when everyone imagines the meal is coming to an end. Then it comes on a tray—a whole duck of magnum size, roasted to a rich, crisp red-brown, sizzling in the hot grease of its fat. There is a moment's startled silence, all eyes in one direction—and then the host smiles modestly and says, 'Won't you have some duck?' The cook then picks up a sharp knife and slices the duck in small, manageable-by-chopstick slices. Each slice is dipped in a dark rather piquant plum sauce, placed in the middle of a dough-pancake, which is then folded around the piece and eaten. Oh—what bliss—and in between each course are the repeated gambeis—toasts given in the form of gulps of rice wine. Everything is toasted—the Association, us, the work, friendships between various peoples etc. I wanted to propose a toast to the duck but I didn't think it would have been appreciated.

We then rose from the dining table and sat at another table, where we were given towels rinsed in hot steaming water. Ah, they felt good. Cigarettes were passed around and tea was poured and I sat back contentedly, ready to lapse into the silence of supreme satisfaction. But soon another tray with bowls arrived—something sweet this time—small white squares which they called almond curd and a few red squares—tomato curd—in thin sweet syrup. To my surprise I managed to eat an entire bowl. And I proceeded to hold a strange conversation on Chinese musical instruments with my next-door neighbour who spoke in faltering English. I don't know what he understood, but at the end of ten minutes he assured me that I must go to a concert of Chinese music—so it could not have been too bad. By then it was 9.30 p.m. and our host turned to us and said: 'You must be very tired.' We hastened to assure him we were not. But he insisted so we took our leave! To be told that, 'you must be tired' was a polite formula used for closing an evening or invitation.

The next day we turned to work. We tried to get an appointment with Dr Xia Nai but were told that he was busy in a session with other officers of the Institute of Archaeology. These we discovered were meetings of a kind of confession and self-analysis, where they spoke about their work and its end purpose and whether the end purpose was being met, as they also discussed their relations with others in the office. Such sessions went on for the entire day. This was a new activity and a departure from the earlier ways of running offices. It had other purposes as well in terms of the Communist Party getting to know the higher echelon of officers in the decision-making level of administration. It was also the channel through which officials were informed of the views they were expected to subscribe to. Above all it was a way of finding out what a person thought about his or her work and the procedures. It sounded like the rectification campaign that had been talked about by people outside China, connected eventually to the flowers blooming and the schools of thought contending.

We were met instead by a couple of others who worked in the same office and we had a detailed discussion about our plans and the schedule that we thought might be appropriate. Some small changes were made but basically it was a clarification of how we were to proceed. That was a considerable help. We did get to meet Xia Nai the following day, when we discussed our plans, and he confirmed the arrangements.

We were to work at two sites that had hosted cave monasteries associated with Buddhism in China. Each had halls of worship that had been decorated with murals and with sculpture of Buddhist figures. We indicated that our study at Dunhuang was to focus on landscape painting. This site has been known for some decades and a fair amount written on it therefore we had made a preliminary study. The other site where we were being taken to first, Maijishan, was a recently written about site and we had little information on it. We were anxious, therefore, to read as much as possible that had been published on it, but little was available. I had the impression that perhaps this site was allotted to us in order to make it better known outside China.

Some long visits in the next few days to the National Museum were a useful preliminary to setting out. I was interested in seeing the objects that I had studied in the course I had taken on Chinese art and archaeology that were linked to some aspects of our two sites, as well as being better informed on what we were likely to see at the sites. The display in the museum is like the display in all Indian museums. Objects are laid out in a line along the four walls of a hall with another row in the centre. The labels are all in Chinese so that is not of much help although Mingo happily undertook to translate those that were especially interesting. The information was in any case limited—as it always is in most museums. It generally consisted of the name of the object, the date and the dynasty with which it was associated, and the place where it came from. Much of the material displayed was from existing museum collections since there had not as yet been many fresh excavations. The artefacts from new excavations tended to be kept temporarily at places near the site where they were found. I was making frantic notes and also marking places on a large folding map that I had acquired, and all this together with the way we looked, raised the curiosity of the occasional Chinese visitor to the museum. Return visits to the museum at the end of our stay were a much more informative experience and helpful to our work.

We called in at the home of the first secretary of the Indian embassy. It was a typical Beijing house—small rooms around a square courtyard—with a lovely red entrance door—all in a tiny hutong. He and his wife then took us to the Bei Hai (North Sea) Park, near the Forbidden City. It has a large artificial lake with an island in the middle, on which a pagoda has been built. The teahouses were closed and the boats were being called in. Pity we were late—I would have enjoyed boating on the lake in the evening. The boats are all rowboats, taking two or four people. Perhaps on our return to Beijing, we might go boating one evening. Considering it was the end of the day, the park was amazingly clean. A few people were still about, mainly couples, sitting on the benches or wandering hand in hand. We walked around the island—quite a walk—and all we heard were our own voices and the voice of the man calling the boats in, which echoed across the water. I didn't expect so many boats, nor so many to be taken out. The Chinese enjoy the good things of life. I say this not only because of the meal in the Peking Duck Restaurant. But generally they enjoy food and drink, they enjoy sitting out in a teahouse, and other such sociable activities. They would probably enjoy the bistros of Paris, whereas Indians would be hesitant, although the dhabas of India are not to be scoffed at. That is another striking thing about a first visit—the remarkable balance between enjoying an act and overdoing it. Perhaps this is overenthusiasm on my part.

4

On the Way to Xi'an

We are now on our way to Maijishan and Dunhuang. The first site is in the general area in which Chang'an (as Xi'an was then known), one of the ancient capitals of China, is located, rich in archaeological remains. It has a major museum so we shall stop there for a few days to study the relevant objects in the museum before proceeding to Maijishan. Our journey out is from Beijing into the heart of old China. From childhood I have loved journeys by train so for me this long train journey of two days is a joy.

The night before I left London, I had listened to a recording of *Oedipus Rex* thinking that that would be the last piece of European music I would hear for some time. Yet here I am now, sitting in a Chinese train, barely a week in China, listening to passages of *Prince Igor* being played on the speaker system in the train. An hour ago, it was the Brahms violin concerto, which sounded equally strange in these surroundings. The man in the compartment next to ours, who may be Russian, and is reading a book in Russian, has a small battery radio. I haven't yet been able to find out whether he was tuned in to a Chinese or a European station. I shouldn't be at all surprised if it was Radio Peking. European classical music is popular in China, and there is much more of it broadcast than from All India Radio. I'm told that most large cities have their orchestras and chamber music groups and concerts given by them are very well attended. I have seen Chinese carrying violins—a sight rare in India unless one is being thrown out of a smart restaurant at closing time and happens to exit together with the dance band.

This is due in part I suppose to their having adopted the European musical notation for their own music too. This is commonly used now for writing any sort of music. In the old days they used numbers to denote the notes of a scale, e.g., do re mi fa so la ti do, was 1, 2, 3, 4, 5, 6, 7, 1. A lower scale had dots placed under the numbers, and a higher scale had them placed above. It was not quite clear to me as to how it related technically to the European system though they use the pentatonic. Writing Indian classical music—the raga—in this notation is not easy although it has been attempted. I heard a few folk songs the other evening in Beijing. We were sitting on Coal Hill, an artificial hill overlooking the Worker's Palace of Culture. To me they sounded very modernized, almost like Cossack songs, but my friends assured me that they were genuine folk songs.

Last night, Mingo sang us a lovely little love song from Xinjiang. Knowing the European music notation she wrote it down. I am waiting now to play it on an instrument and see if it sounds sufficiently Chinese. They frequently use the piano as an accompanying instrument even with folk songs. This I think is wrong. The sound of the piano would seem too alien. I am sure they could continue to have the accompaniment on a traditional instrument, particularly as their instruments are so imaginative. I don't quite understand why they encourage European instruments accompanying Chinese songs. Perhaps it is intended to show that they are sufficiently familiar with Western music and can adapt the piano and the violin to their own system. Or, was it that in colonial times it was thought that the music would be more familiar if accompanied on Western instruments? This would be somewhat parallel to using the harmonium in Indian music. On the one hand there is a tremendous cult of collecting folk music, and then there is the travesty of playing it on a piano. In Europe, the piano as an accompaniment to popular music is common in high schools and Salvation Army gatherings, aside from the recent adoption of the guitar and skiffle instruments. Playing it on its own tends to happen more often in classical music and jazz. Not that I am anti-piano, far from it. But it sounds *so, so* alien in China.

We are passing through a tunnel at this precise moment. There are quite a few in this loess plateau neighbouring the North China plain. In parts it is very dramatic country with the tall cliffs of ochre-coloured loess grown over with trees and shrubs. Where they are bare, they look as if they had been cut away clean with a knife. I remember my geography book at school stating that where the loess soil is soft, people cut into it, making caves in the loess cliffs and living in them. Imagine my excitement this morning, when as we finished crossing the North China plain and entered into the loess region, I saw them, the cave dwellings cut into the loess. Yes, there they were. Some with just a dark hole for the entrance—others were more elegant with well-fitting wooden doors—and entire villages of them, not just an occasional one. In fact, the free-standing roofed houses are dotted about in a more scattered fashion. This type of soil with its constant erosion allowing the formation of very few slopes produces strange shapes that cut dramatically into the skyline. I wish I could make sketches of them.

It must be incredibly difficult to build a railway line on this soil, and more so, to keep the track free from getting hidden by soil falling on it through erosion. In parts, the embankments have been cemented up, in other parts, the soil has been compressed and patted down. The area is naturally fertile. We have been seeing nothing but greenery since we left Beijing. First, it was the vast expanse of fields moving into the horizon and now the loess fields—sometimes large flat areas covered with maize and millet crops, and elsewhere, where the loess has formed hills it is cut into terraces and planted with rice. The planting of trees seems to be taken seriously. Young trees are visible everywhere, either in regular plantations or else as an avenue on both sides of the railway track. Every inch of soil is cultivated. The fields stretch to the very edge of the bank.

I can now hear some Chinese music. They broadcast it over the mike sometimes. It's very pleasant in the dining car—one eats to excerpts of the Peking opera. I was downing sweet and sour pork last night to the accompaniment of the furious dashing of 'A General Saying Goodbye to his Favourite Concubine'—can't say the Chinese haven't a sense of humour. The landscape is now beginning to look like travel documentaries made in colour about the Grand Canyon in America—higher hills with more frequent terraces enclosing a winding flat area that may once have been a river. We crossed the Hwang Ho (as the Huang He was then known) this morning, a huge river, swirls of fast-moving water, thick, muddy, and yellow as its name describes it—frighteningly large, with a single sailboat in the distance. That's all I could see, a huge, flat river and the sky and the boat. I can't think how terrifying a calamity it would be if such an expanse of water should flow out of its course. That is something I miss in Europe, really gigantic rivers which give one the feeling of their actually being the veins of the country and not just pleasant waterways. Yet the irony is that an average river in Europe is much more the vein of the country because, despite its smallness, it's put to greater economic use. The Chinese and the Indians are now beginning to build power stations and irrigation works to use this force but surely some could be organized immediately for purposes of navigation and transport. It seems such a waste—all that water flowing without supporting a human need.

We have just arrived at a small station and there has been an announcement over the train mike telling us where we are. This is obviously a good system as it prevents one having to run around asking. They also announced the length of time the train will stop. This is a wayside station but looks like a smaller version of the larger ones. There is a large main building and smaller buildings on each side. The platforms are generally uncovered except in the bigger towns and are wide and clean. Vendors and hawkers bring their barrows on to the platform but there is little mess or litter. At one of the larger stations this morning I walked the length of the platform. There was the inevitable newspaper-and-magazine stall on wheels, the rest of the hawkers were selling eatables—round bread, bread shaped like plaits, whole roast chickens, bowls of hot noodles, jars of pickled vegetables, melons, apples, plums, pears, boiled eggs, ice cream, tomatoes. The fruit was neatly tied up in string bags of one-catty weight. There was no crying out of wares and no frantic rushing up and down as in India, where buying something on a station platform requires professional talent. It is much more orderly here, in fact orders are so strictly adhered to, that at one station the train had not quite come on to the platform but had stopped and we saw a woman with a basket of pears, but she would not sell us any because they are only allowed to sell things on the platform.

We have just finished eating another delicious meal—I shall grow crazy when I have to stop eating Chinese food every day. It was a lovely evening, the fiery brightness of the setting sun caught the yellow olive of the hills, filled them with a suffused warm pink—quite out of this world—and also caught the grass, the full green fields, with a powder-blue sky away from the sunset. Sunsets in China are like sunsets in India, they have a personality that I never seem to recognize in English sunsets.

Where was I before we went for dinner? Ah yes, at the platform. The one most striking difference which makes it possible for people to alight from a train at a station without losing patience is the absence of beggars. This is a remarkable achievement. China seems to be clear of beggars, where before there were so many. Not only on station platforms but even in the streets of towns. In India, it is an impossible situation—the moment the train stops beggars gather around—maimed, diseased, fakes, all together, with flies flitting from sore to sore. Here one can go anywhere without fear of being surrounded by beggars. We were told that they have been divided into groups. Some have been sent to virgin and unclaimed lands to till the land and settle in proximity to village communities. Others have been put to work in camps and have been given a vocation. I have heard some people argue that if a person chooses to beg, he has a right to do so and stopping it is all much too disciplined, and where begging is a necessity for survival, there this solution is to be commended. This is an argument I disagree with. Begging is unacceptable. Other solutions have to be found.

Talking about flies—it is no joke, the fact is there are no flies in China! China has been cleared of flies. During my entire stay in Beijing I saw only one fly and I did not have the heart to kill it as it seemed so alone. During this journey two or three have flitted in and out as we keep the window and the door of the compartment open. It's quite amazing that they have cleared out the flies so well. After we'd been in the train for about an hour, yesterday evening, the steward came around with a fly swatter for each compartment and asked us to swat the flies. This is an innovation we could well introduce at home. Apart from the absence of flies there is also an absence of stray dogs. I suppose they were also got rid of. Does that also explain the lack of domesticated dogs or cats or other such pets? Not even parrots.

The temperature at the moment reads 93° Fahrenheit, and we are all sweating and feeling very hot. We have had a night and day in the train and have another night and day to go. So far, I don't feel too bored, but by tomorrow I shall probably feel very tired. I slept well last night because I took a sleeping tablet, otherwise I can't sleep on a train. We arrive at lunchtime tomorrow and spend three days in Xi'an. As of now, my kingdom for a bath. The landscape becomes more and more dramatic—large fissure-like openings on the surface, wide as gorges and deep as ravines, keep coming up. What would it be like to spend a few weeks here, living in a loess village and working on a rice field?

I haven't seen many cattle roaming around the countryside—just a few stray ones, all rather thin looking. This does not seem to be an area for 'dairy produce'. China generally, I am told, is not a culture given to consuming milk in various forms. It is not milk obsessive, as we are. In India, one gets so used to seeing so many cows just drifting about that it seems strange to see so few in China. It would appear that they have better control over their cattle livestock than we have. Certainly, no religious prejudice or superstitious public opinion prevents them from adopting a sensible attitude towards cattle breeding.

The following morning, we were in the mountains and it was much cooler. Tunnel after tunnel and in between we crawled along the edge of a gorge. The river (or stream for the Chinese) winds along lazily, the hill slopes are thickly wooded and wherever there is a bare patch it is planted with millet. I have never seen fields climbing up a hill like this. We stopped a few minutes back on an escarpment overlooking a village. It is a small village with a small street and houses and shops on both sides. Small mud or straw dwellings with thatched roofs, just like India, except that the street was also covered with a mud wash, and the houses look beautifully clean. I just stood and looked. How can they keep it so clean? And this was not a station or a regular stop, we stopped merely to let another train pass. Each house has its own back garden growing vegetables and flowers, but the neatness of it left me quite amazed.

The journalist Robert Guillain in his very recent and much-discussed book, *The Blue Ants: 600 Million Chinese under the Red Flag*, writes that there is a regimentation with everyone appearing in the same clothes of standard blue material—it was too ordered and alike and reflected the regimentation of the mind. But what does he say of countries where large numbers of people dress in rags because they cannot get anything better? I find this attitude impertinent and I say this not only because I am an ex-colonial and am therefore still sensitive to the comments that Europeans make about Asians, but because I think it is out of context. He knows what conditions were like in China ten years ago and what conditions are like in other parts of the Third World today. I haven't yet come across a single Chinese who wasn't adequately dressed. Yes, now they are wearing regulation trousers—ten years ago they were wearing regulation rags. Men, women, and children, they all have clothes and they all look clean. I am aware that the women at least don't look so elegant in slacks or skirts as they might look in their traditional qipao—the tight, slit skirt, also known as the cheongsam, but if the new dress is more easily available and affordable, why not wear it? The qipao is always there as the Sunday best for formal and festive occasions.

The good thing about everyone going around in white shirts and blouses and in various shades of blue trousers and skirts, is that no obvious differences of wealth and class are immediately evident. Walking down Wangfujing, the main shopping street in Beijing, it is not easy to distinguish the income groups. But this seems characteristic of many things. They have achieved what might be called anonymity from wealth in appearance, to a far greater extent than even in Russia, and certainly more than any other country I know. It is not displeasing either, as I have not felt bored by the similarity of dress, although I dare say that if I were living here the unending uniformity might wear me down. The faces and expressions continue to evoke curiosity. I don't know whether the picture is different in winter when people wear woollens and winter clothes, whether the same whites and blues are worn in woollen stuff rather than cotton. Women are now being encouraged to dress with greater imagination and a little more femininity, as it is being said that some have gone to the other extreme and simplified their dress too much.

Talking about determining a person's economic class, it is noticeable as to how much actual and practical equality there appears to be in China. It is an applied principle and not simply a theoretical one—it is apparent in the streets, in the theatres and parks, in the restaurants, in the dining car in this train, in the hotel lifts, seemingly everywhere. But, of course, as a casual visitor would I be that discerning? There is also the other question. Is equality only to be judged by access to material goods? There is also the equality of rights that should be available to every citizen.

I have just eaten a divine meal—noodles and aubergines and pork and chicken—all to the sound of a story from the Peking opera. Now I feel almost ready to compose couplets in Chinese on the beauty of the mountains, the soft rain, and the distant mist! The temperature has come down and the air is fresh. Mingo is leaning out of the window singing 'O Sole Mio' in Chinese! Sounds terrific. The train is crawling by the edge of the river again. This is a land of continuous construction and building. Every few yards we see stacks of timber or steel frames of railway tracks, bags of cement, cranes etc., and either there is a surveying team or else a crew of workmen working on some construction. They all wear shirts and straw hats marked with the crest of the Chinese railway. Past the railway tracks, roads are being built, and in some parts stone-lined channels down the hillsides to divert the rainwater to the fields and irrigation tanks, rather than let it soak into the hillside, to no purpose.

We stopped at another little station a short while ago and a woman came around selling peaches—a lovely-looking woman, quite elderly. Her feet were tiny, about 3.5 to 4 inches, and she moved slowly along the platform. The only way she could move faster was with a waddling movement like a duck. I still see some women of the older generation with tiny feet, abnormally small and obviously bound when they were young. It is so pathetic! On one occasion I saw a woman coming down the stairs and it was such a difficult movement for her that I felt highly antagonistic towards a culture that had for hundreds of years permitted this torture and had, in fact, prided itself on treating it as a prized cultural trait. Why was it done—to enslave the woman and prevent her from literally running away and justify this by maintaining that tiny feet look graceful? But I fail to see the aesthetics of it. And they are definitely not in proportion to the rest of the body, they are far too small, even if Chinese women are generally slender and small in figure.

The smallness of the Chinese figure became something of a nightmare for me. As I didn't bring any working clothes with me from London, I had to buy some slacks and a blouse in Beijing. Easier said than done—I hunted high and low for something that would fit me. Even the largest sizes just would not stretch enough to go around my hips! Eventually I found one, just one pair, and even that is constantly at bursting point. When I return to Beijing, or perhaps even before that, I shall have to get something made to order.

It was really hot this afternoon, so I sat curled up in the corner by the window and read *Ulysses*. It seemed so distant, almost as if it didn't belong to this world, as indeed it doesn't belong to *this* world. But then I sometimes wonder whether the rhetoric and the idiom aren't really universal, and the imagery of this book could well be one of the ways of looking at a world seemingly entirely different but perhaps really not so?

I can't imagine many non-Europeans appreciating James Joyce. It is too completely and purely European. I too have problems empathizing with all of it. No doubt Joyce would have been equally amazed to hear that an Indian woman was reading *Ulysses* on a train in China. What made me bring this as one of the books to read on this journey? The idea as I now see it is in some ways rather fantastic, just to think of it leaves me bewildered and puzzled and quite startled by the contemporary world. Am I really a creature of my times or merely a nineteenth-century projection or remnant, living in the twentieth century? I would like to belong to all this: to the Chinese peasant with his new clothes and the fully cultivated soil around him; to the water cascading down the Huang He and being harnessed somewhere and used to drive the machinery in a paper mill. But something prevents me from 'belonging'. Perhaps being Indian and touched however briefly by Europe is making me too self-conscious; perhaps I don't feel all this intimately enough.

Now that it is becoming easier to observe and write about what I see, and I am intellectually beginning to wake up, I may start writing something that may be worth reading. Once we arrive in our grotto in the mountains, I hope to be writing poetry!

For the moment let me return to the mundane and say something about the train. The train is like any other train (not a profound thought); it is a corridor train so that one can walk the whole length of it. In India very few of our trains are corridor trains. Here they don't have classes as such on trains, merely different degrees of comfort (to me it's the same as having classes but perhaps they are averse to using that word). So it is categories of soft and hard berth. We, being state guests, are travelling in the most comfortable type of compartment—a four-berth cabin, two below and two on top. The soft berth upholstery is in dark green velvet that makes it even hotter and leaves me with the wrong associations. But I suppose it is ideal for the winter and since it is cool in China most of the time, they gear their comforts to the cool weather. Otherwise it is much the same as any other. The less comfortable hard berths are wooden without any upholstery. A further type is the non-sleeper, an open compartment with seating arrangements all the way down.

But the really different and efficient thing about Chinese trains is that a crew of forty-four persons travel with each train and are responsible for service and organization. There are two stewards to each bogey who keep the place clean, make the beds, and assist with whatever one may want. Last night, Anil was leaning on the window rail and it came down. The steward was immediately informed, and he brought a screwdriver and fixed it in a matter of moments. In India there are no stewards except in the most expensive and air-conditioned compartments, so we would have had to travel to our destination before anything would have been done about it. The compartments and corridors are swept almost three times a day, which is a great boon if one is doing a journey lasting almost three days through dusty areas, and with a coal engine at that. This is again something that isn't thought of in India where at the utmost one can try and ask a sweeper at a large station to sweep one's own compartment and pay him for it. Here the entire train is swept and cleaned. There is a regular kitchen staff consisting of cooks and waiters. The dining car is again kept pretty spotless even though it is well used by everyone.

Does cleanliness or deftness come naturally to the Chinese or is this a lesson of the revolution? There was a boy of four this morning shovelling a large plateful of rice into his mouth using chopsticks, and at a great pace. When he had eaten and left, I hopped across to see whether he had left half the rice on the tablecloth—there was not half a grain anywhere near where he had been eating. Another thing that amazes me is: how on earth do they teach children to use chopsticks so cleverly? It's much easier for us since we use our fingers. In every compartment there is a large thermos with hot water; ours is gaily painted pink with red and green flowers—quite revolting to look at—also many little packets of Chinese green tea. Each person is given a porcelain mug with a lid, the idea being that everyone can spend the day drinking hot tea. A man comes around with a watering can full of boiling water and refills the flasks when they are empty. Another member of the crew is in charge of the announcements over the mike and the records. In our case it was a young girl of nineteen, a charming girl, who says she has been working for four years now and is not very keen on marriage as yet.

They have a chief officer in charge of them, with whom we had a long conversation the first night. He started working when he was seventeen with the Youth team that operated on the Beijing-Harbin run. Before 'Liberation' he worked in a flour mill. At nineteen, he was transferred to the Beijing-Lanzhou line. His work consists of six days travel, Beijing–Lanzhou, Lanzhou–Beijing, and then he gets six days off, out of which he has to spend two days attending a special institution where he is given instruction in railway organization, politics, and other subjects. Before being selected for the crew, a candidate must have middle-school education and pass a special entrance exam. At work, they work in eight-hour shifts—and if necessary they work overtime for which they are paid extra.

Until last year he lived in a dormitory with other railway employees—I specially asked him if they stick pictures of their pin-up girls on the walls by their beds and was delighted to hear that they do. Last year he married a Chinese girl of his own choice. His mother had arranged a match for him some time back, but when 'Liberation' came, he decided he would marry someone of his own choice. His mother incidentally approves of his present wife. She works in a cotton factory in Beijing. They live in a flatlet built for railway workers which has a bedroom, a kitchen, and a toilet. He earns 70 yuans a month plus overtime earnings and occasional bonuses. The exchange rate currently (in 1957) is 6.7 yuans to £1. His wife supplements the income. His reading, apart from the studying he has to do, consists largely of Chinese and other novels. Much Russian literature is also sold and read. He is very fond of the movies and he saw an Indian film, *Awaara*, about which he made very pertinent remarks. This was not the first time that *Awaara* was referred to. It was a great hit in China largely because of its social message and its catchy theme song. Wherever we went they would hum the tune to suggest that they recognized us as Indian.

He also enjoys the Peking opera, but prefers the less courtly and more colloquial variety. Both he and his wife love swimming and sometimes they cycle down to a large pool in one of the parks and have a swim. He left us saying, in complete sincerity, I am sure, that he was very glad that we as foreigners had come to *his* country and he hoped we'd be happy in *his* country and would like it. He is a good-looking man of twenty-four. They are all extremely young with an average age in their early twenties. It is obvious that as a result of the revolution the young have come to the fore, but that such young people should be given positions of responsibility is encouraging.

We walked into one of the open compartments and there was a Chinese family sitting there, so we started talking to them. They came originally from the north-east and were moving to Lanzhou. The man had been in the army and had been demobilized. He worked for a while in his native town but didn't like it and had now been offered this other job in a factory in Lanzhou—a good 600 or 700 miles from his home, in a completely new area. We asked him how he felt about uprooting himself like this. He replied that since he was doing it entirely of his own volition, he treated it all rather as an adventure and his family felt the same. As for going into a new and strange area, he reminded us gently, and with the utmost courtesy, that for the Chinese no area or part of China was in any way strange.

These are random conversations, but I think they are a pointer to a certain sentiment in the country. The emphasis on building something new and worthwhile is unmistakable. They have set themselves high standards and have certainly got cracking about moving in the direction of where they want to go. Whether they will arrive remains to be seen. Not only does this drive for efficiency include the placing of spittoons in appropriate corners on the train, and reprimanding those that might spit outside the spittoon, but it also includes courtesy and dignity of behaviour that is such a change from other places. I asked myself whether this was taken seriously because it was new. Will it last? I would have to return after twenty years and see. They are a cheerful people and they appear to enjoy life, judging from those that I have talked with, yet it is so rarely that one hears them raising their voice or screaming at each other when quarrelling. That quietness surely must be inbred. I can't imagine any institution producing it overnight among a few million people. Or, alternatively, are the strictures from authority such that they instil this quietness?

The strictures seem to underlie many of their assessments. For example, there is the constant reference to 'Before Liberation' and 'After Liberation'.

The revolution is now a recognized time marker, and the references are to what it was like before the event and after. But this is not just in terms of being a date. It is perceived by those now using it, and is projected by those defining it, as a marker of profound change. Whether it will be that eventually, remains to be seen. The change constantly emphasizes equality and accessibility. People are treated as equal and jobs are accessible. The concept of 'Liberation' has moved from being a time marker to becoming symbolic of a possible new world. The present is registering the initial steps towards it. Whether it will become that remains to be seen. The Russian revolution was also a before and after phenomenon but the dream did take on some of the contours of a nightmare. I wonder whether this would also be the case in China?

5

The Ancient Capital at Xi'an

Arriving in Xi'an was for me an absolute thrill. It was once the ancient capital of the early Chinese kingdoms, but for me it was more than that as it was the location of one of the monasteries where Xuan Zang resided after his return from India in the seventh century AD. It became the focus for early Chinese studies of Buddhism. This was encouraged by his bringing back an elephant-load of manuscripts on Buddhist thought and teachings that were then translated into Chinese from Sanskrit.

I had a little pang of missing India as we arrived at the Xi'an railway station. Something about it reminded me of Old Delhi Junction. I saw the same crowded trains although perhaps not so crowded as the third-class compartments in Indian trains. An occasional person would come and stand close to us and listen to our conversation and I wondered whether he understood English, and was he a government agent, or was he just a curious bystander. Families were rushing to catch their trains, with mothers holding babies and fathers carrying bundles. Even the innate dignity and elegance of the Chinese did not change the picture much. There were crowds outside the station, with similar hawkers and vendors calling out their wares.

My short-lived homesickness was largely due to the feeling that I was missing being among people whom I could understand—literally in terms of language, and by extension through familiarity of signs and symbols—people I could converse with. What I find disturbing is that the Chinese I meet are much like us Indians and yet they elude me. I get tired of making mental observations and yet not getting anywhere. How does one think beyond the obvious? Does it need hindsight?

I was predisposed, I suppose, to like Xi'an but I feel quite at home and comfortable here as it has a feel of familiarity, although I don't know why. The drive through the city was pleasant as it had rained and the dust had settled somewhat. I did not have to cover my nose and mouth with the pallu of my sari. It is a large city and clearly old. We stayed at the People's Hotel, a huge grey stone building with two flanking structures that had roof ends pointing upwards—the usual concession to Chinese architecture! The irony is that the People's Hotel is only for foreign guests and Soviet consultants. The Chinese people are not permitted to stay in this hotel. We entered a hall with large opaque windows and, halfway down, sat at the reception. The terrazzo floors of marble chips have yellow and green geometric designs. The rooms are furnished in green with green-washed walls. The furniture of dark brown wood has gilt decorations. The living room of our suite was furnished with leather upholstered solid-looking chairs. It doesn't take much imagination to guess who designed all this.

The lounge of the hotel was furnished in what I call Eurasian style—commodious armchairs and sofas, with a wooden frame and pink cloth covers with a fringe hanging down. There were large 'famille rouge' porcelain jars with tall flowering plants standing up against the walls. Tables with white tablecloths had the usual sixteen glasses laid out for tea. I never got to know why there are always sixteen. There was one Russian journalist on his way to Rangoon, and I thought that going via China seemed an unnecessarily roundabout way to get there!

One has the impression that the intention is to create a sense of having arrived in the world of the wealthy, but that hardly squares with the world of economic equality for all. Designs of simple furniture would be more effective. We passed through streets with not a single car but there was a fleet of them parked at the hotel. We went to the dining room for lunch and were about the only non-Russians in the room. The overwhelming presence of Russians among foreigners is unavoidable because the Russian experts often come with their families. The dining room had lacquer-red pillars and a green ceiling with murals painted on it supposedly resembling those of Dunhuang. This presumably was a concession to the Chinese aesthetic. But despite all this it was still aesthetically an improvement on the Leningradskaya.

In the evening we heard some music from one of the side buildings and wandered off in that direction. It was a Shensi (as Shaanxi was then known) opera company giving a performance. Having come in the middle we had no idea of what was going on but the costumes were magnificent, so we sat for a while. The singing in what is generically referred to as 'Peking opera' is not my first priority as it is an acquired taste and does require some familiarity with Chinese music, of which I have none. The dining room had a different kind of music played through a radiogram. Mingo and I decided to stay for a bit after dinner to see what was happening.

The atmosphere was just like that of small hotels of the period of the Raj in India, that have dinner-dances a couple of evenings in the week with music from a radiogram. The records were clearly well used and somewhat scratched, and so had occasionally to be helped along manually. They were largely old waltzes and foxtrots of the 1930s and 40s, presumably what was enjoyed by the visiting Russians and thought to be the kind of music that the West danced to. But the atmosphere was remarkably informal and friendly. Russian men would come up, click their heels, and ask for a dance. It was very strange doing a foxtrot with a person one could only smile at but not converse with since neither Mingo nor I knew Russian. After the music stopped the heels were clicked and a thank you muttered, and one was escorted back to one's table. It was the same with the Russian women. What in the West is called 'ballroom dancing' is treated as another form of folk dancing, and this makes perfectly good sense as it is essentially the middle-class community dancing of this century. This probably explains why it is not unusual to see two men and two women dancing as a group together, which I thought made it all much more entertaining.

I got talking to one of the Russian women this evening who knew a little English. The men are largely engineers and are working on the many power stations that are being established, and in the cotton factories. Not knowing the language can be such a barrier. But when they drink some maize wine then conversation is a little easier, I notice!

The presence of Russians in places that had industries involving new technologies was perhaps not all that surprising. The connection is not new for either the Bolsheviks or the Chinese. Prior to the Chinese revolution there had been political diplomacy between groups in both countries.

The Nationalist Chinese were in dialogue with the Bolsheviks, made more complicated by the subsequent confrontation between the Nationalists and the Communist Party of China. By way of an aside, the three Soong sisters who married leaders in different factions were interestingly involved in the dramas behind the dialogues. The Japanese attack on China was yet another factor. But the nature of relations between Russia and China after the Chinese revolution were, of course, different.

We spent our first long afternoon at the museum and most impressive it was in its collections. A Confucian temple in origin, it is now surrounded by additional buildings so it boasts about a dozen galleries and displays some of the most impressive finds from recent excavations in the Shaanxi province. The area of Xi'an having been historically so important, the discovery of sites from early times is no surprise. The director of the museum was a pleasant knowledgeable woman. The displays were well-laid out and supplemented by modern models of what was being stated in the labels, but of course differentiating between the ancient artefact and a modern copy. Explanatory charts, maps, and rubbings of early inscriptions provided additional information. There was much emphasis on the equality of men and women underlined in the cases displaying objects from the Stone Age.

I raised the question of this equality in present times with Mingo but she was reticent in talking about it, whereas a European counterpart would have given her view more readily. I can never decide whether Mingo is being guarded in what she says however informal our friendships have become by now, or whether she is uncertain about the information on the subject, or whether there is not too much concern about the ancient past among this generation of Chinese. Is it perhaps similar to the general interest in India about the past where knowing the dates of events is more important that considering what might have been their causation. There are plenty of explanatory charts, maps, and rubbings in the galleries at the museum that are useful and sensibly displayed. The area seems to be bursting with material remains and the museum will have to be extended in future years.

Today there was something of an intellectual anti-climax, and sadly, in the context of archaeology. We went to see the much talked of excavations of a Neolithic site, Banpo, located a little beyond Xi'an. The site itself was extremely interesting and the director of the local Institute of Archaeology showed us around. The excavations are well cared for and protected from too much sun and wind by thatched roofs. It is also fenced in to prevent curious visitors poking around and disturbing it. Postholes and floors point to both circular and square huts of a familiar Neolithic form with stouter support from the central position. Pear-shaped ovens suggested cooking hearths distinctly different from pottery kilns. Artefacts found there consisted of large amounts of pottery, bone implements of various kinds as well as stone axes and adzes. There was evidence of burial in urns and in graves.

From there we went to the site museum, also with an intelligent display of artefacts, each carefully classified and labelled. The excavations had produced much material of considerable interest. I was delighted with the visit to both places. We then went to the office for a cup of tea and discussion. I asked simple, basic questions just to become familiar with their procedures. I was told that no surveying had been done previous to the excavation as the potsherds were found accidentally when the area was being cleared for the building of a power station. This happens frequently I am told, and fortunately they recognize the importance of such discoveries and the need sometimes to follow them up with at least a brief excavation.

What was disappointing was that there had been little planning of the excavation and no future plans for even those areas that could be excavated. The digging was a simple process of removing layer after layer of earth and setting aside the artefacts so found. The construction workers did the digging under the supervision of students of archaeology. The trenches seem not to be marked by clearly discernible layers and this made the chronology of the finds somewhat confusing.

The terminology used struck me as being rather out-of-date and when I asked about the recommended books, I drew a blank even on the works of Gordon Childe, who as a major Marxist archaeologist and pioneer in archaeological theory should have been known, leave alone others. Noticing my disappointment, the curator excused himself by saying that he was a 'museum's man' and not an excavator, which I thought was a curious remark since the museum was dedicated to prehistory and was a museum at the site of an excavation. Inevitably I did a quick mental comparison with conditions at home, and thought that being well-trained by even a good colonial archaeologist such as Mortimer Wheeler has the advantage that one knows

the technology although theoretical understanding of the cultural formations being excavated may be limited, or sometimes even non-existent.

Later I asked myself whether I was being overcritical. How many
years does it take for archaeologists to move on from just being conscious
of the importance of a culture to understanding why it is necessary to
excavate a site? It is not just to obtain more objects from the past, but to
piece together the past in a sequence of history and as illuminating as the
kind of society that produced the objects. Finding objects accidentally and
then excavating the area and placing the finds in a museum are fine and
far better than not doing so at all. In some places it is referred to as 'salvage'
or 'rescue' archaeology. One wishes that more of our countries with a
rich past of material cultures would do the same. But there also has to be
simultaneously a training of archaeologists in the methods of archaeology,
now becoming more and more science-oriented, so that there is a better
understanding of the cultures they are working on.

A drive out of town took us to another site. The concubine of a T'ang
(as Tang was earlier known) emperor had occupied a group of pavilions
close to Xi'an where there was a hot spring and she could bathe in steaming
hot water gushing directly out of the earth. Mingo told us that her story is
beautifully portrayed in a Peking opera called *The Drunken Beauty*, and that
the famous male actor and singer Mei Lanfang portrayed her role with great
brilliance. Her luxurious sunken bath is still there, as is the large lotus pond
with its small red bridges over which she was fond of talking a walk. It was
a cloudy day and the mountains were partially hidden in mist. When I
looked up, I saw a small tree in the silhouette of this landscape, much like
a Song period painting. The pavilions come alive because they have been
carefully reconstructed retaining their original grace. The refinements of
the concubine's life were enviable! There were two old men sitting outside
one of the gates selling bright red pomegranates heaped high in wicker baskets, which seemed to be a part of the narrative of the pavilions set amidst
the hot springs.

Apart from being the residence of a Tang king's concubine, the place
has a connection with a major event in recent history as the location of the
Sian Incident that took place in 1936. Chiang Kai-shek, the leader of the
Nationalist government who was combating the Communist Party of China,

was arrested by two of his subordinate generals. They were pressurizing him to make an alliance with the Communists in order to jointly fight the Japanese invasion into North-east China. Chiang's resistance to the idea was broken by the arrest and he negotiated an alliance with Zhou Enlai representing the Communist Party. The two political parties together took on the Japanese occupation. It was also a turning point in the history of the Communist Party as it was now able to organize the Red Army with greater facility. This was to play a significant role in the Communist revolution and the eventual overthrow of Chiang Kai-shek and the Nationalist government. The room where he was imprisoned, and the cave in the hillside to which he later escaped before he was recaptured, are now tourist attractions. Poems composed on the incident have been inscribed and placed in the cave.

I had shown an interest in the local pottery, so Mingo took me to the section of the market where a number of shops were selling pottery. I walked into a shop selling baskets to buy a basket for carrying the pottery but was misunderstood and almost thrown out of the shop, followed by profuse apologies when they were told what I wanted. We immediately collected a huge crowd because someone had spread the rumour that the actor Mei Lan Fang was buying pottery. This would be the equivalent of a rumour that Raj Kapoor was shopping in Bombay's Crawford Market.

We passed a man selling postcards of what appeared to be archaeological objects, but after a brief conversation he rather surreptitiously showed us some rather ordinary postcards of Chinese pin-up girls clad in swimsuits. This may of course have been just a hint of what was available, but we showed no interest. I was a trifle surprised that he thought that we two young women would be at all interested, except in the style of the scanty swimsuits the girls in the photographs were wearing.

The pottery shops were a treat. Stacks of roughly made peasant ware, highly attractive with its unfinished look, large storage jars almost Biblical in size, black-bellied wine jars with rounded shoulders and lugs for carrying, oil jars of the same family but a little taller and slimmer, small pots and bowls of all sizes for eatables, teapots in grey-green crackled glaze, noodle dishes with free brush designs in black and brown—so much to choose from. Then there was porcelain but with less striking character. Now and again the potter's workspace with a wheel and what looked like a kiln would be visible in the room at the back. This interested me greatly since I had spent the previous term at SOAS making mechanical drawings and water-colour reproductions of potsherds collected by an archaeologist Raymond Allchin, from a site near Bamiyan in Afghanistan. There were suggestive similarities in the process of their making. On a couple of occasions, the potter was kind enough to show me how a shift of pressure from the thumb or finger produced a variant shape. I found this fascinating.

We spent long days in the museum studying specific objects. My favourite galleries were the ones with Wei and Tang sculpture and some fine bronze ritual vessels of a large size recently excavated. And then came the pièce de résistance for me, the magnificent seventh-century Tang period relief of the horses of T'ai Zong. This was a big surprise because I was under the impression that they had all been transported to the Philadelphia Museum of Art, but it seems that of the six, only two were sent and the rest are here. The four horses I saw deserve all the praise they have received. There seems to have been almost an integration between the artists and the horses! This was a little surprising since the horse in China, as in India, was always imported as a luxury item. But somehow the Indian sculptor never quite became one with the horse as did the Chinese sculptor.

A couple of halls had a forest of stone tablets and inscribed steles, akin to a library of texts written on stone in past times, ranging from the lives of philosophers to the order and activities of the Dowager Empress of more recent times. I felt very envious of Chinese historians who have so much of these kinds of sources to work with. Since becoming more acquainted with the Chinese past I am convinced that the Chinese scholarly tradition had a stronger sense of history than those of other early cultures. They seem to have been more meticulous than even the Greeks in both recording and commenting on the past, although I realize that it is almost blasphemy to say this in historical circles. What little I have read of the Chinese chronicles suggests that we should give them more attention and not focus only on the Greek historical texts. Interestingly these steles that we saw here, for instance, were collated and preserved during the Song period, suggesting a serious interest in knowing about the still earlier past, and perhaps distinct from mythology and literary fiction.

On one of the days when we were returning from the museum, I insisted on seeing the historical mosque in the vicinity. There was some reluctance initially by our hosts as the people there had not been informed of our visit. But it was part of my intention to go unannounced. I said a little sarcastically that surely a brief visit did not require a prior announcement. So we went. We passed through some of the really small backstreets of Xi'an, narrow little alleys. In one a man selling melons had placed his slices of melon well onto the road so we had to wait for him to clear the road before we could go through. Clearly no cars come this way normally. The houses had their main doorways opening directly onto the road so entire families stood at the doorway and stared at us. Some thought we were Indonesians since a few had visited some weeks before. For the children of the locality our visit was a big diversion from daily routine and would be much talked about. They chased after the car shouting loudly and screaming joyfully.

The mosque was hardly recognizable as such. It was built in late Tang times and restored in the Ming period, as was evident from the glazes on the tiles typical of Ming temples. The architecture was Chinese. The outer courtyard had stone tablets and inscriptions in Chinese and only the gateway had verses from the Quran in Arabic. The square interior of the mosque was covered and was supported by red-painted pillars. The ceiling had a recognizable Ming design with intricate forms and unusual shapes in various shades of green. We arrived when the mullah was leading the prayers to a small congregation. He sounded more like a Buddhist monk chanting the sutras. What it did have in common with mosques in other countries was the row of shoes lined up outside the courtyard, and the mullah whose style of beard was unmistakeable despite an otherwise Chinese-looking face. The Muslim population here would have been a small group of traders from Central Asia, but I had not realized that they had settled so far inland, having always thought of them as being on the Chinese frontier in Xinjiang.

The next day we drove to the monastery where Xuan Zang lived and worked on the Buddhist manuscripts that he had brought back from India. The beautiful location of the monastery on the higher slope of a mountain looks across the valley giving a view of the chequerboard fields, some cultivated and some fallow, and the trees sparsely planted in between. Waiting outside the main shrine for it to be unlocked we were all struck by the rich red colour of the pillars and the carvings in wood, indicating that it was well maintained. I was looking idly across the yard at the pagoda-like edifice, which is the tomb of Xuan Zang, when suddenly around its corner there appeared an apparition: an aged monk in saffron robes. I did not realize that the monastery was still used by monks. The shrine had all the familiar objects of Buddhist worship—the small icons, the incense burners, the drums, and the prayer wheels.

In another part of the monastery, a polished granite tablet in memory of Xuan Zang carries an etching of him carrying a bundle of 'sutras' on his back. This has now become the standard icon of the pilgrim monk. We were taken to the room where he is said to have studied the sutras and translated them. The aged monk who took us around treated each object with reverence and explained that he had studied the writing of Xuan Zang with much concentration and had great respect for his scholarship. I assured him that scholars of Indian history and Buddhism in India, not to mention worldwide, were also great admirers of Xuan Zang. The younger monk accompanying the older one was not in robes but elegantly dressed although in the required blue, with cloth sandals that were of the same design as the ones worn by Xuan Zang depicted on the tablet. The design seems to be popular locally! He explained that the two monks supervised the restoration and upkeep of the monastery and they were obviously doing it well. I lingered for a while, imagining the Chinese monk of ancient times planning such a near impossible journey, but urged on by the compulsive need to bring back the required texts to enable the understanding of a new but attractive religion.

It felt uncanny being there, and I had a distinct sensation of what may be called the sweep of past centuries as I stood alone on the balcony of the upper room looking out at the main monastery and down the hill. This was in a sense the moment that crystallized my journey to China. How incredible must have been Xuan Zang's journey across Central Asia and India—a sixteen-year venture in the seventh century AD, and all in search of what he knew of as the true Buddhism—the Buddhism of India, which for the Chinese was the location of the western heaven. He was such an extraordinary person, and judging by his description of the journey, a man with incredible perception of place and person.

Yet no one in India, not a single person, thought of recording the conversations that many must have had with him not only on Buddhism, but specifically on Buddhism in China or even the contemporary philosophies that emanated from China. I have often wondered about what accounts for this lack of curiosity among pre-modern Indians who remained uninterested in commenting on the world beyond their immediate own, yet it was a world that they visited and worked in, either as Indian traders or as teachers of religion in Central Asia or in South-east Asia. Nor did any of them write about any non-Indian who travelled in India, and many came for a variety of reasons, some as Greek mercenaries and traders, or Chinese Buddhist monks or Arab merchants, or Central Asian Sufis. Does it show a curious lack of interest in exploring people and places or were there other reasons for this striking disinterest? It is such a stunning contrast to the Chinese avidly wanting to know about the wider world and writing about it.

As a city, Xi'an is growing laterally and will in future times have the problems of such an urban spread. Many new buildings are located on the periphery of the city of which quite a few are public buildings—a massive new university, power stations, factories and mills and their offices. Included in this construction are lengths of ditches that will go into a large-scale new sewage system. Everywhere there is ongoing building and construction. As one goes past, one hears the rhythmic chants of workers on physically arduous jobs easing the effort by singing choruses in unison. Architecturally the buildings are unimpressive as they are blocks with doors and windows and little effort at decorative or stylistic features to relieve the austere monotony. This style is characteristic of new buildings on a mass scale in many of our countries where quick construction is required. Doubtless the buildings would be adequate, but one wishes that their exteriors were a trifle more attractive.

Even the new museum that houses the prehistory collection is a series of halls, grey-brick outside and whitewashed inside, room after room with woodwork in either polished dark brown or painted red. One is not asking for another Confucian temple as a museum, but the modern museum could be more pleasing to the eye. A barrack-like structure could be improved by changing the elevation of the halls and by arranging objects in ways other than just lining them up against the walls. The Chinese aesthetic is subtle and could attempt visually more complex forms and colours without much extra expenditure. Is this a case of the imposition of an alien aesthetic in the name of progress. Surely progress can be conducive to an attractive aesthetic?

Their less important monuments are in many ways integrated with domestic living, as for instance the Confucian and Buddhist temples that are not strikingly different architecturally. The pagodas, however, do stand out. By comparison temples, stupas, and mosques in India are buildings that are quite distinct from domestic architecture even where they are less important than the major monuments. Adapting institutional buildings to modern architectural styles should not pose a problem in China. But they seem to prefer Soviet-style buildings that perhaps they view as good examples of socialist architecture. Why don't socialist revolutions produce any striking examples of new architectural styles? Is it an obsession with dumbing down everything to the level of those that cannot or do not appreciate the luxury of a concern with aesthetics? Or is it the view that 'style' in anything has always only concerned the elite and therefore is to be set aside when society turns socialist? I don't mean that buildings should look like mock pagodas but the possibility of introducing a modern aesthetic of a different kind seems not to have been of much interest so far.

We passed through a number of villages that looked as if they were part of an Indian rural landscape, the difference becoming apparent only on a closer view. There were a few men going about with a pole across the back of their shoulder at each end of which was a basket for carrying items—a familiar site in many rural areas. Some of these here are actually mobile eateries. One basket has a stove and pans and a hotplate in which soup or noodles may actually be cooking, and the other basket has bowls, chopsticks, as well as other cold eatables. The man carrying the baskets can stop anywhere and quickly rustle up a snack. Some of these villages however are indicators of the prevailing poverty in certain rural areas—a picture not too different from India. One asks the same question as to how far back in time has this poverty prevailed, and what has been the contribution of the colonial attempt to control the economy and thereby impoverish people still further.

Sources from the past do refer to poverty but not to its being extensive. However, one has always to keep in mind that texts from the past were written by the elite and that too by those who were educated enough to write books. They are reflective more of their own lives and living than of those who were impoverished. The difference of course is that we today are more conscious of poverty in our societies and are aware that it not only needs to be removed but we also know how it is to be done. It is a question of whether what needs to be done will be done. Where will the Communist Party of China place its emphasis—on the removal of poverty and on giving all its citizens an equal start in life, or in ensuring that both as a political party and a system, the CPC remains in power? The latent potential, it would appear, is being tapped, so the future may not look as negative as it has been for centuries.

I'm bothered by all the fuss that is made of foreign visitors or even consultants when the economy cannot really afford to keep them in such comfort. It is obviously an attempt in part at saving face. But surely the Chinese citizen must resent foreigners living in relative luxury when they themselves have no access to these hotels and cars. Why can't the experts from outside live in the same kind of houses as do their Chinese counterparts? This might actually lead to the government having to improve the housing of the ordinary Chinese as well. It is galling for those of us who once boasted great cultures to accept being part of the Third World now, and because of our poverty having to seek aid from rich countries. We should however treat it as our right since the wealth of the First World derives to a fair extent from its erstwhile exploitation of its erstwhile colonies, now substantiably the Third World.

On a lighter note, I have to say that my shopping expedition was not successful. Since I couldn't find a jacket large enough to fit me, I hastily sewed up a sack for myself. It is literally a sack, big and loose, as I wanted something very cool and not tight-fitting, and I roam around in a pigtail wearing a pair of regulation blue slacks. I really do look a sight—so different from the petite, slim Chinese women, and certainly a target for whistles from teddy boys, except that there seem to be none of those here. I troop through the entire length of the train to get to the dining car, with men sprawled all over, looking on. A few give me an amused look, but I have not had one catcall or whistle yet. I bet they are very human in what they are thinking, but they are good enough not to make it obvious and embarrass a timid stranger! On second thoughts, perhaps I would prefer a really honest catcall to this respectable silence!

It raises a bigger question in my mind. Curiously it seems that parallel with the movement for the emancipation of women, there is an emphasized puritanical trend, not altogether surprising in revolutionary situations. It certainly appears to have taken root, because apart from obvious things like the disappearance of prostitution, one notices the absence of rowdiness. I wonder if this trend is derived from the idea that one's private life cannot be divorced from one's public life, which appears to be a guiding principle in present-day official Chinese thought. I wonder if this trend will have repercussions perhaps in a decade to come.

6

A Brief Side Trip to the Luoyang Caves

We took the train to Luoyang and arrived to coincide with the mid-autumn Moon Festival. We were fed moon cakes—flat pie-shaped pastries stuffed with chopped nuts and condiments. One has to guess what's in them and they are heavy on the stomach. Many processions carrying banners were moving along the streets in celebration of the festival, with people either joining in or dropping off as they went from place to place. Luoyang was also once a capital of Chinese dynasties, prior to Xi'an.

We were taken not to a small hotel as I had expected but to a large modern guest house, fitted with central heating and mod cons including that which is now beginning to give me the greatest joy—the availability of a hot bath. Apparently, they have many visitors so it was decided to build a proper place for them to stay. I ate my first cooked breakfast in China, an English-style breakfast of fried eggs, bacon and ham, and the radio in the dining room played Beethoven's Fifth Symphony and after a lengthy announcement proceeded to the Sixth. I wondered if they intended to broadcast all nine, in which case by the time we returned, I would get to hear the 'Daughter of Elysium' in the finale to the Ninth.

At dinner we managed to tune into a programme in English probably from the BBC. It was a church service with a sermon consoling the Christian brethren in the Far East who might be feeling isolated and alone, and reassuring them that they were not alone as there was a unity to all mankind believing in the same true God. I wasn't quite sure what the authorities were making of this message. Mingo went into giggles translating it for Mr Chiang, the archaeologist, who was our host and who cannot follow English. Eventually we got to the news and heard it without disturbance. We had not heard the news since coming to China as we had had no access to any

English language newspaper. The highlight was that the Russians had developed an intercontinental rocket that had alarmed the Western world. This news had come to Anil in a letter from a friend two weeks ago, so obviously it was still being discussed. We fiddled again with the radio and got a Japanese station that was broadcasting popular music and we heard a woman with a distinctly Japanese accent singing 'Love me tender, love me true . . .' such a change from Elvis Presley!

The bonus for us was that we were being taken on an extended visit to the caves at Lung Men (as Longmen was then known), not too far away, to see the superb Buddhist sculpture. This was more than a thrill. The cave entrances are relatively open so the sculpture almost comes out to meet the viewer's eye. A river runs between two hills and there are caves on both overlooking the river. During the dry season when the water is not very deep, carts can be pulled through the river as we saw this morning together with the horses drawing them. Unfortunately, there is a coal mine and slag heap nearby, so much of the easily visible sculpture is layered with coal dust and is grey in colour. We had to go further into the cave to see the cleaner part. The caves and the niches with sculpture number more than a thousand. This background of grey and coal was a contrast to the bright orange of the persimmons heaped on the roadside for sale. Mr Chiang said that a road was being constructed on the other side of the hill to transport the coal. The sculptures then will not be covered in dust. The traffic on the road was largely animal drawn and I wondered how much coal such transportation could carry. Surprisingly we saw no trucks.

Much of the sculpture is of the Northern Wei and Tang period of the fifth and later centuries AD, with traces of what seemed to me to be some Indian styles. This is religious art at its best, mature and well-balanced. Bas-reliefs depicting royalty and others worshipping the Buddha were quite exquisite. There is the usual difference in size where the Buddha figure is the largest, royalty a trifle smaller, with the smallest being the common people. A multitude of caves were cut and there are consequently many thousand images. From the ninth to the twelfth century there was a falling off in the excavation of grottos. The limestone is eminently suitable for sculpture. But the real crime here is of modern times and from the activities of international art dealers. Many of the sculptures have had their heads hacked off, an activity that provided the highly priced objects for the international art market in the early twentieth century. Armed gangs were organized by the mafia of the art market who entered the caves with axes and crudely hacked off as many heads as they could.

When returning, we stopped at a temple and monastery built by a local general of earlier times, that have been repaired and redecorated, and now house a museum with sculptures from the fifth to the twelfth centuries. The frequency with which local museums are established is something that needs to be applauded. Such museums do encourage an interest in local history and pride in the objects displayed. This was one of the areas where the ancient Shang culture flourished but much of what was dug up and found, we were told, was taken out of China. I hesitate to use the word excavated, because many of these finds came from accidental digging during road building and the construction of large buildings. The word excavation is used here for this method of finding objects from the past, but it does not refer to a properly controlled and carefully recorded excavation, layer by layer, of a site. A controlled excavation is crucial to interpreting the data. But thankfully at least the objects found in these casual diggings are recorded and placed where they can be studied, so one can't complain too much. In many other countries little or no attention is given to the possibility of obtaining archaeological artefacts from such digging for construction purposes. Most of the objects in the museum were found three or four years ago when the main road was being constructed.

Another surprise was when we were told that a road was being cut through a low hill across a river. It ran straight into a Han tomb. The tomb was 'excavated' and cleared but the objects left in place. We could actually walk into the tomb and see its layout. It was in part a home with rooms and a kitchen well-stocked with jars and pots. Of the connecting doors one had a design of a pelican holding a fish in its beak—perhaps a family symbol. A long, low passage led to just a tomb and we had to walk in single file, each of us holding a candle. This gave it something of a mysterious feel. The archaeological richness of the area seems to burst out of the earth and only a minute part of it has been revealed so far.

Then came the visit to the famous White Horse Temple and monastery, believed by tradition to be the first Buddhist place of worship in China, built in 68 AD when Luoyang was the capital. There is a little confusion about its identity because not surprisingly there were other monasteries in the neighbourhood that also claimed to be the White Horse one. The story goes that a Chinese emperor sent two emissaries to India to bring back information on Buddhism about which he had had a dream. The two arrived in North-west India, probably Gandhara or the frontier region between North-west India and Central Asia, where they met a couple of Buddhist monks and persuaded them to come to China. One version says that the monks came with the sutras laden on a white horse, hence the name of the monastery. The monastery was then built and the two monks were established there and set about translating the texts into Chinese. Historical evidence of the monastery dates to the third/fourth century AD and links the Indian Buddhist monks, Dharmaratna and Kashyapa Matanga, according to some sources, as staying at this monastery. These are regarded as among the finest translations of Mahayana Buddhist texts from Sanskrit to Chinese. It is also said that Xuan Zang stayed here intermittently, after his return from India when he was translating the texts. During the second millennium AD, the monastery suffered damage through fires and had to be restored and parts of it were rebuilt more than once.

The current monastery is well planned around a series of open courtyards along its length surrounded by grounds and enclosed by a high red wall. The juxtaposition of three arches provides the entrance. The icons were part of the restoration and are therefore modern and their quality is a little diminished by their being covered in gaudy colours with ample gilt. The buildings, however, remain impressive rising from a sturdy stone base to the roof, the beams of which carry dragon gargoyles and three-pointed spears as decoration. The individual shrines have not been cleaned in a while as they are decorated with cobwebs. The chief monk looks well-fed and comfortable and is obviously living a life of ease. The monastery is said to be financially well off since in addition to official support it also has the support of organizations such as the Association of Religions, and the Association for the Preservation of Relics. Being a historical monument, the Department of Antiquities also comes to its aid when necessary. We visited what were said to be the tombs of the two Indian monks. It is an attractive group of buildings but I can't say that the ambience inspires respect for the place. The monastery at Xi'an had much more going for it. The monk today was as uninspiring as the monk at the Xi'an monastery was inspiring.

❀

We drove back through a different landscape and I was amazed at the number of small roofed shrines that were scattered across the fields as also the numbers of steles and stone tablets. They sprout like wild flowers all over where there is space. And equally often there are mounds, masses of mounds. Some are tombs as yet unexcavated, and who knows what some of the others may contain.

What has surprised me is that with all this visiting of historical sites and monasteries and temples, there has been so little conversation about religion. It is understandable that contemporary religion would not be discussed because either there is too little of it or else people are keeping it to themselves knowing that it may not be spoken of with ease. Yet I did expect to hear some comment on the teachings of Confucius or the Buddha, or for that matter even some curiosity about religion in India and some interest in Hinduism that is a virtually unknown religion to the Chinese. But there has been no interest in the subject at all. Not even in Christianity when one asks about the influence of Christian missionaries, considering that there were many Christian denominations active in China; or Islam given that there is a minority Muslim community in the north-west of China in Xinjiang. It is hard to believe that religion could have been so efficiently erased from the life of the Chinese in such a short time. Apart from religion there haven't even been many references to Marxism, either as a theory of knowledge or as a political ideology, as I had expected. Admittedly we were more frequently in the company of officials than academics nevertheless there was a noticeable absence of mention of the official ideology. I did mutter something about the Asiatic Mode of Production on a couple of occasions but it brought no response. Considering that it was Marx's theory about how Asian societies functioned, and owed much to the description of what was called Oriental Despotism that was being debated currently in Europe, I was rather surprised that it did not evoke a discussion.

7

Onwards to Lanzhou

From Xi'an we took the train to Lanchow (as Lanzhou was then known), the sort of city that I should have thought only existed in the memoirs of Marco Polo, or the opium dreams of Coleridge. We arrived at dawn and through my irritable drowsiness, as we walked across the uneven floor of the wood-constructed station, and as I stumbled over potholes and across bumps of pressed earth, I felt that I had at last come to China. The hotel in Beijing was the predictable international hotel of any big city, denuded of the personality of the city. But 5.30 a.m. at Lanzhou brought me face to face with another China. Our mountains of cameras and other film equipment were loaded onto a flimsy-looking cart that was drawn with great swiftness and dexterity by the railway porter. Standing in the station yard, waiting for the people who were supposed to meet us, I was once more made acutely aware that I knew the atmosphere of the place very well. It was North India again.

It was still dark but hawkers had established themselves at vantage points, each with an oil lamp, and were quietly calling out their wares— bread, fruit, and other eatables. The city itself lies in the base of a bowl of mountains. I can imagine the romance of approaching it on horseback, to ride over the side of the hills and suddenly see it nestled in the cup of the hills. We found our hosts who had waited four hours at the station because the train was late, and we were driven in a luxurious Mercedes to a newly built hotel—very modern, and especially built for foreign visitors. There is a cushioning off of foreign visitors by lodging them in specially built hotels. As a place it was not too displeasing, with only a few things that can be called bizarre. Compared to its Russian counterpart it shows excellent taste in decoration and furnishing.

I stood by the window and saw the sun rising over the hills, and with each moment the colour of the hills changed. It seemed quite unique! This happened throughout the day, the changing light of the day filled the hills with a change of colour. The most spectacular was the sunset. Fortunately, we were driving out to the technical school at twilight. We followed the riverbank for a while and then it curved along the contour of the hills in the direction of the setting sun. I could hardly believe that the colours were real. There had been a dust storm earlier in the evening and heavy clouds of dust lay scattered in the sky, their natural ashen yellow filled with the reds and purples of sunset. Because this region is particularly dusty the sunsets are spectacular. Against this highly coloured sky the hills stood out in a musty grey colour. Occasionally we would circle a bend and see rows of poplars by the river but most of the time the hills were bare—an almost startling nudity.

On the other side of the river were the new buildings, the factory, the oil refinery, the railway construction works, and the flatlets for the workers. On our side was the old town. We drove through streets that could hardly be called streets, so rough and stone-riddled were they. Old houses built of sun-baked brick plastered with mud lined both sides, and now and again there was a walled enclosure with towers at the four corners. High up on the hill slopes, the dark openings of what were once cave houses were still visible and looked strangely inviting.

The streets were lit by the coloured lights from the shops. All small shops—many selling melons—large heaps of them falling on to the road, dark melons and light melons and heaps of persimmons. And tea shops and eating places where people sat pouring tea into tiny cups or eating steaming noodles. These are streets where cars don't pass all that often, so people walk down the middle of the road unconcerned about the traffic: at the sound of a car horn children and grown-ups scuttled into the open space by the edge of the road and then laughed gaily, and we laughed back and apologized for pushing them off the road. One enterprising couple had settled down on the small island, or policeman's stand, at the crossroads and were doing a busy trade selling tomatoes.

There were many moments when I was strongly reminded of the old North-West Frontier Province, the areas across the upper Indus, especially the parts around Peshawar and the Afghan border where I had spent my childhood—the same bleak grey hills, the dusty roads, the mud houses and the walled structures on low hilltops. I noticed on the train that when we were in Kansu (as Gansu was then known), the villages tended to be more compact, each group of houses was walled and sometimes an entire village had near it a small citadel with four towers, obviously the effect of the imminence of invasions, and so reminiscent of the many pathan-kots, small forts located on the hills in the North-West Frontier of India. This evening I almost expected to see the khaki turrah of the turban of a man from the Khyber Pakhtun clans walking down the street swinging his rifle.

I don't think it was entirely my imagination, but I thought that the facial type differed a little in this area, suggesting some ancestry from Central Asia. The eyes are larger, the cheekbones not quite so prominent. The colour is fairer, and one can almost spot pink cheeks even in this heat. Some faces could almost pass for those from the North-West Frontier of the subcontinent. The children are not so cleanly kept: begrimed faces, running noses, and an occasional wet sore are not uncommon. We met our first beggar this afternoon in the monastery up in the hills. Begging must have been quite a traditional occupation in a city of this sort—I am surprised we did not find more. The clothes are the same as elsewhere, various shades of blue. The women's blouses though are more colourful.

The women are generally more feminine in their dress and behaviour and well they might be, given that the standard of beauty is extremely high in these parts. Nothing short of an exhaustive search would discover a woman who was not reasonably good looking. They combine colour and freshness with their distinctive features. The curiosity of the people is unbounded, doubtless because it is rare for them to see women in saris. Europeans are not so unusual because of some of the Russian and East European engineers, who come to work here and bring their wives.

We tried to go shopping to buy some essentials for Maijishan, but it was impossible, the crowd around us kept pushing and moving closer, till we ourselves could hardly move, and what can you say to them, when they all smile so warmly and regard you with obvious friendly curiosity because you look and dress so differently. So Anil and I decided that we simply had to get into less conspicuous clothes. These, of course, would have to be stitched.

It all started in a very harmless way. Anil and I, not having brought a blouse for our slacks, decided we'd buy some material and get a tailor to sew us a traditional long jacket-like blouse worn by the Chinese peasant women. I like the pattern very much and we thought it would be the easiest thing to explain to a local tailor. We went to a tailor, followed, of course, by our usual procession of about thirty Lanzhovians. The tailor said that he'd take at least ten days, so that was out of the question. We were then advised to buy a ready-made one. We walked into the depths of an old wooden shop followed by our procession who stood around us and looked on, while we turned down blouse after blouse since none fit. The man behind the counter, being most enterprising, told us that he knew of a tailor who would stitch us the blouses by the next evening and we would therefore have them when we left Lanzhou. In all gratefulness we asked him to take us there. But first we must buy the material. He and our guide decided on a nearby shop, so the four of us together with the procession went to the nearby shop and with great speed and efficiency bought some regulation blue—in fact a very attractive shade. Then we went to the tailor.

Since he was some distance away, we went by car. We managed to get rid of our erstwhile procession only to alight in the next street and between walking from the car to the tailor's shop we acquired another equally large procession that flowed into the shop after us. There had been, no doubt, enough discussion about our problems amongst our first little gathering for the word to have spread. However, now the real problem arose. We did not mind being breathed down our necks whilst we were buying our material, but both Anil and I, being somewhat shy about our inches, didn't like the idea of having our measurements announced to the public. The tailor, with Chinese sensitivity, invited us to a back enclosure where we could give our measurements in privacy.

We followed him, surrounded by what seemed to us armies of assistants, but he assured us that they were all young men who worked in the shop with him. Anil was first, she was measured and her measurements noted. She asked if she could possibly have her jacket padded with cotton or a woollen material. The tailor's reply was brief and to the point: 'You will look ugly.' No more was said about the padding. Then came my turn. My brain was ticking like mad—if only there was some way of avoiding his taking my measurements. I started off on a long rigmarole on how I liked my clothes very loose and didn't believe in the modern fashion of women wearing tight-fitting dresses, to which he nodded and smiled, and he later added that in China only men wore their clothes loose. I asked for a pocket on the outside of the jacket. He refused bluntly because it wasn't part of the pattern and either I should have a thing truly traditional or not at all. Then he produced his inch-tape and I began to get pale—neck, shoulder, sleeve, arm-hook, chest, waist, and then I waited in fear—hips . . . 42 inches. His face froze in amazement. I tried to smile, weakly, but it was too late. For a woman in China to have such a large hip size was inexcusable. Already the army of assistants was discussing the matter in great detail, and I'm sure that by the time we emerged from the shop, the news had spread.

8

In the Train to Tian Shui, En Route to Maijishan

It is very still and quiet and the train is moving almost at walking pace across the low hills. It is noon and everybody and everything seems asleep. The others are sleeping around me and I have been sitting by the window, looking out and thinking about Lanzhou. We shall get off at the next stop and from there travel to Maijishan. The sun is hot and we are travelling through hills, sometimes catching glimpses of the Huang He. Where there are low slopes and small plateaus, these are covered with fields—millet and maize below and terraces of rice fields on the slopes.

Lanzhou in ten years will be a changed city. I wonder if the same amount of construction and change will take place in all provincial cities. The long road to Xinjiang, the frontier region between China and Central Asia that was started with the twenty-kilometre avenue leading out of Lanzhou, will doubtless have been completed: a beautiful, broad tarred road with trees on each side and hills, keeping away the dust. The trees, too, will be planted in some parts to prevent dust spreading all over the city. Dust, dust, dust—that is one impression I have—and I've never swallowed so much dust in three days. I wish I were a machine. Then I could have taken myself apart, cleaned up bits of my body, and put them back together again. That walk in the old town in Lanzhou was maddening. The horses that kept going past raising a storm of dust each time and the children that closed in on us, till it was almost impossible to move. And I wanted to spend a few minutes stopping at various places along the road. But I couldn't stop long enough—melons, more melons—sold in large heaps in open shops—the smell of naans cooking in the houses—wonderful, the big flat bread, which I had so much of as a kid in Peshawar: which the people in Lanzhou eat in the same way with meat and raw onion.

A shop selling cigarettes was where a group of young men sat and watched us with great amusement as we coped with the dust and the inquisitiveness of people surrounding us. The houses were all built in the traditional Chinese style. A courtyard surrounded by rooms on all four sides. If one block is not large enough for a family then another block is added and there is a passage from one to the other. This apparently was very convenient under the old joint family system. Indeed it must have been with each son having his own house, yet the whole building functioning as a single establishment. We were told in Beijing that Chinese aristocrats regarded this as eminently suitable too, since each concubine was given an entire wing, so that they were all close enough for the convenience of the lord, yet not so close as to be stepping on each other's toes—what practicality when affordable!

But the old houses in Lanzhou looked sorry and sad. Most of them had a horse or some other animals tethered in the courtyard. Whereas their Beijing counterparts look attractive decorated with creepers climbing up pillars, and large banks of flowering lotuses and miniature formal gardens, these courtyards were treated as usable space. In Lanzhou, a single house was often inhabited by more than one family, and each family would take over one part of the whole. The courtyard was common property and contained all that could not be put into the house. A corner where clothes were hung out to dry, another where beds were being repaired, a third with an open stove, and elsewhere there lay a mess of melon rinds and black seeds. At the entrance of one stood two men with the cut of the beard that one associates with a Persian style, and an old man and a young man, and near them was tethered a white goat. It was almost a cliché taken from a medieval Persian miniature painting.

Coming up the road we saw two men with large sheepskin rafts—so repulsive to look at, but once in the water they are possibly the best thing for the fast Huang He current. The raft is built of light wood and the floats consist of sixteen pigskins filled with air, looking like balloons. These are tied close together and keep the raft afloat. I should like to travel on one of these—perhaps the next time I visit Lanzhou. The current in the river is really fast, faster than the average river—possibly because it passes through many gorges in these parts and this, with the added movement of elevation, gives it speed. It was fascinating to stand on the old bridge in Lanzhou and see these rafts shooting past.

We visited a Buddhist temple halfway up the hill to the south of Lanzhou. There seem to be fewer temples than I had expected and little reference to temple-going. This temple was of the Ming dynasty and surrounded by a series of buildings, beautifully arranged, beside and above it, which were once a monastic complex. Standing on the highest building and looking down the side of the hill over the pointed rooftops of the temple and monastery was a thrill, because one could see a rare sensitivity to space projected almost dramatically. The spacing of each building, the covered passages and corridors between some and the open spaces between others, was so harmoniously laid out that I looked at it for quite a while and decided that I wouldn't have changed it even by an inch. But the buildings look a little shabby, and their restoration should be done more carefully.

The problem that faces all restoration is that of the degree to which something should be restored and with what restraints. Some buildings have been restored to what was thought to be Ming taste—scarlet pillars and ornate designs of cloud and dragon motifs in bright shades of blue, green, red etc. These colours on their own or in other combinations look rich and pleasing, but in this particular juxtaposition are garish and harsh. Restoration is, of course, called for but I fear that the restoration of Ming and Qing architecture in China might mean an enthusiasm for the rather garish than just the colourful. For instance, if the woodwork, instead of being painted over with colour were to be correctly varnished, all the richness of the wood would remain without offending the eye. Fortunately the entire monastery has not yet been restored. It looks bare too—no grass anywhere, just a few trees. Some greenery would give it a kinder look.

The curator of the museum (which is lodged in the monastery) explained that the Guomin Dang (as the Kuomintang was then known) troops had been billeted in the temple, and they had cut down many of the trees. The main temple has a delightful banner across the entrance, over which are inscribed Chinese characters welcoming 'souls' to the blue heaven. There is a colossal bronze statue of the Buddha, standing in the stance of preaching. On its belly was found an inscription of the Ming period. Was that the most practical place for an inscription? Artistically the image is quite ordinary. Buddhist monks also had an instinctive feel for magnificent locations and all the major monasteries that we have been to so far seem to have a connect with the landscape.

Near the temple is a charming little pagoda that houses a beautiful bell of the Song period. This was brought here from a temple in Lanzhou, which was bombed by the Japanese. There is an old Buddhist monk—a dignified man in black robes, with two long wisps of hair for a beard, that seems to be the fashion among old monks, who still looks after the temple and he opened it for us to enter.

I feel heavy and tired. My nose is running and my throat is sore. Too much dust?

My heart aches, a drowsy numbness creeps—
As though of hemlock I had drunk . . .
But I must write now, or else it will all be left behind . . .

The museum at the temple is the local art and archaeological museum. We had a long session with the curator, Professor Ho, who was once a professor of epigraphy and history. He looked the image of a Chinese scholar as conventionally depicted. A delicately built man, not weak—just delicate, with a white goatee beard, sharp, quick eyes, and long fine fingers—earnest in his conversation and fluent. The museum had a large collection of prehistoric pottery, Han bronzes, porcelain of all periods, and later Song and Ming paintings. I was particularly interested in the prehistoric pottery that had all been collected within the last five years. The museum had only recently come into existence. We were told that most of this pottery was not collected from organized excavations, but was brought in by people working on construction sites, i.e., new factories and railways.

When the new areas are dug, many objects are unearthed and these are brought to the museum—again what would otherwise be called 'rescue' or 'salvage' archaeology. Archaeologists and students are divided into groups, each attending to an area according to the most important project underway. For instance, if a new railway is being built nearby, one group will be sent there. On an object being found by a workman, it would immediately be given to the archaeologist to note the particulars, and the object would be taken to the museum. At present, students of archaeology at Lanzhou work in well-defined and coordinated groups, some on the railway lines being built such as the one linking Lanzhou to places in Xinjiang among others, some in the cities where construction is under way, and some in other places in the province of Gansu.

Scientific excavations are not common at the moment because they have such an in-pouring of objects from all over that they need the students to build the museum, and they feel that for the present they should concentrate on collecting enough for a really good museum since there was absolutely nothing before. The students have to first be trained in recognizing and handling objects and therefore, the more objects, the better for them to become familiar with the artefacts. I can well understand this point of view, but at the same time I think that merely collecting objects is not the way to train students. The technique of excavating, too, is important and is the really scientific part of archaeology, and I hope they will have more of it soon.

Sometimes presentations are made to the museum. But this is rare. Asked why there was considerably more archaeology now than before, we were told that previously the Kuomintang/KMT government was not interested in preserving ancient objects and in fact often wilfully destroyed them. I wondered about the correctness of this since the fashion for Chinoiserie and collecting Chinese objects began some decades ago and the KMT carried away an enormous amount of art objects while fleeing to Taiwan. But obviously the Kuomintang has to be linked with anti-social activities to create the propaganda against them. We were told that now there is a tremendous enthusiasm for reconstructing the past of China as fully as possible. Under the old regime archaeologists could not get jobs, and the only line open to them was teaching. But now Chairman Mao has encouraged archaeology in order to 'discover the richness of China's past, and to correct historical mistakes'. Previously, it was the ruling class that wrote history and it, therefore, had a slant that was often incorrect. Now the archaeologist must fill in the blanks and discover the truth.

I listened quietly for the most part but when the questioning within me got the better of me, I did ask some questions. How does one assess true history? Is this being taught as a method of researching history? We know that even the new interpretations of history can be misleading if the evidence is not properly examined for reliability and the interpretation based on logical argument. The most important aspect of teaching history is to learn how to test the evidence for reliability, to ensure the logical basis of

TO TIAN SHUI, EN ROUTE TO MAIJISHAN • 113

causal connections, and to raise every possible question before coming to a conclusion. I had the feeling that stock phrases were being repeated although this may well have been all in good faith. But despite my making several requests that we meet with some archaeologists and historians of ancient China to discuss their methods of historical analysis, my requests were ignored. I was never quite sure whether this was deliberate or whether there was a genuine inconvenience in trying to arrange such meetings.

After further questioning I discovered something a little nearer home. Our informant explained that the students were most enthusiastic and some of them after working in the Lanzhou Museum go to the Research Institute of Archaeology in Beijing. The percentage of archaeology students is not high compared to students doing other subjects, but this is also because archaeology comes under the department of history and does not as yet have an independent status. The students love the subject, we were told, because they love their country. And also, because British and American archaeologists have always maintained that Chinese culture originated in Xi'an, which view the students of Gansu want to disprove (Xi'an being in Shaanxi province and not in Gansu), and hence the eagerness to dig! This, despite its limitations, seemed to me to be perhaps closer to what is being propagated than Chairman Mao's directive.

Some excavations are held during the summer vacation. The latest move has been to interest the Institute for Nationalities of the North-West (as the North-west Minzu University was then known), as many finds are being made in areas where there is a large population of what are called the national minorities. The latter are the people who trace their ancestry to non-Han populations of earlier times that would naturally be more easily found in the frontier regions. Among them for instance were the Uyghurs in Xinjiang whose ancestors had migrated from across the border and their religion was Islam. Local reports of archaeological discoveries are sent to the central body—the Academy of Sciences in Beijing. Here the material is collated and that which is the most important is published in a journal called *Reference Material on Antiquities* published by the Ministry of Culture as a monthly. Archaeology and art history both come under the Ministry of Culture.

In China, as in Russia, a sharp distinction is made between scientific archaeology and art history, and the two departments are separate.

Obviously there is a spurt in archaeological interest, even if the interpretation of excavated material is sometimes viewed from an extreme nationalist perspective that may even on occasion give an incorrect reading. Nevertheless, enthusiasm prevails. The most encouraging thing is that even on a local level in distant parts of the country, there is an awareness of the scientific perspective involved in archaeological research although it may not be applied, and this is more than can be said of many other Asian countries. The great need, judging from Lanzhou, is for buildings to house the objects. Coming away from the museum, I saw a collection of very interesting greyware that had surfaced a week before at a local site. It had been efficiently mended, and neatly labelled, waiting to be exhibited—but the professor looked at it sadly and wondered where he would put it.

The objects exhibited are kept in glass cases, shining in their new polish. They are well labelled, each one distinctly and separately. The only lack is that in the early sections the approximate date for each object is not given. Broad labels, such as New Stone Age, are used. A chart in each room explains the period, giving a chronology. Another problem is that dates are given as 5,000 years from today, i.e. the present, and this I find imprecise. Some system of reckoning, the Christian era or an acceptable Chinese era should be used. 'Today' is not precise enough as 'today' moves forward in time and with each move the chronology changes. If a historical sense is to be promulgated among a people, even though the Chinese are thought to have had it to a high degree, measuring historical events and objects in time should be more precise. This system of dating from 'today' is, I fear, another manifestation of dividing recent history into 'before Liberation' and 'after Liberation', although this division is rooted in dateable historical events.

It was much the same in the other museum that we visited the next morning, the museum on the history of Gansu and its natural resources. A third section, yet incomplete, will depict socialist reconstruction in Gansu. The historical side had been imaginatively handled—the archaeological side was good as far as charts and maps and explanatory models went. The emphasis right through was on art objects and I felt that in showing the history of a province, much could have been made of local cultures, and in Gansu with all its many minorities, partly because of its proximity to Central Asia, this could be a particularly rich section. The indication of implements, such as agricultural implements in the section on agriculture, would be an added attraction. Similarly, working models of machines in factories and industrial plants would create an intelligent interest in an already interested public. The division into sections was useful and the one on natural resources was well presented. I should have liked very much to see what they would do with the section on socialist reconstruction, but unfortunately it wasn't ready. The workers in the museum were mainly historians and people who had studied the classics. This is both a qualification and a limitation that is common to museum curators in many parts of the world. Some looking after these museums had been to Beijing to various research institutes, others had worked at the local university. A course on museology was not available locally.

The most frustrating thing about meeting Professor Ho and the director of the museum, and others, is that I cannot talk in depth with them, because I don't know Chinese and they don't know English. The interpreter is very good but nevertheless conversation becomes stilted, else I find there is a tendency to give facts and figures, rather than to discuss questions. For instance, I raised the question of terminology with Professor Ho but he sidetracked the question. I don't believe that this was done deliberately, but perhaps because in the process of interpretation he may have misunderstood the question.

Similarly I mentioned the recent thinking on the theory on the common homeland of various peoples in Central Asia and the migration of tribes but he merely smiled and changed the subject. I have a lurking suspicion that this is also due to the fact that provincial archaeologists can only conform to earlier knowledge since they do not always have access to contemporary published material. This is common to many parts of the Third World, and this is why some of us keep insisting that the accessibility especially of specialized academic journals and to crucial publications is absolutely essential to any research and to assessing knowledge in any field. Colonial scholars understood this only too well and hence the enviable availability of sources in the research centres of Europe.

This situation here parallels that of India, where not only provincial, but often archaeologists even in central institutions are limited to an Indian context, owing to the absence of access to sources of other areas. There is a failure then to link cultural activities to and from the outside world, where such activities go beyond the current national border. For instance, we have hardly any academically recognized tradition in India of scholars trained in pre-modern Central Asian or South-east Asian archaeology, history, and language studies, areas where there has been an impressive Indian presence. There is just a bare scatter of individuals who are given little encouragement. Nor is there scholarship in the pre-modern history of areas other than India. With us, too, this is largely due to research centres lacking libraries with up-to-date journals and publications, necessary to this scholarship; not to mention the recognition of the importance of this scholarship to Indian cultural and religious studies as well.

The afternoon at the monastery ended delightfully. Professor Ho and Mr Lan invited us to tea in the garden of the monastery, where we sat amidst the stares of many Lanchovians, young and old, and ate melons— melons large, melons small, melons red, melons yellow, melons green, melons white—an orgy of melons and we sat there making up couplets about melons, about the people of Gansu, and were initiated into melon eating— the way it should be done.

We drove out along the river in the evening. A startlingly colourful sky made everything look unreal. We were taken a good 20 kilometres out of Lanzhou to the Technical School, which was originally founded by Rewi Alley. He was there that week, so we were going to meet him. I didn't know anything about him, except that he was a New Zealander who had come to China many years ago and had started a school to train technicians, and had worked with the Liberation Movement—as it has now come to be known—on this. He also translated Chinese poetry into English but I heard that he was less successful at that.

He is a big, somewhat bluff man. At first I did not take to him. He reminded me of British colonels in the Indian army being condescendingly nice to the natives, calling them chaps and fellas, etc. But gradually I began to see that that was just his way and not meant otherwise. Thirty-one years in the north-west of China, in the very thick of the fight, can take the raw out of anyone. Gradually his brusqueness appeared in the proper light, as, in fact, the politeness of a very busy man. I objected to his serving us Nescafe in glass tumblers and ordinary sponge cake badly baked. Why, I thought, why not serve Chinese tea as something everyone is used to. I wanted to ask him so many questions, about why he chose to settle in this part of China, what made him join the Liberation Movement, and such like, but it seemed absurd to ask such questions in a brief half-hour; besides, answers to personal questions put by strangers are hardly ever honest. He may not have been self-conscious or afraid of us mocking him as I would have been had it been me, but nevertheless he would have been polite or dismissive. I envied him his dedication; I envied him his thirty-one years of living for a cause and it would have been worth drawing him out to speak at greater length—but then perhaps he would not have done so.

At the same time I felt a little cheated. This was the great legend of the north-west, the man whom people have trekked hundreds of miles to see. I remember something about this vaguely in Santha Rama Rau's *East of Home* and various other books. Every recent book on New China mentions him. Isn't it all a little exaggerated? Or again is it simply that one assumes that accomplished people are always surrounded by glamour and that when one sees such a person without it, it is unacceptable? Besides, half an hour's conversation about handicrafts can hardly convey anything. I must read some of his writing, although no more of his poetry translations. More especially I must reread material on the north-west and the Liberation Movement here in the early twentieth century. Now being slightly acquainted with the region it will be more meaningful.

The bare almost martial-looking room of Rewi Alley was such a contrast to the tea garden of the monastery, in the Park of the Five Fountains, where we ate melons and talked about the legend of the park, how couples who wanted a son came to the fountain and tried to pick up a pebble from the floor of the fountain and so forth...

I wondered when we would be taken to a cooperative farm, and the very next afternoon we were taken to the Yen Tan fruit and vegetable cooperative. Only the Chinese, I am beginning to think, can mix sensitivity with practicality and avoid discord! Yen Tan means 'the bird/bud on the river' and what could be better as a name for a fruit and vegetable farm on an island in the Yellow River. We drove through the dust clouds of old Lanzhou and arrived at the farm. We were first taken to the main office and were received in the Committee Room, decorated with large pictures of Mao, Zhou Enlai, etc., and large pink and yellow silk banners with lengthy inscriptions. There was a photograph on one of the walls, which reminded me of Indian institutions. It was a long photograph, at least three feet in length, showing hundreds of people sitting or standing in rows. The photograph was of the 'Heroes of

Labour' taken in Beijing where they had been given awards. One of them was from the Yen Tan farm.

This farm provides the greater part of the fruit and vegetables for Lanzhou, that is for a population of nearly 700,000. The total area of the farm is 4,600 mou where 1 mou is 920 square yards, out of which 500 belong to a government experimental farm. The farm is run by 691 families, and therefore has a population of about 3,500 people. Before Liberation, 400 families lived on the land occupied by the present farm. With the coming of factories to Lanzhou some of these families moved away and about seventy families came in from other parts of China. The mobility of populations is impressive and one wonders what the incentive may be. In 1951, the cooperative movement was started, and by 1956, the area was organized into one large cooperative farm. Membership of the farm is permitted at the age of sixteen, and at present, there are 2,100 members working. The farm also has 91 cattle, 800 poultry, 300 ducks, and 400 chickens. The farm is divided into eight sectors and each one has its own team of workers.

The daily output is 60,000 cattys (one catty is about 500 grams) of vegetables that are sent to Lanzhou. Working hours during peak periods are ten hours a day, but off-season there is much leisure time. People of both Han origin and 'national' minorities live on the farm. We asked about leisure-time occupation. Handicrafts and cottage industries don't seem to exist. Here I think Indian agrarian organization has scored: in organizing handicrafts as a supplementary income for the peasant and in encouraging traditional crafts. But this is a very minor point in the context of the entire agrarian situation in both countries. A certain number of hours each week are kept aside for discussions and study groups. At this time the young and old peasants gather to discuss their problems and give suggestions. Study groups include technical education, to enable each member to keep abreast of new developments in his own sphere of work. I should have been most interested to visit one of the study groups, just to see the level and determine the interest of the people there, but unfortunately there was no time.

There are four schools on the co-op: two are financed by the government and two by members of the co-op. These schools handle the primary education of all the children on the farm, and much of the middle school education too. Some of the younger members we were told occasionally leave to work in the factories, but the co-op continues to support them, till they are secure in their own work. This I must confess seemed a somewhat idealistic statement. I can't see 691 families agreeing to support young men and women who had left the farm and were working elsewhere, in entirely different jobs. On the administrative side, there is a committee of twenty-nine members, six of whom are women. In fact, one team leader is also a woman. We enquired as to whether there was any difficulty about accepting women in important posts, but were told that there wasn't. Of course it would be much easier on a farm, where a woman working is nothing extraordinary. Altogether 1,030 women were working on the farm and had exactly the same pay and rights as the men.

Work was distributed according to ability. The only way one can judge such a changed situation is by living for a while on such a farm. The actual employment of women is not in itself enough to give them status. Most of the workers in bidi factories in Bombay are women, yet that does not alter their position in Bombay society. The new marriage law in China was considered a progressive step, both from the point of view of creating a more elastic society and also contributing to the general elevation of women by giving them basic rights that they had earlier lacked. On the production side we were given many figures. Were we expected to believe that before 1951 production was low, in 1954 it rose by half and by 1956 it had doubled?

After we had finished questioning them, we were in turn questioned. There was considerable interest in and sympathy for the Indian peasant. Later we discovered that the Indian film, *Do Bigha Zamin*, on the plight of the Indian farmer, had been shown by a mobile cinema unit, and this had created further interest in the present-day agrarian situation in India. One questioner wanted to know how co-ops in France are managed, and Dominique hastily explained that they hardly existed in France, except for some vine growers who are organized in co-ops.

We were told that the farm already had 100 new houses. We saw a house made of sunburnt brick, plastered with clay and mud, and built in the traditional way. It was neatly designed with luxuries such as glass windows and wooden doors. More finished buildings they hope will come soon. In recent years, bicycles, watches, and pens have become popular. We walked through an apple orchard and I asked somewhat diffidently if they had tried any experiments along the lines of Lysenko in Russia. Oh yes, I was told, they had a laboratory where they experimented with improving seeds and types, but of course they had not and probably would not try grafting pears onto apples. At this the person who was showing us around smiled broadly.

We walked through melon fields and large cauliflower patches, and vegetable gardens growing tomatoes, green chillies, egg plants, and eventually arrived at a lightly wooded area by the river. Above and beyond was a tea-house, where some of the co-op members were relaxing over little pots of tea, and in the far distance a man was down on his knees saying his namaz. We sat on a bench under the trees, full of melon, apple, and peach, some of which we had been offered in the Committee Room. While we were waiting, we asked casually why we had halted under the trees. We were told that it was just a little break to eat a little melon!

I wondered how many such cooperative farms had been set up in China and whether they were as successful as this one appeared to be. Were they going to take over agricultural production? I also thought it would be worth comparing them with the kibbutz in Israel which in a way combines the organization of production with a strong ideology, in theory somewhat similar to what was happening here.

To complete the picture of modern life we were also taken to an oil refinery at Lanzhou because it is a big plant that would be largely responsible for the industrial importance of Lanzhou. Crude oil from Xinjiang and Yumen will be refined and oil for factory purposes will be supplied all round. The preparations began in 1953 and a committee was set up and a site selected in 1954. The people living on this site were moved elsewhere and were given land on the other side of the plain. Cadres were asked to start work. Groups of workers were employed and sent to other refineries to get training whilst the refinery was being built. Over 100 workers were sent to the USSR and other countries. In every refinery in the country, there are workers from this refinery being trained.

In April 1956 construction was started with a team of eighty members and the number went up by the end of the year to 2,000. The first part of the plan was the installation of pumps, followed by the building of houses, water and sewerage arrangements, all being made by the Lanzhou admin-istration and these became blueprints for other factories as well. The

From the train, travelling from Beijing to Xi'an

Cultivation in areas where there are loess cliffs is carefully demarcated.
Terraced fields at the upper levels are used mainly for rice.
The cultivation of other crops such as maize and millets is often at ground level.

Huang He River

It is a fast-flowing river, and, if one is coming downstream, mechanical propulsion is not essential. Goods that can be more easily transported are placed on bamboo rafts kept afloat by air-filled pigskins, rather like heavy-duty balloons. The rafts are easily constructed.

Huang He River

For heavier transportation, the rafts are sometimes tied together to provide a balance
and these can then be used to transport larger loads.

Xi'an

Visiting a historical site, we met some children who were delighted to be photographed with our interpreter Mingo, and were intrigued by Anil wearing a sari.

Xi'an

Rooftop decorations placed on a tiled roof convey and idea of those living in the house.
Sometimes the forms and figures on the rooftops are there to ensure blessings upon
the house and its occupants.

On the outskirts of a village near Xi'an
Pedicabs wait for customers.

Near Xi'an

A section of the temple to Confucius. The geometrical pattern of this architecture is most impressive.

Near Xi'an

A village in the loess area. Natural elevation is provided by the hillside, and marked by either the floors of a house or independent houses built on the slope. The structure and form of the houses change somewhat as they go up the slope.

Near Xi'an

A village near Xi'an, with its kitchen garden producing a good crop of vegetables.

Xi'an

A small child in his locally made pram. Such prams are widely used, especially in places where the modern version manufactured in a factory is not available. The structure is basic, although it looks complicated.

Xi'an

Display in the museum. The object is a bronze vessel of an early period. The decoration on the vessel is traced and shown as a flat surface, so that it is more easily visible. This technique is used very effectively in the display of various kinds of vessels.

Xi'an

Sculpture displayed in the Museum. Placing sculpture within a glass case was necessary for the security of the sculpture or any other valuable object, but it does create a further distance between the onlooker and the object.

Xi'an

A fine example of the architecture of a pagoda located in a monastery complex.
It is interesting how the shape of the sacred space in Buddhism changes from the
semi-circular stupa to the elongated pagoda.

In a village near Xi'an
Our young friend was initially shy but soon curiosity got the better of her and we started chatting through Mingo as interpreter.

In a village near Xi'an

More of our young friends and this time showing off their pet rabbits. The one with the black rabbit seemed quite happy to do so but the one with the white rabbit appears to be a trifle suspicious.

Xi'an

The elderly monk and his acolyte in the monastery that once was home to Xuanzang. The monk's robes are rather different in style from what the Buddhist monks wore in India. The dress of the acolyte is close to what some of the peasants wear in that area.

Xi'an

The White Horse monastery that is famous as the place where Buddhism was received in China and various Chinese and some Indian Buddhist scholars resided off and on. The horse is a distinguished symbol of the entry of Buddhism into one of the many locations in China.

(ABOVE) **Near Lanzhou**

Dominique Darbois, our photographer who photographed the murals and the sculptures at the two sites where we worked. She is seen here with people from the co-operative farm.

(RIGHT) **Near Lanzhou**

At the co-operative farm, we chatted with these three young women who were working there. They were dressed in skirts with cheerful designs and spoke to us with absolute confidence.

Lanzhou

Children leaving school and rather surprised to see us. This was still a time when children were not over-burdened by heavy rucksacks full of books.

Maijishan

A view of the landscape from the monastery. Cultivated fields in the foreground present a different picture from the uncultivated slopes further up and back.

Maijishan

A local peasant with his donkey loaded with firewood. He was taking this load either to his home or to the village for sale. Clearly, the use of firewood was still common. The hat worn by the peasant is in the local style.

Maijishan

The stream flowing along the valley as viewed from the monastery. This was the
stream in which we finally bathed one afternoon.

Maijishan

A view of the Maijishan hill with the caves on two sides, as viewed from the monastery. The shape of the hill is extraordinary and stands out in the otherwise usual landscape.

Maijishan

A view of the monastery taken from the caves. Its quadrangular structure is clear. The closeness of the forest explains the fear of wild animals that would obviously wish to investigate the monks living there.

Maijishan

The entrance to the monastery with its elaborate pattern of superimposed roofs and stylized animal figures. The frame of the structure was in brick, and the intervening surface was in plastered-over brick plastered in order to have a smooth surface.

Maijishan
The caves and galleries at a higher level. The galleries gave access to the caves within which were located the shrines.

Maijishan

The galleries giving access to the caves abutted onto the vertical surface of the hill. Large holes were cut into the hillside into which wooden slats were fitted and wooden boards were placed on these, which provided the gallery surface. The careful alignment was impressive. Built-in stepladders connected the different levels.

Maijishan

A gallery that still has to be built in order to give access to the caves. The site would not have had even these rudimentary beginnings when it was first located.

Maijishan
The gigantic figures on the outer surface of the hill amid a row of caves. The original sculpting of these must have taken an immense effort on the part of the craftsman.

Maijishan

Our friend Wang, the resident monk at the monastery. He normally wore the dress
of the peasants. The robes were saved for rituals and special occasions. We had to
persuade him to wear them for the photograph.

Maijishan

A mural depicting the Buddha had a surround of a series of halo-like forms on which were painted bodhisattvas and monks as is evident from this and the following photograph.

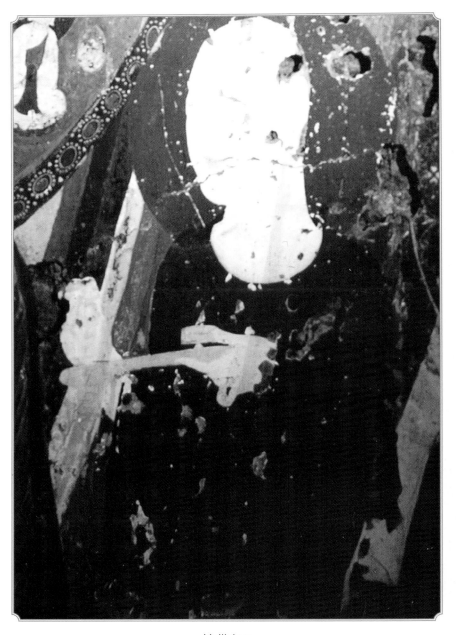

Maijishan
A mural that claims to be showing the monk Kashyapa in a painting surrounding that of the Buddha.

Maijishan

Sculptures from the caves. On the left, interpreted by some as a patron and by others as a worshipper. On the right, an image of a bodhisattva or a Buddha-to-be.

Maijishan

On the left, an image with the characteristics of the Buddha with Indian and Chinese imprints. On the right, an image of a seated Buddha. The variation in style is noticeable. These images seem to suggest the presence of craftsmen from various places, although the difference in time would also account for deviations in style.

Near the Great Wall

Local camel herders lead a pastoral life and provide animals for transportation.
These were widely used for carrying goods in the Chinese–Central Asian trade.

The Great Wall

A local dressed in the typical peasant's jacket was employed to carry stones required for the repair of the Great Wall. This may have been only in one part where repairs were being carried out. It did seem a little surprising that the readily available donkey was not being used for this purpose.

The Great Wall

A view of the Great Wall winding its way over the hills, following their contours. Built for greater security, it also had regular bastions for further defence. The upper surface had the width of a narrow road and was possibly used as such for short distances. The effort, the labour and the finances that must have gone into the building of this wall would have been mind-boggling. Yet it was built, and, when completed, was in some ways a memorial to the Chinese emperor Qin Shi Huang

On the way to Dunhuang

An airfield in the desert with the hills barely visible at the back. Such airfields were not used commercially; they were used more for the work required to set up the oil fields.

Dunhuang

Landscape near the Takla Makan desert, to the west of Dunhuang. A scatter of small oil derricks dot the low-lying hills.

Dunhuang

The surrounding landscape: the edge of the Gobi Desert to the east, with its plains of sand in the forefront, and the mountains further back form a contrast.

Dunhuang

Near the site of the cliffs with caves and murals. Small shrines across the river
are dedicated to monks who were associated with the monastery at Dunhuang.
The shrines continue to be visited by the occasional visitor and the individual monks
are remembered.

Dunhuang

Two small niche caves in one of the cliffs. Most of the caves open onto the front, and one can walk into them as one walks along the outer pathway. Occasionally, where there is space, a small cave was cut into the cliff and housed icons.

Dunhuang

A view of some of the caves cut into the cliff with the sand piling up in the front. The sand was blown towards the caves by the desert storms. Preventing the sand from covering up the entrances to the caves and clearing it requires continuous labour or the construction of a barrier. This is part of the reason that the caves were hidden from view for so long.

Dunhuang

(ABOVE) Cliffs, caves and a retaining wall. The precarious condition of the caves at the site required a retaining wall to prevent erosion. The wall was also useful in preventing the sand from piling up and covering the entrance to the cave and sometimes to the cave itself.

(BELOW) The condition in which some of the caves were found. The repair and reconstruction of such caves has to be done very carefully, so as not to destroy the murals that come up to the edge of the cave as is shown in the photograph. Significant amount of repairs were required in many caves.

Dunhuang

One of the taller cliffs with caves and shrines built into it and open to the front. The many levels can be seen in the top left of the photo. Stairs on the side allowed visitors to climb to the top. The unrestored front can be seen in the top right corner.

Dunhuang
A small farm, at the edge of the oasis, cultivating vegetables rather than cereal crops.

Dunhuang
Women and children at the local market.

Dunhuang
Woman selling grapes and melons in a market at the edge of the oasis.

Dunhuang

The local optician selling spectacles by the road. This must be the quickest way of finding a pair of spectacles—just trying a number of them and seeing which gives the maximum visibility.

Dunhuang

A street in the oasis where the local village cobbler was busy mending shoes. The board on the side referred to the kind of repairs and the estimated cost.

Dunhuang

A school in the oasis. A group of children at play during a brief break in the school time-table. Attending school is virtually compulsory.

Near Yumen

A more complex form of the fortifications that were built in the North-West and in the desert as a defence against the raids of the 'barbarians'.

Near Yumen

A fortified watch tower on the edge of the desert. Such towers are found along the major routes between North-West China and Central Asia. They were necessary to keep a watch-out for invaders, traders, pastoral nomads and migrants. The Chinese borders were thought of as vulnerable and had therefore to be well guarded, especially against the 'barbarians' as many non-Chinese were described.

(ABOVE) **Near Yumen**

A hut near the oasis. The large jars are used for storing a variety of things, from liquids to pickled vegetables. The roof is used for drying vegetables.

(LEFT) **Near Yumen**

On the route to Dunhuang. The area is being widely drilled for oil. The desert landscape is of the kind often associated with deposits of oil.

Shanghai

A building boom in one part of a modern city where the old and new towns are mixed. The architecture is not noticeably Chinese and can be recognized as such only as one comes close and sees the decorative features of the buildings.

Beijing

Apart from the more well-stocked grocery stores and the large markets selling fruit and vegetables, there is the sale of these and other small items of food on the push-carts of street vendors.

Beijing

The new housing that is rapidly being constructed by the state in some of the more populous cities. The most commonly used transportation other than city buses are bicycles. But the donkey-carts also have a presence.

Beijing

A fruit and vegetable market in the suburbs. Peasants bringing in their produce do not always find space inside the market, so they put up awnings on the side of the street and place their baskets of produce beneath these.

Beijing

A more open space to lay out baskets of fruit and vegetables for sale beneath an awning. When located near the local market, the vendors would perhaps lower their prices in order to get the better of the competition with the stalls within the market.

Beijing

Celebrating the Revolution.

(ABOVE) The ritual of paying homage to those projected as responsible for the Revolution. The huge portraits of the founders of Marxism were accompanied further down by those of the major personalities of the Communist Party of China.

(BELOW) As with the pattern followed elsewhere, the march past began with a show of military strength followed by floats on various aspects of Chinese culture accompanied sometimes with local music and dance, and the release of balloons. The firework display was held in the darkness of the late evening.

Beijing

Government buildings were decorated with the portraits of the top leaders of the Communist Party of China. The railway station, for example, has a portrait of Mao Zedong.

Beijing

A wing of the old inn that we visited. This was located in the older part of the city with buildings very close together.

Beijing

Part of a building in the Forbidden City. This was the royal area of the old city with a spectacular layout of buildings linked to royal functions. The red of the walls contrasted with the yellow of the roof tiles, and gave it a resplendent appearance.

Beijing
Anil de Silva and our interpreter Mingo Wong seated comfortably on the sculpture of an
iconic and heavily decorated Chinese tortoise in the Forbidden City.

Beijing

The Summer Palace. Built by an empress of the Qing dynasty in the eighteenth century, it is particularly noted for its landscaped gardens. The islands in the lake have attractive pavilions and bridges.

Beijing

Scattered across the landscape of the Summer Palace are some rather large and unusual sculptures.

Beijing

(ABOVE) The unornamented roofs of some of the buildings that were not part of the Summer Palace and recognizable as such.

(LEFT) A peasant woman rides comfortably on her donkey as she goes past one of the life-size animal sculptures that line the avenue of the Ming tombs. It would seem from the figure of this elephant that the sculptor did not perhaps have too great a familiarity with the animal being sculpted.

Near Beijing

Standing figure of a nobleman near one of the Ming tombs. The physiognomy is strong and the decoration on the dress unmistakeable.

Near Beijing

Detail of a highly stylized sculpture at the Ming tomb, as part of the architectural features of the building style of the period.

Near Beijing

Terraces in one of the buildings near a Ming tomb. This area of tombs has figures of men in different costumes and of familiar animals with an occasional building set back a little. The avenue of tombs lies at a small distance from Beijing.

workers on the sites doubled from 8,000 to 16,000 between 1956–57. It was expected that the refinery would produce 1 million tonnes of crude oil when completed, though eventually it would be increased to 2 million tonnes. In 1959, they would be refining 100 tonnes of crude oil. I wondered if these figures and the speed of construction were for real or were they aspirational. It would eventually be the biggest refinery in China, and would be twice as big as the existing ones. The oil would be brought from Xinjiang and Yumen by train. This meant considerable railway construction—the line from Yumen has already been completed, that from Xinxiang would soon be ready. Most of the machinery is automatic and controlled by switchboards. The tanks are built underground along a length of 700 kilometres.

Steel to the tune of 50,000 tonnes was needed during the construction. Every workshop would be air-conditioned with fire extinguishers and lifts to upper levels, operating tables to ensure security, changing rooms, and bathrooms for workers. A special dining room was set apart for national minorities, i.e. Muslims. Each family would be allotted a flat, albeit a small one, with kitchen, bathroom, WC, and bedrooms. Amenities such as nurseries, hospitals, schools, cinemas, and shops would be provided. There are 400 women, married or unmarried, on the staff, doing office and tech-nical work. Some are graduates of schools of technology where selected students undergo a four-year course. In addition they study politics, Chinese language, and maths. Soviet experts have designed the refineries on the lines of the refineries in the Soviet Union and are here to instruct. Czechoslovakia and Poland have also provided assistance.

So much for the official information. I was interested in some of the people we met. Miss Xian, the secretary of the office, was twenty-three years old, and obviously very competent. She was trained as an oil engineer in the Soviet Union—she appears to be accepted as a highlight in the place, together with her fiancé, another oil engineer and two or three other young people. Their youth doesn't stand in the way of their being given responsible work and being treated with the respect they deserve. I suppose one could call her young and dedicated. She took us to her room in the women's dormitory, very simple and bare. The books were largely on oil, and a few political books, a radio and a gramophone, a writing table with a small photograph of her fiancé. I sat on the bed, while Dominique took some pictures of her as an example of a young Chinese scientist. I felt very envious of her. She had nothing to be angry about, as she was working on something of great value to her. This whole project, this expansive laboratory—was hers to work in—the work was so full that she hardly had any time to question the fundamentals, and I daresay a young person in her position would hardly question fundamentals. There was no need to.

We went into another room occupied by four girls, again very simply furnished, with posters and reproductions on the wall, bright, cheerful girls, of whom only one was politically inclined. One of the girls was sitting on the bed reading—a lovely girl of twenty. She worked as a draughtswoman in the planning section, and she was reading a textbook. She comes from a village some miles away from Lanzhou and at first she had no training beyond middle school. She spent some time at the technical school and was trained in planning. I asked her what her parents thought of it, and how they let her come away, considering how convention-bound society in the north-west is. She smiled and said her parents were pleased when she decided to work in the refinery. We met the other girls too, who came in shyly, all between the ages of eighteen and twenty. Some came from Gansu, others from as far away as Shanghai. This astonished me, why did they come from so far? But it was the same as the workers from Shanghai whom we had met in the factory. They smiled and said, yes, obviously conditions in Shanghai were better, but since the north-west was in need of workers, they had volunteered. From the north-east alone, each year some 800 senior-school students volunteered to work in the north-west. I did wonder whether so many had volunteered, and if so what was the incentive, or was this a euphemism for being sent to work in this area?

At the technical school, we saw some of the students playing basketball. I thought then of the industrial apprentices in England, to whom I lecture once a month at Essex. As with the apprentices in England those here were also given a course of lectures on other countries as part of a liberal educa-tion. But the ones in England have the possibility of finding jobs in other countries. Another difference is that for those in England life revolves around rock 'n' roll and football. For these boys it is perhaps something more focused on formal learning. But would it be the same if they were left to their own devices? I think so, because the awareness of having a cause outside of themselves is evident, possibly some of them may laugh at it and disagree but for the large majority it seems to exist. For most of them the opportunities inherent in the situation both personal and public were in themselves a big leap forward in terms of expectations.

The refinery itself did not interest me as it hadn't started functioning as yet. There were machines, some still lying under cover of packing, some being assembled. Dead machinery leaves me quite unmoved. The place is huge and sprawling. Once the refinery gets going, it would doubtless be more impressive.

In the afternoon, we saw the director and all the office and administrative staff working with spades and clearing a load of bricks. This is the application of Mao's directive that, one afternoon a week, the administrative staff must work as workers, in order to avoid their becoming too bureaucratic and divorced from the conditions of physical labour. This struck me as rather farcical. They probably treat it as a Saturday afternoon exercise. I couldn't see how bureaucratic attitudes could change merely by the office staff shovelling stones, once a week.

From the oil refinery we were shot across to the power station. We asked about living conditions. The workers live far away and come by bus, these being largely Škoda-made buses from Czechoslovakia. Trained largely in the north-east of China, a third are from various parts of the country and two-thirds from technical schools. They are given the fare home for themselves and their families for two weeks' annual leave. Those who bring their families can also do so—and the factory pays the fare. Model workers and teams exist as exemplars and are lauded and encouraged. Factory workers earn 60 yuan per month as do building workers. Engineers earn about the same initially, but the salary increases at a faster rate and eventually goes higher. Rent and water are heavily subsidized and so is electricity but less so. Education is free from primary school located on site to middle school in the city.

Later in the evening, after supper, we had a farewell speech from Mr Lan and we in turn had to give speeches! He was a playwright and president of the Gansu Writers' and Artists' Association, and our official guide in Lanzhou. As a young teenager he was one of the 'little Red devils' in the Eight Route Army. These were peasant teenagers who were given rudimentary arms, if at all, but became soldiers following the Red Army and were active as peasant guerrillas in the mid-1930s. A handsome man, always very well dressed, elegant and smart, smoking continuously and spitting with real gusto—fortunately always into a spittoon! This was apparently the first time that he had taken foreign guests around Lanzhou, so he did everything with great thoroughness, starting with a brief introduction to the history of the city on the very first morning.

I tried to visualize the situation elsewhere, in India, for example, in current times, a local and respected playwright acting as guide to four women for three days, and taking them not just to sunny spots but to farms and factories. Considering the number of people who visit Lanzhou, it must be a problem for him, with little time to write, but he said he found time all the same. His plays are about the army, representing the army to the people, that being his longest experience working with the Red Army. He is also an official in the association. This doesn't give him much time to indulge in eccentricities. But because of his official status he now has a respected position even among the bureaucrats.

I thought of his equivalent in Delhi, of any well-known playwright, putting on his plays. No one would bother him. Such a person could spend his time in various parts of the country or even abroad, doing what he liked within the limits of his status in his society whatever it may be, and the ever-present fear of not being able to have things his way. Lan has security and is respected. What is the degree of freedom that he can express? One does not think of absolute freedom since that is a non-starter in any society. There are always some categories of curbs on absolute freedom. What would be the curbs here?

Lan was the first writer I met in China, and I was interested in what he said. I noticed a tremendous pro-Soviet feeling that is common among a few Chinese in his position. They don't want an overt criticism of the Soviet Union because they feel that that was the first socialist state and, as such, mistakes cannot be avoided. Besides, Soviet help to China has been tremendous and the Chinese, or rather the Communist Party, know that without it they could not have done so much. The feeling of friendship towards the USSR is loyal. Lan's constant stress was on the fact that 'we are a very young country' (which inevitably made me smile—China a young country?)— 'we want to show our construction work because we want people outside to know that we are really working and trying to build a better place...

we want to show our defects too, because we want to improve, we invite foreign criticism, constructive criticism.' I believe he meant this quite sincerely. With him it was not a question of mouthing pretty phrases. He believed in the future of China as a socialist society. When we got talking about writers in the new society—he said quite firmly that, 'to be a writer one must be a politician and a scientist'. I would have qualified that statement and said, to be a writer acclaimed by the state, one must be a politician and a scientist.

I wondered if his plays consisted of percentages, so much per cent of humour, and so much of pathos to produce the right catharsis. But perhaps he has more vision than to write formula plays. It was a bit strange hearing him say this, particularly in the light of what is happening to Ding Ling. She has been accused of rightist tendencies, because she asked authors first to get to know themselves, before writing for 'the people', and she also stated that in her experience, politics, and writing do not go together. Writers, if they are to be of any value, should be free, not of political comments, but of political requirements. That coming from a well-known novelist, and red-hot revolutionary, must have startled quite a few Chinese.

9

The Work Begins at Maijishan

At first the Writers' and Artists' Association at Tian Shui decided that living at the site of Maijishan would be too difficult for us. After all we were three women who did not give the impression of being able to rough it. How could we possibly live in 'primitive conditions'? So it was decided that we would live at Tian Shui and drive in by jeep every day. On asking for explicit information about the travel and living conditions we were told that the travel on an impossibly bad track would take us three to four hours each day but we would be spared having to stay in two bare rooms of the monastery. We consulted and decided that so much travel time would eat heavily into the time that we had to work on the site, and none of us was averse to a few weeks of tough living conditions. We simply had to live at the site. We argued with Mr Li. By then we must have sounded earnest enough as Mr Li eventually agreed. One of the four wings of the monastery was cleared and the two rooms previously occupied by Wang and Xian were given to us, and they moved into another part of the building.

So the next morning we set off on our expedition in great style. At dawn we piled into a large 15-tonne ex-army truck. There were the three of us and Mingo, Mr Li, and another woman, Yingmen, who was supposed to look after us and who, in fact, has turned out to be doing nothing and could well have been dispensed with. The four of us were seated on a padded bench at the back. A fat cook accompanied the large wooden box with provisions. It reminded me of what we used to call 'dry rations' in our army households. The cook explained that it would have been impossible for us to eat what the monks eat, therefore he had been sent to cook for us. They also provided two men, 'bodyguards', to come with us. They were to help us carry our equipment up to the caves during the day, and sleep outside our rooms at night armed with guns, since this was an isolated place and wolves and bears were known to come down and crawl around the monastery at night. Wang is very particular about locking the main monastery door soon after sunset and no one is allowed to wander into the woods at night. During the day he insists that at least two people should go together even in the area surrounding the monastery. We were warned that if we heard people walking during the night, it was only the guards—but I've been sleeping too well to hear anything at night.

To return to the truck—apart from the people in it, we had our suitcases, Dominique's array of cameras, bedding, a large wooden box containing food supplies, and four chickens. There was only one thing lacking to complete the picture, a goat. And thus we bumped and jolted along the narrow road, past sleeping or just-awakening villages, full of the smell of frying oil, and sleepy faces of children sitting casually all over attending to their early morning needs—on the road, by the hedges, in the fields—and we came up the winding lanes of the mountain raising a storm of dust. At the end, almost climbing up the mountain, we stopped after three hours at the monastery door. The mission had started. At last we were at the first of the two sites that we had come to work on. This did mean a mental sliding back into the past untouched by much of what we had had to try and comprehend of the present in the last two weeks. Having been given an exposure to a mix of some history and some development work, we were not unprepared for the site of Maijishan.

It had been a slow journey as we had to negotiate the rather substantial bumps. The road left much to be desired and it was more frequently just a track. The landscape slowly changed from the rather dry flat cultivated fields of the valley to the green foothills and then the higher hills with their varied foliage that began to cover rocky hillsides and worked its way up to the mountains in the distance. The green of the hills was a striking change from the loess flats that we had become so familiar with on our train journeys. The almost sharp blue of the sky was a contrast to the soothing heavy foliage of variegated greens. I, at least, almost forgot that I was being jostled in the truck as we negotiated the many bumps. Our route followed in part the Wei River Valley. We arrived at the monastery almost without noticing that we had arrived. It is a small monastery, located at the base of a

hill, recognizable by its little gateway with a sloping roof that had animal sil-
houettes along the rib of the roof—so common in many Chinese buildings.
An elderly monk greeted us. After a brief exchange we were led to the section of the monastery that we were to occupy. This consisted of two rooms
that had been cleared and we settled in. The cook got busy elsewhere with
preparing a small meal while we took in the surroundings.

The monastery was the typical cloister. It had a couple of rooms on each
of the four sides with a courtyard in the middle. The rooms were sizeable
as was the courtyard. There were four monks in residence, but not permanently so, and they occupied the rooms on the three sides of the courtyard.
The fourth side was given to the four of us with strict instructions that we
were to enter and exit from the outer side and not enter the courtyard, since
the monks were on no account to be disturbed. It was a great concession to
us that they had cleared one wing where we could stay. Keeping our distance
was reiterated and we were reminded that we were four women.

But everything became non-existent when we looked up at the site.
Maijishan is a hill in the Gansu province of North-west China, an area
closely involved with the centuries-long trade across Eurasia. The name
literally means 'the mountain in the shape of a corn-rick', a reference to its
resemblance to the large haystacks that farmers build after the harvest.
The hill rises up sheer and straight and four-cornered, prominent in an
otherwise undulating landscape of valleys and gentle hills. At the upper
levels the four sides slope inwards. Soothing green foliage covers the background area with an occasional bare hillside at its upper levels.

The monastery was located at the foot of the hill, almost tucked into its
base. The hill towered above us. It was a single hill among a cluster of others
but stood out dramatically. There were caves on two sides of the hill and
fairly high up so accessible only when there was a gallery attached to the
side of the cliff and connected by ladders to the base. The caves were where
the monks meditated or where they placed their icons and painted their
murals of the lives of the Buddha and the bodhisattvas, and the parables
and myths of Buddhist belief. Our project was to study the icons and the
murals and assess the caves as shrines pertaining to Buddhism: and this in
the context of both Indian and Chinese history and the trade across
Central Asia.

The caves are cut from about a third of the way up the hill and continuing to the top one-third. There is no slope to the hill until the top one-third and its face on all four sides below this is a sheer drop. Therefore, entry to the caves is through a series of wooden ladders that provides access to wooden galleries that abut on the caves. Thick wooden square slats were fitted into holes just below the threshold level of each cave and planks of wood were placed on the slats and nailed in. These were the narrow wooden galleries that hugged the cliff and provided a small platform that acted as an entrance to each cave. On the outer side there was a railing that saved one from plummeting down to one's death. It was rather scary walking carefully on the wooden planks and looking down on the unobstructed drop far below. One wonders why such an impossibly difficult location was chosen as a site for Buddhist worship, although it was a dramatically beautiful location. Understandably it would be good for meditation but lay worshippers may not have been easily attracted for normal worship.

This had been the arrangement since the time when the caves were first cut. But the galleries being made of wood were liable to catch fire or rot in parts and had to be rebuilt. This acted to preserve the caves since replacing the galleries took more time than it would have, had the caves been easily accessible. Even now only the galleries of one side had been reconstructed. The fortuitous impact of an earthquake and a fire that burnt away much of the wooden galleries did however help to preserve the caves from too much enthusiastic restoration of the murals and sculpture in the later period that often damages the original rather than restoring it. Some of the caves thus became inaccessible and some were sealed by the accumulation of natural debris at the entrance. This helped conserve their contents. Earthquakes however, brought rock fall that damaged and brought down the galleries.

In 1952–53, Chinese archaeologists first surveyed the site in detail and repaired what they could. We were virtually the first group of non-Chinese working there. The rock was relatively softer than in the surrounding area and therefore it was easier originally to excavate the nearly 200 caves. A sizeable population of monks and lay persons had earlier inhabited the vicinity, attending to worship at the site and its maintenance. The existing monastery at the foot of the hill was small with just a few monks. Of the galleries, those giving access to the more important caves had been repaired and the repairs followed the still visible outline of the earlier galleries.

Originally the site was not in an isolated area. Its location was just a little off the Central Asian routes that fed into what has been called the Silk Route. The route went from Chang'an (as Xi'an was then known) to Lanzhou to Dunhuang. Maijishan would have been a stopping point in the first part of this route. In those times it must have been sufficiently populated to maintain a major monastery. Despite patronage from the nobility such monasteries did require substantial local support. Prior to the Buddhists taking over the site, when the area was sparsely populated there may originally have been a few accessible natural caves that may have given the monks the idea to excavate further caves at a higher level, although the idea of having cave monasteries was common to sites all along the route.

Starting with Bamiyan in Afghanistan, the pattern was similar at many sites along the Takla Makan and further east to North China. A cliff face was chosen, the rock of which was not impossible to cut into. Caves were excavated for habitation, meditation, and as shrines for worship with murals and sculpture. Outside the caves and clinging to the cliff, there were usually some three or four gigantic statues of what became almost a Buddhist pantheon. The pattern was recognizable at many sites. Possibly some of these caves may have been used in rituals connected with earlier forms of worship and this may have given the Buddhists the idea of establishing bigger centres at these sites. Buddhist monks may not have been averse to taking over an existing sacred site, as was frequently done when new religions were replacing the old. This happened in India where some Buddhist stupas with the relics of the dead are proximate to Megalithic burial sites. And there were many chaitya caves, used as halls of worship, spread across central India and the Deccan. Some of these were later converted into Hindu temples.

Maijishan was first marked out as a site for Buddhist worship in the mid-fifth century AD when two monks with their disciples made it their base. It was not too far from the then capital at Loyang. Presumably patronage from the local king or authorities enabled them to employ people to excavate the caves for them if they did not excavate the caves themselves. There must have been some craftsmen present as well, some local and some from elsewhere, since the sculpture in these caves, if not brought from elsewhere, was impressive and some had a touch of the Gandhara style that initially evolved in centres in North-west India and in the Oxus region. It is unlikely that the sculpture was transported all the way from the Oxus plain. Other important sites were Longmen and Yungang where the rock was limestone and again somewhat easier to work. This was the period when low relief on steles was frequent with such sculpture often illustrating a narrative.

But all was not smooth sailing. Buddhism competing to establish itself faced periods of opposition, some leading to persecution before it finally found a foothold in China. Inscriptions of the sixth century suggest a more established situation. They refer to the excavation of certain caves carried out with the help of lay families. This is reminiscent of inscriptions at the Bharhut and Sanchi stupas in India that also refer to the support of artisan and merchant guilds. Whereas cave shrines became important and were created even in difficult terrain, stupas tended to remain small in Central Asia and North-west India as compared to those constructed further south in Central and South India, or even the larger ones in Sri Lanka and South-east Asia. A king of the Sui dynasty wished to emulate the Mauryan Emperor Ashoka and basing himself on the Buddhist legends built a large number of stupas.

A fairly extensive attack by Tibetan forces in neighbouring areas and also in this part led to another period of the persecution of Buddhists by the Chinese rulers. But in the tenth century the support for Buddhism improved and in the next century there were attempts to revive the cave shrines at Maijishan. However, more earthquakes brought down more galleries and one wonders why there was a repeated return to a site threatened by natural disasters. Obviously it was regarded as particularly sacred. New galleries were built, new caves cut, and the monasteries enlarged.

In this uneven history, there were times of trouble again in the thirteenth century because of a famine connected no doubt with one of the many peasant revolts. Grain supplies were forcibly taken away from monastic holdings and the cultivation of monastic lands was supervised. What Max Weber referred to as monastic landlordism seems to have been prevalent. Monasteries were granted large areas of cultivable land either already under cultivation by peasants or with peasants being settled on the land. Again it is not entirely clear as to who were the new patrons except that later in the sixteenth century there was a revival under the Ming dynasty that is referred to in literary texts.

But the time of troubles was not over. In the eighteenth century there had been a political problem and some rebellion in the neighbourhood.

Political refugees fleeing from Gansu found a place to stay in the Maijishan caves, and passed their time scribbling on the walls of the caves. Presumably, some of the galleries were intact for them to reach the caves. It was not until the mid-twentieth century that it was properly recognized as a site of major significance to the history of Buddhism in China and it then received considerable archaeological attention.

The caves are of various shapes and sizes although most are square. Some are small enough not to need the support of internal pillars whereas the larger ones have built-in pillar support where the pillar is cut from the rock, its top and base being attached to the rock. The caves open onto the cliff-face and the gallery. The form of the ceiling varies from flat ceilings to those slightly curved or domed and some that are in an inverted V-shape. The sculpture is in part cut from the stone but there is also some free-standing sculpture that is not of local stone and may have been brought from elsewhere. Hoisting it up into the cave would have been quite a feat. But much of it is in clay, and some in stucco, perhaps influenced by the same medium that was used in the production of Gandhara sculpture. Stucco, in this case, was clay mixed with various other ingredients and sculpted both when semi-wet and half-dry. When it solidified it was refined and coloured. Some statues were sculpted in stucco over a wooden frame.

The entrance to one of the more impressive large halls was guarded by dvarapalas—doorkeepers—one on each side. The rear wall had a seated Buddha with his favourite disciples—the monks Ananda and Kashyapa—on either side. Mahayana Buddhism was popular here. There were also the usual bodhisattvas, the cult having been popular in Gandhara and had travelled with the trade to eastern Central Asia. The focus in Mahayana Buddhism was more on the Buddha with the bodhisattva Avalokiteshvara and Guanyin, the latter being worshipped as the goddess of compassion, in later times. The Buddha is often recognizable as Sakyamuni and he is shown sometimes in the company of the Buddha to come, Maitreya, also popular in Central Asia and North-west India. On one side of the hill are gigantic figures associated with Mahayana Buddhism that appear to be attached to the hill. It is amazing as to how they were constructed on the sheer face of the cliff under incredibly difficult conditions.

The murals are effectively in the style of Chinese painting and the style varies from early to later periods. The earlier ones have some elements of what is thought to have been an Indian style. However, this changes fairly soon, becoming more and more distinctly Chinese as does the physiognomy of the men and women. Because the murals in these sites were painted during many centuries, virtually a millennium, these cave sites are like museums of Chinese painting and to some extent of sculpture as well. The subject matter of the paintings draws on various texts. Some are the presumed biographies of the Buddha, some are *Jataka* stories about the previous births of the Buddha, some relate to what was popularly called the Lotus Sutra, and sometimes there are scenes from contemporary Chinese courts showing royalty in acts of worship.

The depiction of the Buddha underwent something of a change from being recognizable as an image from Gandhara with Indian origins to gradually becoming more and more suggestive of a greater degree of Chinese origin. The change was familiar to us from the variation in the sculpted Buddha images from Gandhara when compared to those from Mathura and further south such as Amaravati. The attempt it would seem was to show the universality of the Buddha with the implicit statement that the Buddha was always one of us, wherever he was being worshipped.

Our routine of work was regular. We would go up after an early breakfast and work in the caves until lunch, then nip down for a quick snack after which we would go up again until evening when we came down for our daily wash and a hot dinner. Taking photographs was not easy given the problems with creating light inside the cave. Reflectors of various sizes had to be used and carefully placed at angles to each other. Sometimes the murals in a deep corner were shrouded in darkness and had to be studied by torchlight. Taking a break meant sitting uncomfortably in the gallery. But this afforded us a clear view of the monastery down below and occasionally the activities of the monks, which on the whole tended to be rather mundane. The occasional visit of a local peasant family would make a change, and especially if they were persuaded to come up to the gallery and enquire as to what on earth we were doing there. We kept strictly to the rule of not trying to converse with the monks, although it did seem a bit odd that we were living in close proximity yet not even exchanging the day's greeting.

This changed some days later when I heard the regular sound of a ball hitting a hard surface repeatedly and then a pause. I guessed it was a game of what we as children used to call ping-pong, in other words table tennis. I enquired from Mingo if my guess was right and she laughed and said that there was a roughly made-up kitchen table in the courtyard and the monks and their occasional visitors played on it for amusement. I promptly asked if I could join in. Anil was not so sure as we had been requested to keep clear of the monastic side. Mingo decided for us and said she would speak to the monks. Back came the reply from the monk Wang, 'But of course and right away'. So we trooped into the courtyard to play ping-pong. We were told that the courtyard was now open to us and we were welcome to come and sit there in the evenings. In the first game I played with one of the monks, he won which I thought was a good omen!

Some nights later we sat in the courtyard. It was a clear night, a little cool, and drowned in moonlight, with the moon coming up from behind the hill at the back of us. The Maijishan hill with its east face reflecting the steely light of the moon looked distant and inspiring. It looked then like an early engraving of a south Indian temple, or like a drawing published in an early report on a temple, in the days before the structures had been cleared and restored, when stunted trees growing out of the structure were an almost expected feature in the older monuments. The shape of Maijishan hinted at some passing similarities. The shapes of the cave entrances and the narrow wooden galleries, somewhat blurred in the moonlight, were reminiscent of heavily ornamented exteriors of gopurams or temple entrances. But as its name is said to suggest, the shape of a haystack built up after the harvesting of the corn seemed the most appropriate.

But last night I sat there with a couple of people who had come from the local village to help with odds and ends. Xian was trying to teach me to play the erhu, the lovely little two-stringed instrument that I had picked up, played with a bow that is drawn between the two strings. I was supposed to be playing the Shaanxi folk song that Mingo taught me in the train, but the notes I produced sounded more like hens cackling. But my little audience laughed uproariously, obviously enjoying it and encouraged me vigorously. Each time my erhu squeaked, I stopped to join them in their laughter, and every time I produced the right note, they would clap with great gusto. It was the sort of evening that I call a spontaneous evening, one of those rare moments when there seems to be harmony in all ordered things. It doesn't happen often and one can't predict it, it just happens—but it made the next few days for me. I wasn't even distinctly conscious of it then—the strangest thing of all was that I didn't know the language and had to express myself through an interpreter; or was it because of this that the nuances evaded me and I could perhaps imagine all that I felt.

I wondered what I had in common with this little gathering. I was sitting on a low wooden plank-bench with the erhu on my knees. Xian was sitting by me and laughing with me when the squeaks became intolerable. A little way off was the tiny kerosene oil lamp in splendid isolation, ignored, because the light of the moon was so strong that the lamp paled. And the circle of faces around me—that's all I could see—faces set on squatting or seated bodies—Li's sharp delicate features and broad cheekbones; I wonder if he writes poetry, he fits my picture of the modern Chinese poet to perfection— even his short black hair that always seems to be standing up.

The cook, big and appropriately stout, who found it such an effort to climb to the caves the first day that he keeps well within the monastery now, lest he be inveigled into going up again. The man is impossible—he has a fixed notion that because we are not Chinese, we would prefer what he calls Western food. So he produces the most awful hash by way of a special favour for us. We have requested, we have pleaded, and now, I think, he has begun to notice that the food returns comparatively untouched, so he is beginning to give us Chinese food, which of course we finish with great relish. Poor man. No doubt, we have shattered his illusions about foreigners and he must be annoyed at not being given a chance to show off the versatility of his culinary skills, but we prefer to go native, at least as far as food goes.

Another face—of the young man who is one of our bodyguards—I don't believe he is older than eighteen, though he insists that he is in his late twenties. Maybe—it's incredible how young the Chinese look, and it is not just that they are of a different physical type from me. I cannot guess or imagine their age. And then the man with the bulbous nose: my first impression of him was negative but gradually I began to see a shy wholeheartedness about him that makes me think of the Hunchback of Notre Dame each time I see him. Dominique thinks he looks like a Bourgogne, with his large red nose like the nose of people who drink all the time. But I am beginning to find him more sympathetic. He looks after our needs with an almost maternal care—and he was certainly very encouraging about my playing the erhu!

Wang—not the monk—who was asleep till our commotion started, woke up and came and joined us. He lives here permanently and looks after the caves. Before 1952, he had worked in the cultural and educational office at the village of Kangjian. When the Maijishan survey began he joined the archaeologists as he was always keen on history and archaeology—now he intends to stay here permanently and work on the caves. He must surely have been a Mandarin in his last birth—he has all the quiet dignity and modesty of a man devoted to some particular work. I asked if his wife who stays at Kangjian with their son objects to his being away. He explained that in a year's time when his son goes to middle school, his wife will join him here.

And Xian whom I liked from the very beginning because of his smile—his smile that seems to accept the whole world—and he too is happy in his work—he was a primary school teacher teaching history and Chinese—but I feel with him, that his real sensitivity is for art; I saw some of his sketches, still groping but full of strong potentiality. He uses a soft pencil for portrait figures—this is a foreign medium for him as the brush comes more naturally—but he explained that it was easier to work with a pencil when he is in the caves. So he is trying to get accustomed to this medium. All I hope is that he does not completely forsake the brush, because the brush is the right medium for drawing in the Chinese tradition.

The first day when we arrived at what were to be our rooms we saw some bowls of various shapes and sizes arranged in one room, they were the base of some really beautiful dry root and stone arrangements. These, I discovered later, were Xian's experiments in arrangement and design. He came to Maijishan because he wanted to study at length the Buddhist art of various periods as it exists here. Fortunately for him, he was allowed to do this and is now employed as one of the three workers whom the archaeological department keeps here essentially as guards and, on the rare occasions when there are visitors, as guides. As the evening wore on they started singing other folk songs—a love song from Xinjiang, a harvest song from Henan, and a couple of 'modern' songs, songs composed recently about new China—even the black and white dog that strays around the monastery joined us—so it had to be time for folk tales and fairy stories.

At the moment there is only one monk living here permanently. He is well over fifty years, and lives and works while the archaeological survey comes and goes and produces reports on the art historical aspects of the place. A couple of monks join him for a time. The monastery dates back to the Northern Wei period and has been continuously repaired. There is a reference to the monastery in a story dating to the Song period. One of the monks found a very precious herb called Lin-tse-tsao or Lingzhicao (which literally means rejuvenating herb) on the top of Maijishan, which he sent to the emperor who in turn gave the monastery the name of Ray-yin. In the Northern Wei period there were three big monasteries in the area, and each one had many monks. T'an Shao was a monk of Maijishan who was very well known as a preacher and was said to have had 300 disciples. In the period of the Western Wei the monastery was even more popular. One of the empresses lived in the monastery and later became a nun here. She was at first buried in one of the caves but her body was later disinterred and buried at Xi'an.

The monastery underwent major repairs under the Ming and Qing dynasties, but gradually lost its patronage and was in the end reduced to a small group of derelict buildings—which were recently repaired and are now in use as the present monastery. It was also during the Ming and Qing periods that fires destroyed the wooden galleries abutting on the rock that were the only access to the caves. The galleries on the east face were rebuilt, but not those on the west. This for art historians was perhaps just as well, since the Wei sculpture and the early Sui and Tang have not been tampered with and remain unspoilt on the west side, whereas the same early sculpture has been re-crafted by Ming and Qing restorers on the east side.

The earliest caves were rough-hewn and possibly first cut and sculpted by local monks. Later aristocratic patronage seems to have been responsible for some of the aesthetically more decorated chapels. A story illustrating this is told about the Hall of Scattered Flowers. Owing probably to a happy accident, the cave has been cut in such a way that it produces a suction movement of the wind, so that flower petals thrown over the gallery into the air float in mid-air for a few brief seconds and are then drawn up and inwards, back into the cave, creating a beautiful effect. We are told that in the period of the Northern Wei, Li Yun Xin, a high official decided to build this hall, also known as the Seven Buddha Hall with its seven images, in order to gain merit for his dead father. This story is reworded in the writings of a famous contemporary author who inscribed it on a tablet and buried it at Maijishan, but the tablet has not been found. A Ming tablet containing the story was found in one of the caves. Maijishan was also the subject of a poem by a famous poet of Tang times.

I am surprised that it has not been written about more often. The landscape around here, although not extraordinary, is nevertheless quite distinctive. The others say it reminds them of Switzerland in parts, but it doesn't to me. It has far more personality than a Swiss landscape. I am sitting for the moment on the veranda-like projection of our rooms and I can see in the distance the blue mountains, not very high, about 6,000 feet. Nearer lie the lower hills, thickly wooded to their very summits. Dark masses of low pine trees clustered together, producing an unruly matted surface, and against them, to offset the dark green, is the occasional paler green of the weeping willow. That is all, mountains and trees all around and such a deep silence. I can hear the carpenter in the distance quietly sawing wood. He uses the little outhouse, which was once a stage, as his workshop. Nearer me, the wasps are buzzing in the wooden beams, building a hive, large black and yellow wasps moving along the rust-red beams, and, of course, the hum of the crickets in the grass. Last night when I snuffed out the candle, and looked out through the window, I saw a firefly—I haven't seen one in so long.

The upper wing must have been a later addition to the monastery as it's on a slightly higher level. Sitting here I look directly onto the roof of the building in front of me, a tiled roof with a raised and ornamented portion in the middle—a scroll of dragons intertwined with flowers, and surmounted by a procession of little animals—below which comes the roof itself. The animals and their poses show a delightful sense of humour.

The buildings consist of large, sturdy wooden beams placed on stone supports. This framework is filled in with a mud-and-straw mixture on the outside, as is used in local villages, and a wash of plaster on the inside which has been whitewashed. The roof is built largely of wooden beams laid in a triangular fashion, and over this the exterior is tiled. The rooms become a little damp at night, especially with the windows closed but we dare not open them, else Wang will threaten us with wild animals! The beds are most unique. Some are just broad wooden trestles, but these are the moveable variety. The fixed beds are built into the rooms—platforms of rubble enclosed in bricks about 1.5 feet off the ground and the usual bed size attached to the wall. Over this is placed a wooden board and then the bedding. They are a bit severe on the back for the first couple of nights if one is used to soft beds, but one soon gets accustomed to them.

The monastery in itself is quite an adventure, as every now and then one comes across a wall with an inscription on stone embedded in it. One wing of the monastery is used as the museum which houses bits and pieces from the caves and also objects such as pottery etc., found nearby and dating back to a few centuries.

Working at Maijishan follows a simple routine that does not leave time for much else. I wake up grudgingly at 6.30 a.m., and we have to be at work by 7.30. It is pleasant walking through the dewy grass in the early morning and looking down over extensive fields of tall maize and sorghum—the latter is the base for Kaoliang, the popular liquor. The village is about 15 kilometres away so all I can see from here is a hamlet over a distant hill and nearer us a farmhouse folded into a hill. Whilst we are working in the caves, all we can hear is the wind in the trees and water rushing down a little mountain stream, way below us; and of course, our own remarks as we creep in and out of some of the low, back-breaking caves. Sometimes, looking out over the gallery, one can see an occasional peasant riding a donkey or going along the track down in the valley. The donkey is the local beast of burden, carrying men and children, crops, basket-ware, baggage, and in fact anything that can be carried.

The climb up to the caves is a little tiring because the initial wooden steps are steep—but thank goodness they have them. Somehow I can't see myself going up by a rope. Since the caves were cut into a sheer steep surface, these wooden stairs and narrow galleries were necessary from the very beginning. Over the last 200 years they have been in a state of disrepair, so that pilgrimages to Maijishan became more and more infrequent. In 1952, when archaeological and preservation work started on the site, the stairs and galleries had to be rebuilt. Here and there when I place my foot on a loose plank, I wonder what would happen if . . . It is a drop of 100 metres.

Having completed their work, the archaeological survey team left Maijishan. The preservation and care of the site has brought with it the beginnings of a limited tourist interest and the scenic beauty adds to the attraction. I do hope that the place won't get spoilt, part of its beauty now is its isolation and silence—but to see it swarming with tourists would give a very different impression. So far, what little we have seen of Chinese tourists has not been unpleasant. There were a few Chinese army soldiers living here until yesterday—holidaying for three days. This, I thought, was a particularly enlightened touch, to bring soldiers here and introduce it to them quietly by way of a holiday. They didn't intrude in any way—in fact, I personally was sorry when I saw them drive away in two large lorries. They had enlivened our evenings—one of them played an accordion, so we were entertained with songs after supper, Chinese folk songs and Russian folk songs. We found that the one who sang had picked up the Russian songs from members of the Russian Red Army choir, which had been visiting and giving concerts in China. It was not quite in harmony at first to hear Cossack melodies in a Buddhist monastery, but we soon began to look forward to it.

Another reason why we missed them was because one of them was a keen ping-pong player, and I had some good games playing him. The old kitchen table in the courtyard had been smoothened and fitted with a net. One has to know, of course, the location of the cracks in the table that divert the direction of the ball, but once the topography of the table is mastered it is possible to play with great enjoyment. On the first day two of the soldiers were playing and the others were sitting around. On an impulse, I walked up to them and asked if I could play. They seemed genuinely pleased and followed the game with interest. After half an hour, I went to have lunch, and they smiled and invited me to come and play again. I thought then that if they had been a group of British or French or even Indian soldiers, I would have hesitated to ask if I could join them in a game of ping-pong—and even if I had, there may well have been an excuse to dismiss the request. Yet with this group I did not feel at all awkward.

Do Chinese men have a natural distinctiveness that sets them apart? Surely not. Or are they just trained to be on their best behaviour with foreigners? They seem to now accept women, or they have to accept women as more or less equals, and this acceptance changes and improves their attitude toward women. I've noticed it everywhere—I have felt quite relaxed whether be it in the streets of Beijing, on the train, in the refinery at Lanzhou or here at Maijishan. And it doesn't seem to be just my reaction. I've noticed the same with Chinese women—they are friendlier and less on edge with their own men than women in many other parts of the world. This, of course, would not have been so in earlier times and one has to concede that the norms introduced by a revolution have some advantages. But will it fundamentally change male attitudes to women? Or is this going to be a momentary historical aberration, unless the revolutionary changes, what are described as post-Liberation changes, have come to stay?

The very occasional day-picnickers find their way up to Maijishan—but there are no orange peels and greasy bits of newspaper strewn all over. One would never believe that anyone had been around. It is possible that the Chinese have a conscious sense of cleanliness that is not just a post-Liberation conditioning but perhaps a matter of traditional social discipline. No doubt the present regime has worked on it with quite impressive results. I am not the sort of person who goes about with a can of DDT and a mask preaching hygiene all over the place, but when things get as out of control as they have in some remoter parts, even my romantic instincts of leaving the remote untroubled, are in revolt—I approve of some degree of forced cleanliness. One can now walk down the street of a Chinese village, or at least some villages, without having to constantly sidestep or hop over heaps of offal.

I took the morning off today to catch up with some writing and recording more extensive notes on the caves. This is probably going to be my chorus throughout my stay in China. I can hardly believe that I have been in this country for only four weeks. There are many moments when I feel it is all so familiar to me that I must have spent many months here. Is the entire East really so much alike in spirit? I now feel that I don't want to return to Europe for many months yet—I want to live here longer, and I should like to spend many months in South-east Asia—Vietnam, Laos, Cambodia, Thailand, Malaya, Burma—a whole new world of which I am only just beginning to become aware. In moments of enthusiasm, I feel the future lies here with us.

How easily I associate myself with 'the East'. I am referring to the future not in an opportune way but in a substantial and almost inspiring way. On the purely building level the Chinese are facing it far more squarely than we in India. But the intellectual side of it worries me. I find a tendency towards oversimplification. They say it is necessary in the early stages of socialist reconstruction, but I feel scared that once it comes it will stay. This is what happened in Russia. We might forgive their mistakes because Russia was the pioneer and was inexperienced, but what if it is repeated in China? Is it perhaps necessary to any revolutionary change? I do not find much awareness here of the faults of the Russian revolution. There seems to be a complete readiness to overlook the glitches. And then, sometimes I wonder if the fault doesn't lie with me? Perhaps I fail to understand the problems of China.

I could live in Maijishan for many months—I could write here and read here—in fact, I am beginning to envy Wang and Xian. Perhaps I like it even more because this is the first time that I have been in quiet surroundings since some time now. The days before leaving London were too full and fast—and then Moscow and Beijing and Xi'an and rushing here and seeing this and that, and meeting so many people and the conversation always being polite. It exhausts me. I like a quiet life and I often prefer my own company to that of others, yet the contradiction is such that I find myself being whirled into an extroverted existence. I wear out my energies in activities on the fringe and therefore I can never be strong enough to be dynamic in isolation. But enough of self-pity. I shall bask in the quietness of this place while it lasts. It is not often that one can spend time in a Buddhist monastery. If only I were alone here—that would be perfection.

Working on a site such as this has one big snag. The best hours of the day are spent in the caves. We arrive at the caves, up into 'Heaven', early morning and we work there till noon. Then a rapid descent to the monastery for lunch—a 'swallow' of warm hot sunshine, and we are up again and in the caves soon after. Melons continue to haunt me even in Maijishan. In the afternoon they bring a melon up for us—it makes a welcome break.

Working on the west face as we are doing these days means a snatch of sunlight in the afternoon when the sun strikes the west side—else it means continued work among spiders' webs, bird droppings, and bats' remains, until the setting sun or almost when we finally come down. Our work in the caves is relatively straightforward. We examine and identify the murals and the sculptures and decide on what we want to photograph and write about in our studies. At this point, Dominique would prepare the taking of photographs—both in colour and black and white. I would take detailed notes and discuss these with Anil.

By the time we have washed and eaten our evening meal it is dark and after an hour's chatter by candlelight or a letter written with straining eyes we find ourselves under our quilts and within our little mosquito net tents. And then the mice start their Ascots and Derbys in the rafters and since the ceiling is thin I can hear the entire proceedings. I regret the fact that we have no time to spare—I want desperately to be able to write each day or at least to read a little. *Ulysses* is stuck at page 207 and at this rate will probably see me all through China—what of *Varouna* and *The Brothers Karamazov*? And my book on *Teach yourself Chinese*?

Yesterday I had the bright idea of memorizing an ideograph or two in between work in the caves. It is a source of amusement to me and prevents me at the end of the day from feeling stale. By the evening I managed to produce one sentence, 'I do not know whom I should call', and I was quite pleased with myself—otherwise it becomes tedious to be constantly making notes on the sculpture and taking down film numbers. The real hard work for me will begin when we start to write up the material we collect here. But these long hours are necessary since we have only a short time here. I wish we'd been given more time. But the Chinese were so certain that conditions here would be too hard for us, with no electricity and running water, and no sanitation. I feel that they still regard us as visitors rather than doing field work. That I suppose is in part the fault of the sari—it makes a woman look feminine and graceful—irrespective of whether she is or is not—and, from the point of view of working in caves, so helpless, that I don't wonder they thought we wouldn't be able to stick it out. Besides, our Chinese counterparts wear slacks all the time and look far more determined and efficient. I have taken to wearing the peasant outfit that I had had stitched before coming here as it does make it far easier when climbing ladders and creeping literally on all fours, in and out of some of the caves.

There is one thing missing here and badly so—something I have felt the need for desperately and which I know will be impossible until we return to Lanzhou—a good bath. To have to clean one's body within the limitations of two small basins of water is real torture. The stream is at the bottom of the valley and since we come down from the caves so late, there is not enough time to go and bathe in the stream. We are perched practically three quarters of the way up the valley. One afternoon we shall go down and have an orgy of bathing.

I was most amused this morning: Anil came to me and said she thought Dominique was looking tired, and she did not want her to overstrain herself, so we should persuade her to rest for a while. Ten minutes later, Dominique came along and said she thought that Anil was very tired and that we should persuade her to rest this afternoon. I had a quiet little laugh and by lunchtime when we had all persuaded each other to drop work for the day—I was even more amused.

So we took time off today—it is one of those warm drowsy days. I have been moving from chair to chair and have done nothing: perhaps each day is like this but I don't feel it in the caves where it is cool and instead of smelling the sun in the pine trees and the morning grass, I smell bat droppings and the humidity of damp grottoes. Anil and Dominique are sitting near me and discussing the beauty of being white-haired, and the words are drawled out with difficulty and are interspersed with wide yawns—ah, the energy of the day's work. Is this the outcome of really hard work? If the sun were a little warmer I would go on strike this afternoon and would go down to the stream and bathe. But it is a little cloudy and sometimes even cool—the fact is that I am too lazy to go down the valley to the stream. The crickets again and the buzzing wasps, all else is silence—except of course for the discussion on white hair which continues.

Yes, I should like a bit of quiet, undisturbed quiet. Life in the monastery is conducive to gentle relaxation. The cook has been complaining that he has only one kettle and not enough cooking utensils, that he has very little oil, that we have eaten up all the meat and half the chickens that we brought from Tian Shui—and now what could he give us to eat? This morning I saw him poking around the hillside with a large stick—was he looking for herbs or mushrooms to feed us on? We kept saying that the truck was due in from Tian Shui any moment, and it would bring us provisions—but he refused to be hopeful and insisted that since we had bought all the chickens that were on sale at Tian Shui a week ago, what more could the truck bring? However, it did come and brought masses of stuff—

just as well. I can't somehow believe that we ate quite as much as the cook says in these last few days. I suspect that he is given to exaggeration or else that others are also being fed, which, of course, would be perfectly normal.

The coming of the truck is an event of great importance for us at Maijishan. It comes on every fourth day or so, bringing food etc., and is also supposed to bring our mail. Needless to say, the day the truck is due, we all eagerly wait for a packet of airmail envelopes. It is coming again in another four days—and we all feel absolutely certain that this time there are bound to be some letters for at least one of us. Anil wants a letter from her agent, Dominique from her mother, and I from a friend in London giving me sage advice on what to do in China, while Mingo smiles at each one in turn and promises to do her best next time. I was thinking last night that to be a month behind news can be trying. I haven't seen a single newspaper since coming to China and I thought that wouldn't bother me—but at this moment if I were given a copy of the *Sunday Observer*, or the *Manchester Guardian*, or the *Times of India,* I would read every word with infinite pleasure. I miss the *Observer* in particular, and the intellectual stimulation that it provides.

Perhaps, if I could now and then have a really scintillating conversation that would add to my pleasure. I can't spend all my time being frivolous and light-hearted—I must have something substantial to bite into. I resent not being able to read for an hour each day—but it would be futile to try and explain this resentment, it would merely create a misunderstanding. Reading is not always sufficient—I like to talk about what I read and hear and imbibe—I am presently so full of impressions—both enthusiastic and dubious—and I want desperately to talk about them, at length—a week in London or Bombay or somewhere where I could talk almost non-stop. This is not to suggest that I am bored with my life here and the study we are doing—but only that I would be happier if I had a little more intellectual stimulation—in whatever form I want it. Fringe living is exhausting, but given that it is temporary, I am happy to make adjustments.

I should like, for instance, to travel in China for a few weeks as did the French explorer-cum-archaeologist whom we met on the train. And if one is alone one's perceptions are heightened. Much of what is lost or frittered away in the easy security of being with two or three people is retained when travelling in isolation. No doubt it can also lead to many misunderstandings of a country and its people, but with a basic intelligence and knowledge, there is much to recommend it. Modern living seems to have little time for such activities. Besides, the thought of having to rush back to London in a couple of months and start work on the thesis all over again is somewhat daunting.

On rereading passages of what I have written, I realize it sounds very much like journalistic reportage—or the story of a car that runs so many miles to a gallon. Places I have been to and things I have seen. But I have a camera for that. It sounds self-conscious and awkward—I get like that sometimes when I am pushed from place to place and made to see things— the rush of it gets to me. And, also when I am unsure of my relationships with other people. Basically I am a cautious person and until I have determined my position in relation to my environment, I feel self-conscious and awkward. I have been in China for almost a month—and I don't really know myself in this new context yet—nor my companions. In another couple of weeks it will work itself out, and then I shall be a reacting body and not just a camera. Yet it hasn't been all that tough. Anil is such an easy person to be with and ready to explore situations that it has allowed us to follow trails that might otherwise have remained buried. Mingo in her own quiet way of talking has opened up so much of China that otherwise would have just passed me by.

There is a fly sitting on my mosquito net, a very persistent fly. I shall have to wax it like the one we waxed last night. I saw a new and terrible use to which a candle can be put. A half-dead fly—one that has been swatted but is not dead—is non-messily dispatched by a drop of hot wax from a burning candle to fix it. Leave alone the fly it did rather transfix me. Last evening was another unexpected evening. We were all very tired as we had tackled the two troublesome caves two days running, 133 and 135, and we ate a little later than usual, and by the time we came around to the dessert— dumplings with ample helpings of golden syrup—it was time to light the candle. And as we sat about idling, chatting, Wang appeared on the steps outside, sat quietly on the bench and started playing his flute, a long bamboo flute of a soft tone. We drifted in his direction, Anil and Dominique on the bench beside him, Cao near the door, Mingo and I sitting on the raised threshold of the door, while Li and Longmei chatted inside. Cao who sings all day in the caves felt embarrassed when we asked him to sing, but eventually we got him to sing something from a Peking opera. Halfway through he was overcome with shyness and he got up and ran off but later crept back slowly.

Wang played a Qinghai love song that was particularly beautiful and also the ballad of Su Wu the exiled chief—and then the Mao Zedong song, that everyone sings and the words of which I simply must learn. Cao's brainwave was greatly appreciated—he dashed down to the office and brought the gramophone which Li had sent from Tian Shui specially for us and a collection of scratched records—some folk songs and some music from Canton (as Guangzhou was then known) which is different from North Chinese music, somewhat in the same way I suppose as Carnatic music is from Hindustani, and involving the way semitones are used. They even produced a Chinese version of the song, 'Awaara Hoon', from *Awaara* that was a superhit in China. The Chinese version of the lyrics sounded weird but the tune was recognizable! Apparently it was such a hit in China that they had to bring out a Chinese version. And again I kept asking myself, what is it that gives the Chinese this supreme ease of manner? Or is it just particular people? Wang and Tsao seem to me to be like people whom we have known and worked with all our lives.

It's a long, long time since the days when I used to sleep at 8.30 p.m. But here I am tucked beneath a mosquito net and rolled up in a large eiderdown. The candle is on a chair just by my bed and I am writing in the faintest light. Why I am still writing at 11 p.m., I don't know except that I felt the need for something to write—I have just had a large mug of Ovaltine, I wish we'd thought of it earlier—and that too after a huge dinner with rice and two large pieces of steamed bread—and despite all this I still have hopes of being able to buy myself a pair of slacks. I feel rested now—and elated, I don't know why, almost in the mood for writing poetry!

Dominique and I walked for hours this afternoon down the road over the fields and across to the farmhouse at one end of the valley. It was really quite comic. We crept out of the monastery, hoping everyone would be asleep, and we'd be able to roam at random. But Longmei saw us and before we reached the bottom of the hill, poor Cao was chasing after us. Then we crossed the next hill and by then Li and one of our bodyguards armed with a gun were with us. Apparently the bears are quite daring in these parts and it is absolutely forbidden for anyone to go about alone. We were later told that one of the five rules of the monastery is that people should only go out in groups and there must be one person with a gun each time. Our little procession was regarded as quite mad with the five of us walking single file over a rough track.

The Maijishan hill looked most inspiring from a distance. I took some photographs, but I wish I could have painted it—particularly later in the afternoon when the rain clouds gathered grey behind it and against the blue and green of the hills surrounding it. It stood out upright with its rough tan to red-brown surfaces. Seeing it thus for the first time I felt its real beauty and realized why the monks who originally lived here chose this particular place. It can be breathtakingly beautiful. Beyond the farm we met the stream higher up, so we sat soaking our feet and eating walnuts from a nearby tree.

It rained in the evening—it was like a release. And now it is cool and fresh, almost as if something oppressive has lifted. I am glad we did only half a day in the caves as I needed time to look around and feel the ground under my feet, and the trees around me, and the mountains stretching out and reaching into space. Tomorrow I shall work with a feeling of dedication.

There was so much food last night and so much wine: apple wine and plum wine, and the deadliest of all, maize wine, which is a typical Gansu liquor and really good. We had a farewell feast—everyone at the monastery, and we were all a little high. I felt sad leaving, and leaving in a hurry too. I was sad at leaving Lao Zhao, who, if this does not sound too Victorian, reiterated my belief in humanity. He amazed me with his complete friendliness and guilelessness in his attitude towards us as women. We sang ourselves hoarse in an exchange of folk songs. It was an evening of careless abandon as far as shouting and singing went, and I was gently reminded of New Year's Eve parties—all we needed were whistles and balloons to complete the picture. But, of course, the similarity is superficial and it would have been a different picture altogether.

It had been a tiring day. We climbed to the top of Maijishan in the morning—to see the landscape from a height. It was an arduous climb up a steep path where the ample spread of dry pine needles made it quite slippery. I was clutching Wang's hand all the time, and he guided me and helped me along with the easy and graceful movements of a ballet dancer, if I am allowed a mild exaggeration. There is a pagoda in stone on the summit: it has the usual stone slab with the names of various visitors scratched on it. The climb was well worth it; the crazy quilt pattern of the fields rushed up the hill slopes in rich shades of green and brown with an occasional patch thickly wooded. Behind the hills in the distance was the circle of blue mountains covered in a heat haze. We saw the Stone Door peaks, the two sharp peaks over the exact middle of which, we were told, the moon rises every year on 15 August. We smelt the pungent scent of the small dwarf pines around us, and in between grew large bushes that resembled stunted oaks. There was a profusion of nettles and thorny plants along the paths. This was unpleasant as we met them when we put out our hands to clutch at something whilst slipping. A wild holly turned up around every corner.

Through the thick green shrubbery shot flowers of many shapes—most of them of a purple hue—either pale or dark full-petalled or in clusters of small efflorescence. The region is not particularly rich in wild flowers— the emphasis is more on greenery—which makes the shaded hill slopes very cool and fresh-looking. The courtyard of the monastery was full of cultivated flowers—a blaze of bright yellow-gold chrysanthemums—quite stunning as you walk in—deep reds in dahlias and hollyhocks—and a mass of yellow daisies. It made a great contrast to the unalloyed green all round. Possibly because we stayed at Maijishan towards the end of the dry season we did not see so many wild flowers.

We did only an hour's work in the afternoon—just to round off the loose ends. I could have spent the entire afternoon in the caves. I feel that now at last I am getting to know the sculpture and that it was beginning to have more meaning—but now we are to leave. Perhaps the more I think about it in retrospect the more I shall enjoy the quieter, unobtrusive pieces—the little seated Buddhas in the niches on the rock surfaces—the tiny caves into which I had to crawl on all fours and stay down because I could not stand up, and after a few minutes of looking vacantly into the darkness my eyes would begin to see the shape assume familiarity again, and I would recognize it as a bodhisattva or a Lohan—then the frantic search for details—did it have a circular nimbus or a pointed one—any flying figure above or around it, did the head have a topknot or some other headdress, and did it have long ears as do some early figures? Then the next thing to be noted was inevitably the drapery that invariably leads one on a wild goose chase through the various dynasties of China, and the various art styles of neighbouring countries.

What was the stance—was it seated in the usual way—the position of the hands was important—many of the figures had no hands, so that was eliminated—and then the question: was it late Wei or early Tang?

Sometimes I wished that I had a tape recorder: our spontaneous comments would have been of great interest to art historians! The figures would then be gently brushed with a large brush to remove a minute fraction of the dust of a century—and occasionally we would awaken a sleeping bat by doing so. Then while Dominique set the tripod and prepared the flash I would open my notebook, to record what was there with comments on the pieces seen—and the cave would be slowly documented. This sort of work becomes mechanical after a while. I soon found myself rushing from cave to cave behind Dominique and applying the questionnaire, without pausing to consider my aesthetic and emotional reaction to the statue in question. I then slowed the pace deliberately by taking longer notes that gave me time to get a sense of what I was seeing and why I was describing it in a particular way. I began to wonder whether this was the way art historians work when in the field. It was a good experience for me to work in a different way and not confined to a library. In a sense, it prepared me for similar work at archaeological sites in later years. We had had just enough time to finish the west side, with some Tang and some Song restoration.

The east side, largely Ming and Qing restoration, was somewhat different and the more I saw of it, the more sad I became at the 'restoration' but I suppose Ming aesthetes thought they were doing a service to Chinese art. The large mural was partly worn. Some parts offer interesting comparisons with what I have seen from Dunhuang in photographs, but most of it is too damaged for any efficient study. The question that remained unanswered was why was there this interest in restoring the shrines of earlier times. Was it largely an act of piety, was it an interest in reviving the aesthetic and the artistic styles of previous centuries, or was this an effort to provide a historical connection with the past and thereby ensure some legitimacy for the present?

Yes, yesterday was a day of many events. Later in the afternoon, we actually did manage to get down to the stream and we bathed, the first proper leisurely bath since we left Lanzhou, and goodness did we need it. The feeling of being able to sit in a stream for half an hour, splashing water, was indescribably pleasurable. I felt clean and cool for the 'feast' in the evening.

We drank many toasts at the feast. Again I was taken aback when Lao Zhao in all earnestness and with real feeling toasted the ending of the hydrogen bomb—that I think is real consciousness, much more than the speeches made in the Lok Sabha in Delhi or the Central Hall in Westminster. Dominique muttered that night that she found such gatherings a trifle meaningless since one cannot speak the language. I see her point but at the same time I thought this suggested a limited consciousness of place and time, reflecting an inability to reach out to something that cannot be seen but can only be felt. The journey so far has been interesting from this point of view, the difference in European and Asian reactions. Dominique has some European notions about Asians—they remain subconscious, and most of the time she is unaware of them. In many ways she is detached from European inhibitions and won't admit that she has these notions until she is made aware of them. But it is cruel to do that. In some ways, the Chinese are as alien to her as to me, and yet I am at ease with them far more quickly. But this is also a personal predilection. The experience of other peoples and other ways of life do not automatically add to our perceptions. One has to consciously want to understand how the other person functions—whoever the other person may be. Travelling in remote places and among 'exotic' people and photographing them can be an end in itself, and a form of going around the world and being entertained by what one sees. But having the sensitivity to see beyond the obvious perhaps makes one a different kind of person.

10

On Our Way to the North from Tian Shui

We all climbed into the truck last morning and sadly left Maijishan. Lao Zhao kept singing rousing songs—the Red Flag and songs of the Liberation Army—some of which we tried to learn in hopeless confusion. The fat cook was happy to be going back, where he could work in an efficient kitchen again. We passed the same familiar villages where they were still threshing, where the ducks were still bathing on the edge of the river, and people were still sitting in their doorways drinking tea—the same maize and sorghum fields. We came to the same dry riverbed—but here, within a few weeks, they were starting to build a proper road across it. China is surely a country of constant building—we passed the tall loess cliffs with two trees shooting out—like a Song landscape painting—the long avenue of acacia trees—the village with the open market on the roadside; the maize fields, the peasants with loose flapping trousers and large-brimmed straw hats, some riding a donkey, others walking along the road, some carrying large baskets mounted end to end on their backs—willow baskets, no doubt. Willow trees are in abundance and many little farms have a row of willows or a few dotted nearby. The open market was as markets are—colourful, with farmers riding in on mules with rich red designed quilts with lace trimmings as saddles. Small square awnings like garden umbrellas beneath which sat fruit and vegetable vendors—large heaps of green and yellow melons, the purple of shining eggplants, the red of tomatoes beside the bright green of capsicum— and more melons, more and more melons all over. Stray dogs wandered casually across the road, children in their slit knickers careered around corners or shot across the road at unexpected moments. Young and old men sat in groups, smoking their long pipes, glancing up on hearing the hoot of a truck. The women in blue and white peasant jackets—their hair plastered back and pulled tight into a couple of plaits—or a bun among the older women—the size of their feet indicating whether they are young or old. The really older ones belonged to the era of binding women's feet.

We jolted along, narrowly missing melons and eggplants, dogs and hens. We wanted to spend some time at a village and asked if we could get the jeep one day to wander around. They hummed and hawed and made many excuses—eventually we were told we could go this afternoon. So we set off in the afternoon—through acres and acres of maize the jeep went in the hot sun and the dust. The road was like any one of our roads connecting villages, roads only used by carts and full of ruts and ditches. A jeep alone could navigate them. The carts here are made of wood just like our carts, but are drawn by donkeys, mules, and occasionally horses, and not by bullocks. Most of the ones we passed on the road were carrying large pieces of timber or packs of firewood. Some timber is brought from the lower hills and is used as firewood since there is a strong campaign against using cattle and horse dung as fuel. Dung and night soil are now placed in compost pits and used as fertilizers. At one place near the river there had been a landslide and we had to cut across a field.

After many kilometres we came to a stop in front of a brick-built building and were told that this was the granary of the village. We were greeted by three farmers who obviously knew Lao Zhao and Lao Li—I felt annoyed because I realized we had been brought to a co-op farm and not just to any village as I had wanted. Why? They knew we had already seen a co-op and that we wanted to spend as long as we could watching the daily doings of an average village. We were received in the village schoolroom—tea, cigarettes, melon—the ritual. The melon was very welcome as we were hot and thirsty and our mouths were full of dust. There was silence for a few minutes and all that could be heard was the shirr-shirr-shirr of people noisily eating and enjoying large slices of watermelon. Then followed the history of Tian Jia Zhuang. Originally sixteen families lived here and owned 2 mou of land each. Now there are over 100 families. In those days they produced about 600 cattys, now they are supplying 30,000 cattys of maize and apples. It sounded like a well-rehearsed spiel.

We were particularly interested in the women's movement in the village, as two out of seven co-op committee members are women and the vice president is a woman. I was impressed by the confidence with which they sat among the men and, when questioned, answered directly, without turning to the head of the co-op. One of them looked particularly bright. She had been married at the age of thirteen (and was glad that the average age now is eighteen!). She has three children. At first her husband disapproved but gradually she won him around to accepting her new role in village activities. The average family consisted of a couple and three children. When questioned about birth control, they looked very bewildered. She explained that there is a separate women's organization, which decides who is to do what work and which appoints an older peasant woman to look after the children of a particular quarter of the village, while the younger women are away at work. This organization works in conjunction with the co-op committee. The head of the village is distinct from the chief of the co-op committee, though both are elected. Minor cases of justice are dealt with by the co-op committee; more serious offences are taken to the court at Tian Shui. I asked casually if we were the first foreign visitors, hoping they would say yes, but alas—many Soviet friends had already visited!

I was then taken by the hand and led out into the village by one of the peasant's wives. She was a short woman, middle-aged with a small head of set features—and very pleasant to look at—small tiny feet that obviously had been bound once and she was neatly dressed in black trousers and a white jacket. She took me from house to house; in each place we were greeted by smiling women, some hastily getting into their jackets on seeing us arriving. The village was beautifully clean—streets, courtyards, houses. I noticed the ground still retained broom marks. Was this cleanliness usual or did they do a special rushed spring cleaning on hearing that we were coming? I prefer to think it was normal.

We wandered pretty well all over the village and at random. The houses, mostly built of sunburnt bricks and plastered with mud and straw were designed in the traditional way—four blocks around a courtyard. Normally three to four families occupied one house. The central room of each house, the room where we were taken, consists of the 'kang', the raised portion spread with mats where the family sleeps, and the rest with the objects of immediate interest to the family. In every case there was always a table with an incense burner on it, and behind it on the wall hung the red banners with silver inscriptions—the requisites of ancestor worship. In one room, there was a spinning wheel, rather like an Indian charkha and a loom. The thermos for hot water and small tea cups were present everywhere. The courtyards were on the whole empty, most had small bundles of hay where possibly some domestic animal is tethered at night, and a few stray chickens and rabbits. The main entrance intrigued me as it was a large sturdy door, ornamented with a traditional design, as apparently it always is.

To me it seems absurd to try and judge the prosperity of a village after a brief three-hour visit. I would have to live at least a week in such a village to find out. Who were the group of older peasants sitting outside the school who seemed almost to resent our coming when we passed that way? Were they older dissidents who were unhappy because they no longer owned their own land? Or was it all my imagination and were they just a group of tired peasants who had returned from work and were enjoying a quiet smoke and a joke? But apart from the orderliness and cleanliness of the village—the obvious thing must be accepted that the co-op village was more prosperous than the others we saw. Apart from the figures about the number of cattys per acre—there is no denying the greater sense of purpose and ambition, incentive, in short, among the farmers of a co-op. I also had the impression that the feeling of the village as a unit is much stronger. To see the women confident and sure of themselves was a treat—and I would say that the co-op is worth it for that alone. One can see it in the faces, as the difference between the women we saw at Kangqian, where we stopped one afternoon, and those at Tia'n Jia Zhuang. We were told that with the new organization of the co-op, it was possible to use tractors—and when we had walked past the cattle bin towards the jeep, I saw the tractor.

They gave us some maize at the village, and that delighted me. I walked into the kitchen of the hotel and toasted it, to the great amusement of the cook. He explained to me at great length, and after much effort when my few words of Chinese came to my rescue, I realized that he liked to smoke bidis—he had once been given some as a present by a visiting Indian.

We all went to the public bath at Tian Shui after dinner. The hotel has only one bath for Muslims so that they can wash before praying. Non-Muslims are not allowed to use it as that would pollute it. The public bath consists of a series of cubicles—each has a bed to rest on after the bath, a long stone tub into which they pour boiling water from wooden buckets, and a pair of wooden clogs. Presumably the Chinese have an art of bathing. Anil and Dominique examined the bath minutely and decided that since they couldn't see whether the water was clean or not, they wouldn't bathe. I don't think I have enjoyed a bath quite as much as I did last night. We walked back through the streets, it was 9 p.m. The shops were still open and even the barbers' shops were doing a brisk trade. Corner shops flooded with the smell of frying oil were well patronized—and heaps of melons everywhere. It might have been a bazaar in any North Indian town at night. People sitting on the pavement, smoking, and gossiping; sleepy-eyed children tiring themselves out playing their favourite games. Cyclists tinkling down the road, weaving in and out of evening strollers, in a hurry to get to wherever they are going, and idle faces staring, without really caring too much. The moment we were recognized as foreigners, a little army of people—children and young people mostly—closed in on us, eager, interested, curious faces peering at us—wanting to know who and what we were. We never dared to stop. If we had done so, it would have been impossible to move all night.

Arrived at the train station and boarded the train for Jiu Quan. We have been chatting with a young Russian, an adviser on power stations, who is working for a few months in China. He mentioned that a major plant is coming up near Xi'an and was telling us about it. We in return told him about the archaeological sites and the ancient monastic centres that we are interested in. There is a kind of continuity in the narrative that is becoming a familiar theme. This is symbolic of one of the most striking aspects of China—the insistence on collecting and preserving the artefacts of the past and understanding them in a historically rational manner, and then these being juxtaposed with an equal insistence on providing a foundation for the future. I found this unusual and worth thinking about.

I spent the rest of the journey recalling the Qinghai love song that Mingo taught me, the dream of a shepherd with its slightly forlorn melody:

In a place far away, people pass the tent of a pretty girl
They all pause to look at her, unwilling to go away
Her smiling face, like the red sun
Her beautiful bright eyes, like the bright moon of the night.
I wish I were a lamb, always at her side
Her slender whip patting my body each day.

11

Into the North at Jiu Quan

I have just eaten! Some bread—delicious though cold—wheat bread, sprinkled with sesame seeds cooked like a roti. I also ate corn on the cob, steamed the Chinese way—all this from a vendor on a street corner in Jiu Quan. I loved the bread. I wish it was used more in Chinese cooking. We sat in a corner of the park drinking tea from small vessels that look like miniature teapots. It was a very pleasant park, sufficiently non-cultivated to retain its personality—and dotted with odd tablets and small monuments—some dating to the Han period.

This morning I was again faced with the full force of the Chinese past. The truly obvious things are often what I find most inspiring: we visited the western end of the Great Wall. We drove across a desert-like landscape in the direction of the snow-covered mountains. It has been quite cool today, with a cloudy sky. All around is complete flatness till the far distance where the mountains start. The lower ranges are a brown earthy colour, the distant ones a blue-purple, the latter colour caused not only by mist and snow, but also the reflection of an abundance of a local purple stone. This is a stone desert and not a sand desert. We didn't meet quite as many trucks as we had been warned about and had been dreading because of the dust they raise. The country is bare for miles all around but for the telegraph poles lining the road. Here and there the sources of water can be spotted since they host oases of poplar trees enclosing a small cluster of houses and vegetable patches. Mirages are frequent and the trees appear to be reflected in large lakes of water.

This is obviously a land susceptible to invasions. Houses are built close together and enclosed by sturdy walls interspersed with strong squat towers. The whole atmosphere breathes the possibility of uncertain life and constant movement. Then in the distance there appears another enclosure—a square wall with two large gates, covered with a terraced pagoda and roofs and four towers. The walls are built from the same material as all the villages in the region—sunburnt bricks covered with mud and straw and clay plaster. From here the Great Wall traversed the north-west, north, and beyond Beijing into the north-east.

We drove in and stood by the entrance to the courtyard. One look around at the landscape and it became obvious why the wall was built. There is complete openness all around—not a stone would stir to hold back an invader. Earth and stones, earth and stones—so much of it that the poplars looked out of place. The mountains are hazy, covered in mist, and can hardly present a forceful obstacle. To the east is a closer range that rises and descends in a gentle curve, leaving many passes for determined conquest. All one can hear is the wind moving in and out among the old ruins and the doves in the eaves of the upturned roofs. Then, quite unexpectedly, two woolly hump-backed camels rose up from their sitting position to stretch themselves to their full height and ambled off at a leisurely pace towards the hills.

The dust cloud of a passing truck in the distance is the only other sign of life. I thought of Kafka's satire on the inarticulateness of humanity disguised as an incident in the building of the wall and the many other reproaches of inhumanity heaped on Qin Shi Huang. But despite the consciousness of many hundred lives lost in the process, I felt an obstinate sympathy for the man of imagination and daring who believed he could hold back what he saw as the barbarian hordes—as no doubt he did to some extent. Walls may keep out the barbarians, although this is always doubtful, but they also close in those on the near side of the wall and this has other consequences often detrimental to the empire so enclosed. Are empires vast open spaces that receive a range of ideas and actions or are they enclosures with sealed frontiers, always fearful of what may be on the other side? The ambitions and frustrations of the emperor are almost visible in the structure of the wall as it goes on to ride up and down the contours of the hills. It is most impressive although perhaps less as a monument and more as a political and psychological document.

Was this massive wall effective in keeping out the barbarians as the Chinese saw them? Initially it might have been, provided it was backed by strong armed strength to meet the threat or the actuality of the invaders. Wasn't there a contradiction between treating the nomads as a threat but at the same time trading with them and keeping them at bay, as it were, with bolts of silk? Eventually the nomads were successful since some of the major dynasties of China in the second millennium AD, such as the Yuan and the Manchu, had a Central Asian ancestry. Interestingly so did the other parts of Asia that had hung on to connections with Central Asia, such as the Mughals, Ottomans, and Safavids. Central Asia played a greater role in Asian history than we have conceded so far.

The notion of boundaries, of course, has changed through history. In the past there were frontier zones that straddled a chunk of territory and were often associated with a natural landmark such as a river, a mountain, a forest or a desert. People were more familiar with frontier zones that were intermediary areas of a no man's land where anything could happen and where authority was uncertain and could change repeatedly. There was a multiplicity of frontier zones across Central Asia. The attempt at marking a precise physical boundary was also what resulted in the Great Wall. And yet today we mark boundaries as lines on a map, demarcated to the last mile and made sacrosanct.

But how sad must be the spirit of Qin Shi Huang amid these ruins— desolate, deserted, and badly kept. It has been a monument to China's history since the beginning—the constant change of hands—under imperial garrisons and Central Asian hordes. More recent history has seen the famed bandits of the north-west using it as a stronghold—and later still, the Kuomingtang troops. Yet it stands unkempt. The two tall gateways have been reinforced with bricks, but the courtyard and the walls are in a bad state of disrepair. There was something about the courtyard that reminded me of a mosque. Was it the square form, the simplicity and the dignity? How old is this form in Chinese architecture? We walked along the rampart behind the turreted walls and looked out at the stretch of desert, at a small village near which some horses were grazing on the solitary green patch.

Beside the gate is a temple dedicated to a famous general who lived and fought during the period of the Three Kingdoms. The walls are covered with some excellent frescoes of the Ming period depicting his life. But again they are in extremely poor condition. Rainwater channels running down, chalk scribbles all over, and numerous scratches. It really is quite maddening

to see good painting badly preserved. Apparently the present government is doing something about it, by at least keeping the doors locked and
allowing visitors only when accompanied by the local warden. But so much
restoration work will have to be done before they can be presentable. I was
interested in the style of the Ming frescoes: they evoke enlarged Persian and
Indian miniatures. If the paintings date to a later period, to Qing, this idea
becomes even more interesting. It might be worth pursuing the migrations
of form and style in all these murals.

I am now beginning to feel the excitement of approaching Dunhuang.
Aurel Stein, Paul Pelliot, Langdon Warner, Irene Vincent are coming alive,
and the pages of *Ruins of Desert Cathay* keep flashing through my mind
each time I see an old tower or just the expanse of the desert. The thrill of
going to Dunhuang is beginning to grip me. I keep visualizing Stein visiting
it half a century ago travelling in a cart and the travel taking four months.
My only regret is that I cannot ride here as this is ideal horse country. A few
kilometres on horseback each day would be the way to travel. The carts here
are good fun, driven by three horses, with wheels as large in diameter as the
body of the cart. Possibly they would make one sore after a few days.

We went for a walk this evening, Dominique and I. This was the first
time we went alone since leaving Beijing. The desert breeze was very fresh
and we sat in a sand pit for a while, and the earth seemed to move with the
sky—perhaps the effect of walking along a desert road—even the sand in
the pit seemed to move with a circular movement. Another thing we noticed
was a changed sense of time and direction. Direction is understandable
because things seeming near are really very far—but the sense of time
was strange—hours seemed to go by very quickly. I enjoyed being quiet—
and not part of a crowd being conducted around. The trouble with an
invited trip is that I become irritated at being shepherded all the time. The
Chinese have been extremely kind and have taken so much trouble over
our comfort, and yet—I wish I could be alone for a week, just to wander ad
lib. If I had my own form of transport I would love to do that.

I have just picked up a handful of shards, a small surface collection of
pieces of tiles and glazed vessels, from the surface near the Great Wall. It's
crazy, taking them by air, but I should like to know more about the glazes
and some of my Sinologist friends in London might be interested.

Thinking about monuments, I feel that this is one aspect of the past where we in India have to be thankful to the British colonial government. Curzon's policy, 'to dig and to discover, to cherish and preserve', was indeed a happy one—even if the readings of what was found were faulty, as was to some extent the motivation to discover. The preservation of monuments in India is so much better than the condition in which one finds Chinese monuments. No doubt the Chinese have had only a few years to work on them. It is difficult to do much in so short a time, especially as there are so many monuments. But certain obvious places like the Great Wall at this place require more careful attention.

12

To the High Point of the Journey at Dunhuang

I've been lying on my bed petrified that I may be going in for an attack of appendicitis. I had a nightmare in which it was so, and I was trying to fight it. The nausea that I have been feeling off and on for the last couple of days may be the beginning—I feel weak and tired today, yet till yesterday I was full of spirits. I shall never forgive myself if it does turn bad and I have to be rushed back to Lanzhou. But at least I shall have seen some of the caves at Dunhuang and even that will be enough to last me the rest of my life. We went around this morning to the caves and I was overwhelmed. The painting is indescribably more beautiful than what one imagines from photographs, but my mind is too full of fear of a burst appendix for me to write at all about the murals.

We set out the day before yesterday and slept the night at Jiu Quan. It took us twelve hours yesterday from there to reach here. We drove in a Land Rover, stopping very briefly for lunch. It was the first time I have driven through such an extensive desert. At the start we drove alongside a railway line, and in the distance we passed the Yumen station near the newly dis-covered oilfields. Mountains closing in on both sides reminded me of the passage through the Red Sea. The road is not tarred but is nevertheless amazingly good, so we had quite a comfortable ride. Doubtless this is because a good link to the oil fields has priority. It is dusty, of course, and we passed endless numbers of trucks in the course of the day that enveloped us in never-ending clouds of dust. Every complaint about this led me to remind them that in previous times we would have travelled by cart. Imagining what that would have been like kept us cheerful. It is a stony desert with occasional patches of scrub and, very infrequently, an oasis of poplar trees. Halfway to here the desert becomes even more arid and dry, with large banks of sand piled up against the hills, the work of frequent sandstorms.

The road then follows the hills more closely. These are more like large boulders and rocks thrown together in a heap with their jagged edges jutting out alternating with great pits and hollows. In part they reminded me of photographs one sees of the surface of other planets. It has the feeling of a place without life where humans cannot live—of impossibility and hopelessness. The unkind sun, and the mirage, coupled with the lurking suggestion of some unknown malicious force is somewhat depressing! We travelled on, secure in the Land Rover at 30 kilometres an hour. By the time we came to think that it was a never-ending journey, we found that we had very quietly and almost unnoticed, glided into what was once the sacred oasis of Dunhuang. There was nothing sudden or dramatic about it except that we found ourselves driving into a rich expanse of green grass. Then we turned off the main road and drove on towards the hills. All of us peering out and trying desperately to spot the caves. This went on for the entire 11 kilometres till we turned a corner and a cluster of trees was visible and beyond that was the extensive cliff face with the caves; driving over the dry riverbed, we had arrived.

We are here at a small government institute set up to study the caves and the murals. The small staff is involved both in recording and restoring the paintings. We have been put up in their guest house. As I lie here I can see the cliffs on the other side beyond the small river and the grove of poplars and willows. It is infuriating to have to lie in bed holding onto my stomach waiting for the pain to go when I would so much rather be sitting outside with the others talking to Dr Chang Shu-Hung, the director of the Dunhuang Cultural Research Institute, established to restore and protect the caves. I sat out for half an hour after supper this evening—it was an enchanting evening. The grey-brown of the hills was a contrast against the clear increasingly intense and darkening blue of the sky, partially dotted with clouds. Small single pagodas lie scattered across the sand dunes and some are lined up against the hills. One is a tiny room-like shrine of the monk whose body was cast in clay immediately after he died. The dark colour of the wooden gateway is offset by the pale green of the willows on each side, its roof-ends turning up, with the long clapper bells in the corners, which ring when the breeze hits them. The lower level caves are hidden behind the thick rows of poplars that are embedded in silence when there is no breeze, and when no one speaks. Almost invisibly, just two figures, a man and a woman, walked slowly across the dunes and into the hills. I can't describe it, I just don't have the words.

Yesterday afternoon was four hours of unabated terror for me. It started with a pain in the region of the appendix and I assumed it was an attack of appendicitis. What was going to happen? Would I survive twelve hours of jolting in a jeep, then staying overnight, and finally being rushed by plane to Lanzhou; or would the appendix burst before then causing untold complications? Anil would have insisted on coming with me, and that made me feel even worse, since Dunhuang was a dream come true for her and I felt I would never forgive myself for depriving her of this visit. Between the pain and the anxiety I was in a pretty bad state. Fortunately, Dr Chang came by in the evening hearing that I was unwell, and told us that there were doctors and a fully equipped hospital in the oasis town of Dunhuang 15 kilometres away. What a relief. To know that if necessary I had only to go 15 kilometres to the hospital.

The doctor arrived at 10.30 p.m. last night, and after examining me he suggested it might be an inflamed intestine. I went with him to the hospital this morning and he did a blood test and diagnosed intestinal trouble and not the appendix. I am willing to accept the doctor's word so as to allay the anxiety of the others, but I am not at all sure about it myself. The symptoms are too much like appendicitis. But I may well be wrong despite my dream! However, my only hope is that it will be dormant for the next two months. The gentle-mannered doctor inspired confidence.

I went to the out-patient department of the hospital; it was a small place, rather like the military medical inspection rooms of cantonment hospitals in India. Up till now I have always had a prick on a finger to obtain blood for a test—but apparently in China it is customary to take the blood from the lobe of the ear. It is certainly far less painful, but I must find out if it makes any difference. A woman in the lab gave me an injection—she was not very efficient, knocking the top of the capsule all over the floor, and fumbling with the syringe—perhaps she was nervous. There was quite a little audience standing around the door whilst I was being injected. But these are minor things that will undoubtedly improve. The main thing is that a competent hospital exists—and this because there is a depot of transport workers in connection with the oil field in Xinjiang, not far from here, demanding the presence of medical facilities. The sheer relief of knowing that there were medical facilities close by made me feel very much better.

Let me try and forget about being unwell and write about the site. A frequent conversation was about the history of Qianfodong, 'Caves of a Thousand Buddhas', as these grottoes were called, and the many stories about how it all began. Such stories are, of course, expected at renowned sites such as this. One that is recorded in an inscription relates that a monk travelling from the west in 366 AD broke journey at Dunhuang and rested by the cliff-side. At sunrise he saw a vision of myriad Buddhas over the Three Peak Mountain nearby. What is narrated as his vision does inevitably have variations! The vision convinced him that it was a sacred oasis so he proceeded to hack a cave in the cliff where he meditated. This was the first shrine. The oasis near the cliff was strategically situated between China and Central Asia, so with the growth in the silk trade it became a flourishing commercial centre with merchants using it as a central point for exchange since it was the meeting point of many routes. Increasing wealth led to the Chinese kingdoms laying claim to it and defending their claim by posting frontier garrisons of Chinese soldiers to the oasis.

With the spread of Buddhism in these parts Chinese monks travelling to the West, seeking greater knowledge of Buddhism and bringing back Buddhist manuscripts, stopped at Qianfodong and the neighbouring oasis. Owing to its exceptional fertility and location, the oasis became politically important and extremely wealthy. It hosted a range of diverse peoples from the Iranians and Sogdians, from the western part of Central Asia, to the Uyghurs and Tocharians from the more eastern parts, and the Chinese from further east. Wealthy merchants joined the local nobility in donating caves as shrines. It reached a peak during the Tang period when the cliff was studded with caves and there were monasteries in the vicinity. The river was large so there was no shortage of water.

As in Maijishan, so too here, the murals focused on illustrating themes from Buddhist religious texts familiar to most Buddhists anywhere. The biography of the Buddha was an important source especially the crucial moments in his life that led to the making of his teaching. Narratives from other Buddhist texts were also illustrated. Among them were the popular *Jataka* stories of the previous births of the Buddha; or stories from the *Tripitaka*, the teachings of the Buddha. They were taken from the early Mahayana Buddhist texts that had been put together in the region of Gandhara close to North-west India. When the mythology of this religion developed further this too was represented. Stylistically there was a gradual shift inevitably, from a greater Indian imprint to a great Chinese imprint. But neither imprint was definitive and final. So when Buddhism morphed into Vajrayana Buddhism under the influence of Tantric ideas, this too was reflected in the murals. This change was also partly linked to the increasing Tibetan influence in this area.

The Tibetan invasion and occupation in the eighth century AD was a setback for the site, its becoming less impressive both economically and in artistic effort. During the subsequent period there was a revival under the rule of a local governor who ousted the Tibetans and reasserted Chinese control. Patronage from local governors was to become something of a pattern. The Cao family controlled the oasis for almost a century. The bigger caves were cut and painted during this period. An initial marriage with a princess from Khotan, to the west, brought in both new patronage as well as new artistic styles. She is thought to have brought artists with her that might have introduced styles from Khotan and Kucha into the murals at Dunhuang. The family later also married into the Song dynasty thus bringing in Song patronage as well.

Despite the unrest in Central Asia at that time, the oasis remained calm. The Cao family founded an academy at the site to encourage the painting of murals. Possibly by this time it also attracted other artists from more distant places in China. The admixture of folk motifs was a recognized contribution. Manuscripts dating to this period found at the site refer to many aspects of local living. One refers to visitors from Xinjiang, and another lists the account for expenses on paints and other requirements for the artists. These are important documents for the social history of the period. Where the artists came from remains a little uncertain, except when their names are clearly Chinese. They could have come from as far away as Gandhara or more likely other places on the trade route.

The Song emperor Hui Zong founded a school of painters that is said to have influenced the artists at Dunhuang resulting in the rather stylized Song style. This was different from the paintings of the landscapes that appear to have been influenced by Chan Buddhism, the name Chan being derived from Sanskrit dhyana. Anil's project at Dunhuang was focused on landscape art, and its evolution at the site, therefore we spent time in the specific caves that had examples of this. In a later period, the family in control was primarily interested in Vajrayana Buddhism and Tantric forms and these began to be included in the painting. The Ming era saw the imprint of Tibetan styles. By the nineteenth century, just a couple of monasteries were left at the site and the caves had degenerated for lack of maintenance.

The establishment and spread of Buddhism both in these oasis towns and inland in China did not have a direct trajectory. In the Tang period it did get rooted as reflected in some of the best writing and translations as also the finest sculpture and murals. The ninth century AD persecution did stop the patronage to Buddhist institutions, but the religion survived and made headway in subsequent centuries. However, the threat seems to have been present at least in the frontier areas as that may explain why an enormous of number of manuscripts and paintings were hidden in a secret chamber in one of the caves at Dunhuang in the eleventh century and the cave was bricked up and sealed.

Ironically it was a Daoist priest, Wang, who agreed to maintain the surviving caves provided he could take the donations that were left at the caves by visiting pilgrims—even if the latter were few and far between. It was in the process of cleaning one of the caves that a major discovery was made that transformed the history of the site as also much of Central Asia as involved in the trade. Wang inundated a cave in order to clean it and the wall on one side cracked, revealing another room within. It had been a bricked up wall. An enormous number of manuscripts lay within the sealed room and were well preserved in the relatively dry climate. Some of these found their way to Xinjiang where Stein who happened to be visiting recognized their value. He visited Dunhuang and persuaded Wang to sell a huge number to him for a song. The manuscripts found their way to Delhi and London, and later elsewhere.

Stein's discovery brought Pelliot, Warner, and others to the scene, all searching for manuscripts and hoping to bring specimens of the paintings to museums in Europe. In the process of doing so, some murals were severely damaged. This activity aroused the interest of the Kuomintang government but they did little to renovate the site. The caves were occupied by soldiers from garrisons posted on the frontier, by local bandits, and by White Russian refugees fleeing the revolution, all of whom scarred the paintings in various ways sometimes resulting in irretrievable destruction.

Dr Chang arrived here fifteen years ago and started making painted reproductions in an effort to preserve the art. The present government has appreciated the importance of his project and has sanctioned the setting up of an official art institute that will no doubt be built in slow stages. He now has a group of artists working under him, men and women, who are making copies, photographers recording every shrine, and research assistants maintaining the archive. The aim is not only to make a thorough study of the site but also to present it as a special kind of museum of Chinese painting from the earliest historical times. It is in many ways a unique site given that the murals were painted over a period of a millennium and reflect the changing artistic forms. This makes it an impressive history of painting in China.

The work going well in the next few days, and my having resumed work, we decided one morning to visit the town of Dunhuang, accompanied by a little retinue, including the cook. It is a small town, mud-brick and dusty. Being Sunday, it was crowded with people dressed in various shades of blue and printed materials. We went down the main street, hooting past clusters of people crowded around hawkers and vendors who had spread out their goods on the edge of the street. This included a dentist who squatted on the ground with a large sheet spread before him. On it was a collection of human teeth that he claimed he had extracted, everything from small canines to large molars—a line of bottles and jars filled with powders and liquids of various colours, and on each end were books, opened at photographs and sketches of the human mouth, showing the dental system. Presumably he was persuading the crowd around him that it was pleasurable to have painful teeth removed. Another similarly spread-out cloth had a variety of spectacles and customers could try them all and see which pair suited them. Nearby was a man selling rattles and bird-whistles, rather like the ones excavated at Mohenjo-daro. The grocery shops I noticed were very well stocked—with everything from crude soya beans to tinned pears and bottles of beer.

As usual, wherever we stopped people hustled and pushed to come closer, to find out who we were, what we looked like, what we were buying, and what we were saying. But it is a friendly curiosity, and whereas in the early days I was a little irritated by it, I am now quite immune to it. Many people rode down the streets on donkeys. Donkeys are certainly the cheap means of transport in the oasis. Often peasant women sit astride a donkey with a small child in their arms and another older child mounted behind— and the donkey moves at quite a quick pace. It has a blanket of a thin quilt over its back, and onto this is fitted a wooden saddle, and on the saddle is placed what appears to be a pillow or a cushion so that the mount is fairly comfortable. Some ride with short stirrups, others let their legs hang.

On the way back from the town, the cook had the jeep stopped and hopped out hastily because across the road he had seen a man walking with a couple of chickens, which he obviously wanted to sell. Then the little play-acting began. They bargained for a while, and as the owner refused to accept the small price offered, the cook turned as if to leave, so did the owner. So the cook laughed, paid the man his price, and returned with the fowls, and we continued our journey back to the caves. The town of Dunhuang has possibilities: I must see more of it. I cannot help but visualize it as a grand caravanserai on the old Silk Route.

The bells on the gateway have been clanging for a while now as there is a strong breeze blowing. It sounds like the movements of a camel caravan. Perhaps if I were to shut my eyes tight like a child, I could will myself back into the Dunhuang of ten centuries ago...

I spent the day in the caves today, pain and all. I didn't care. It was like a vision, a revelation, I don't know what. I could have sat there forever in caves 286 and 323, looking at the walls. How poor, in comparison, are the photographs of Paul Pelliot, how unlike the real thing, and to think that we have to study the murals entirely from books and reproductions. There's a desperate need for new publications. I am amazed that no one has thought of it in the intervening years. Subsequently, Langdon Warner came here and in the crudest way tried to tear off some of the paintings from the walls, damaging the rest. What he and his ilk did can only be described as vandalism. Yet such people are applauded for their contribution to Chinese art.

The restorations by the monk Wang from the money paid by Stein are quite monstrous, especially in Cave 323, where there is a regular stage décor background to the shrine with butterflies and miniature bridges and the lot. The unrestored murals are magnificent. I was as stunned today as I was on the first morning when we went around. It is like basing one's knowledge of human beings on a corpse and then suddenly meeting a living person. Fortunately we are doing only a small study here so I shall have plenty of time to look around at an easy pace—provided my digestive tract permits me to. Too much melon—an inflamed intestine—it's all bosh, I must get myself seen to properly. I can't go about with this ailment.

Today, we went to Dr Chang's office to see some copies of frescoes from the caves here and from Kucha made by his wife and various other artists who have been working as a team and as a part of the project. Kucha is in the northern part of the Takla Makan Desert in the Tarim Basin. Some of the copies are quite breathtakingly lovely, and when compared with the originals, are incredibly close. These copies are a real achievement. We asked him to send an exhibition to Europe, and he said, only if there was a demand from organizations there. We must try to create an interest in such an exhibition—not only in Europe but also in India. People need to be acquainted with the work that the Chinese have done in their studies over the last decade. The work is not generally known.

The other day, Dr Chang was asking us about publications on Chinese art in France and England, particularly journals dealing with research on the subject. He wanted to know about the new perspectives on Chinese art. Obviously art historians here don't have access to these journals, as indeed European archaeologists and art historians are seldom acquainted with the latest Chinese views as expressed in Chinese publications. It seems so absurd that even in this century there should be important groups doing research on the very same subject but in an entirely unrelated way. Why can't there be some interchange of ideas at least on this level? An exchange of publications and visiting exhibitions are surely not all that impossible. If a man like Dr Chang could work in Europe again for a year, it would be of immense advantage both to Europe and to China.

There was an open-air film show at the institute this evening. I went for a short while. They were showing a Chinese film, the story of an opera from Anhui, *The Princess Who was Beaten*, all shot inside a studio, and obviously so: long melodramatic movements with lengthy scenes. I don't think the opera style and technique is suited to films, but even apart from that it was unimaginatively handled, very much like a Hindi movie screening a historical romance. Technically they made the same faults and that I found very curious. But it was odd sitting on a bench beneath the poplars with crowds of little children all around—the families of those working in the institute were there, but the larger number was that of families from the oasis.

Looking up—it was a dark night with a clear sky full of small stars— the stars look small from here unlike at Maijishan where they looked huge. Before us was the screen, up against the wall of a building, and behind us in the darkness I could see the façade of some of the top caves. All this at Dunhuang. I cannot get used to it. I have a slight conscience about being here, as I cannot help but think of those friends in London who have been working on Chinese art all their lives and who would probably understand this site much better—and who certainly deserve to come here. I particularly wish that my friend Mary Tregear were here. She did the course with me and has since specialized in Chinese ceramics. But this is the way of the world—I come here as an amateur and they remain in London looking at Pelliot's photographs. It is an injustice, and I can see now why so many envied me this visit, including Mary. Perhaps in the next generation, when travelling across continents will be as easy and as cheap as travelling to the next town, this will be remedied.

I worked in the caves again today. The pain was less, but I felt much better for the work, so tomorrow I shall stay longer, inshallah! The new style on which we worked today fascinates me. It seems to be an effort at portraying early Buddhism, but doing so in an impressionistic way. Is this un-Chinese? But it is not the influence of Ajanta. It was painted at the turn of the eighth century, well after Xuan Zang's return and he may have brought back some small paintings. I can recognize hints of an Indian presence and the Buddhist substance, but why in that style? Personally, I feel more and more certain that the solution is to be found in Tibetan banners of that period: the Tibetan invasion was not far off, nor were the murals of Central Asian sites like Khotan and Kucha. It was a visually exciting and thought-provoking afternoon.

After supper I walked across the bed of the river to the sand dunes and stupas opposite us. It was another beautiful evening, even though the sky was overcast. It had rained for a few moments in the afternoon, a small drizzle lasting hardly ten minutes, and yet within that time there was a small stream moving rapidly down the dry riverbed. In the silence of the evening I could hear it slashing and murmuring and lapping—a soft, sensuous sound. The wind was strong across the hills and on the dunes. I felt it fresh and cool against me. I sat out and watched the sky changing colour and the reflection of the light in the hills and the sand. The desert gives off a companionship at such moments that is as strong as the presence of mountains. In the silence I felt an intimate closeness to the desert.

I am resting. The others are all sitting in the room next to mine, the door is open, and I can hear the conversation. They probably think it rude of me to be lying here and writing, but I felt too exhausted. Dr Chang is here. He comes around practically every evening. He really is a gem and quite the right sort of person to be working here and directing the work of the Cultural Research Institute. He has lived here for fifteen years and made this his life work. I envy a man like him who has found his objective. He came here after staying a while in France as an art student. In those days this was a real wilderness, and a decision to work here must have been a decision to accept the worst possible conditions, requiring complete dedication. There is something about him that makes him much more accessible than some of the other officials we have met. Is this because we can speak directly to him in French, or is it his long years in Europe which have given him an attitude of mind which I, at least, find sympathetic? He has the right degree of directness with just the right amount of politeness to make a conversation really enjoyable. The Chinese refinements in him show even more strongly because he is such an approachable person. Perhaps these are all personal characteristics and have nothing to do with his being Chinese. Four or five years ago I would have thought living one's life in a place like Dunhuang somewhat trying, but now I wouldn't hesitate if given the chance. There is so much to be done. If only we could repeat this at some of our sites. Ajanta, now alas, attracts too many tourists and has been worked on quite consistently. It has to be caves in an oasis in a desert—foolish romanticism!

This is the following evening and it is cold. There is a fierce wind blowing outside and within a few hours the temperature has dropped. I dread it being cold as I haven't brought enough warm clothes. We've had to close all the doors and windows. I do hope tomorrow will be a fine day, as Dr Chang has promised to take us for a walk in the desert. He was here till 10.30 this evening together with Professor and Mrs Li. I was feeling better so I joined them. He talked at length about the more recent occupation of Dunhuang—the Russian refugees fleeing the revolution, and his early work at the site before Liberation, with the constant fear of attacks by the Cossacks. The more legendary side were the stories associated with objects in the museum. The more I get to know him, the more I like him— he has a feel for the place, and that is what makes it so appropriate to his being here.

This morning I climbed to the top of the huge image of the seated Buddha—six flights of steps up to the top of the cliff. I sat there for a while, trying to accustom myself to taking in the murals. Oddly enough I didn't tire of them, even after three hours. In a museum, I can only take in enough for a couple of hours. Perhaps here is because it is all so startlingly good. It is not normal, I still feel overwhelmed by it. Another thing—quite by the way—each cave here is worth a study in itself, and whatever I see sets my mind buzzing in ten different directions all at once. I could with perfect ease spend a year here and even that I would consider far too short a time for even a preliminary study.

My only regret is that at some moments I feel even more cut off and as if enclosed in unknown parts of the world. I was very restless today, as I was yesterday too—but this morning I felt something was wrong somewhere and I was cut off. Perhaps it is just the desert around me, and the seclusion of the place, that brings on this mood. It is over a month since I heard from home, and three weeks since I heard from Europe. No newspapers either. I have no idea as to what is happening anywhere—even here since the newspapers are in Chinese.

The next afternoon was again extraordinary. I climbed up to one of the top caves. A large one with a huge figure of the reclining Buddha in stone— the nirvana scene, rather like the Buddha in Gal Vihara at Polonnaruwa in Sri Lanka. A group of mourners is painted on the right wall standing with an assortment of headgear. But the outlining of these figures was most impressive and I wondered about who had been the artist. Obviously someone of genius—yet we don't know who or what he was—we merely have the painting. I remember seeing an exhibition of Goya's line drawings—quite masterly. This reminded me of them, except that the work here is on a far larger scale. I was standing there, looking dumb, when Professor Li walked in so we spoke about it. After a while we went to look at the neighbouring cave, which had a marvellous panel on one wall, depicting the emperor's hunt, and on the other wall, a jour de fête for the empress with all the array of imperial carriages of the Tang period.

The hunting panel is quite remarkable. Those strong, well-fed Tang horses, like the six chargers of Tai Zong—all symbolizing the prosperity and opulence of the period. But more than that, the artist must have had a real love for horses. I remember now reading somewhere that the best horses in China were bred in these parts, in and around Dunhuang. But the even better ones were imported from Central Asia. In fact, there are legends about the fabulous blood-sweating horses of the Ferghana Valley further west, from where Babur, the first Mughal king, came. The wild ones were caught with the greatest difficulty using a decoy. Langdon Warner has a very prosaic explanation of 'blood-sweating'. He says that when made to go fast, or overworked, these horses suffer from sores that ooze blood. I prefer to think of them as naturally wild and beautiful horses, sweating blood in their wildness—much more romantic. Of course, there is no doubt about this being a region for horses.

In around 1920, about 900 White Russians fleeing Russia after the revolution occupied these caves. Some of the paintings had gold paint and low relief work in gold, as for instance on the carriages painted in the murals. The Russians gouged out the gold from the wall in order to sell it. Now all that remains of the carriages are their outlines marked as deep channels cutting right into and across the mural plaster. It is quite infuriating to see this in some of the best painting, and I wonder if the gilt they thus collected was worth anything. Other caves where they lit fires have been completely blackened with smoke. It is hard to restore such painting as the plaster has imbibed the soot. In any case, it would take a very long time to clean.

Professor Li and I had a long talk on Chinese painting as of today and its future. Happily he speaks French, having been a student in France in 1933 at the same time as Dr Chang. I was worried in Beijing when I was told that the director of the Art Academy was condemned because he was in favour of oil painting and the European tradition. That this constituted his 'right-wing tendencies', as proved by the rectification campaign, seemed to me to be completely uncalled for. Li is a professor of fine art at Lanzhou, and he explained that the general attitude in China today is to train art students in the technique of art as craftsmen, which they are primarily at the level of technique, the technique being both European and Chinese, or only one if the student so wishes, with which I agreed. It is then up to the student to choose his/her own medium, whatever allows the best self-expression, whether it is oils, brush or ink, watercolour, crayon, or anything. Further, whether it is a foreign medium or a traditional one, he must experiment with it and find his own style gradually.

What appealed to me greatly was the consciousness in Li for the need to experiment and not merely to copy the existing tradition in a new medium. He was firmly against copyists initiating a new style. He spoke of his realization that because style is a social force plus a personal force, it cannot arise in a year or two and may well take fifty years. So that even if the large majority of contemporary Chinese artists fumble for the next twenty years, it should not cause anxiety. A style will emerge, as at Dunhuang: even though seemingly isolated from art centres and great artists, the style of each period is abundantly clear. We talked at length. I was interested also because of the similar transitional stage in India. He seemed to be the sort of man who spoke because he really believed in what he said—not because he wanted to make an impression.

Today I feel exhausted. It has all been rather overwhelming and I need to be quiet and to reflect on it. The thought of having to pack up and leave here in thirty-six hours makes me most unhappy. I want to stay longer. I am only just beginning to realize what the murals are—but we must go. I want to return here—but how, and to do what? I don't know enough about Chinese painting to do an independent study. Being here has decided me against attempting such a thing until I know far more, if I ever acquire such knowledge. But a year at Dunhuang would be a really dedicated year for me, except that that will never happen.

Maybe I'm just physically tired—I've been doing so much the last few days trying to make up for the days I was ill. I spent the afternoon at the site-museum making rubbings of the tablets. Dr Chang has asked the official 'rubber' of the Art Institute to show us the Chinese method: with dampened rice paper, and using either a pumice stone or a pounce, with black ink. It is quite different from the European process of rubbing bronzes in churches. I insisted on being taught how to do it, and made half a dozen, which was tiring. One of them, an inscription with a statue, has come up particularly well, and I am delighted with it. I am now just itching to get on to doing some more—but I doubt if I'll get an opportunity in China again.

I have just been to see my favourite caves. I shall be quite heartbroken at having to leave. I remember the first evening we arrived. I was thrilled because I was at last going to be alone in a room, so that I could read and write how and when I liked. I would be able to sit quietly and stare at the mountains and maybe even write some poetry to capture the moment! And that crazy little conversation with Dr Chang when he spoke about the mountains in Greece resembling the mountains here and went on to ask me a question about modern Greece, to which my reply was a look of complete bewilderment. And then it dawned on me that he was under the impression that I was Greek! How he came to that I don't know, as I was wearing a sari. Obviously India is quite unfamiliar to many Chinese, as is Greeece!

This morning I again climbed to the top of the cliff, to the highest part above the caves and there I sat for quite a while. It was so quiet, so still, only the purple mountains, the sun in a blue sky, the mirage of a clear stretch of water beyond the sand. And I wondered about the first monk who came here. Why did he come to this particular oasis, why did he paint murals? Did he paint them himself or did he ask an artist to paint them? How did the community grow? Why did the monks leave the ordered society and live in isolation? Was this oasis frequented only by monks, or did it become a place of pilgrimage and how did it attract the patronage of emperors and aristocracy? Did it become a staging point for traders from China going west or for traders from Central Asia going east? Some of the answers to these questions are known some remain as speculation. One can become one-tracked about the art and disconnect it from everything else. We know that royal families were among the patrons, they are painted on the walls, but this was in the Song period, or a little before. What of the Wei period, who were the patrons, and did this patronage change? Was the life at

Ch'ien Fo Tung (as Qianfodong was then known), 'Caves of a Thousand Buddhas', a strictly monastic one, or did it gradually become a community of artists supervised by monks—a strange mélange? Was it always aloof, or did it attract many people in the heyday of trade along the Silk Route? I tried to imagine the site in the second half of the first millennium AD.

In the afternoon we returned to the cave with Tantric-inspired murals. They were a curious mixture of what seems to be later Buddhist painting merging with a Tantric cult. Tantrism intrigues me historically, because of this inherent mélange with other forms. What would have been the sources? The ladder up the cliff to the cave was somewhat terrifying, with rungs half-broken and with large gaps. I was doing the splits going up and down.

We climbed up the cliff after that and onto the desert to collect pebbles—some beautiful stones, shaped by the wind—some unusual colours, grey, white, and pink mixtures. Dr Chang came with us. I must say he's very active for his years—climbing up cliffs and ladders. We walked away from the cliffs, and I took off my rope shoes and walked barefoot, letting my feet and toes sink into the soft sand.

There was a farewell dinner for us at night with Dr Chang and Professor and Mrs Li. We toasted everyone present in red wine from Xinjiang that tasted like sweet vermouth. If only it were possible—I was almost in tears this morning, when we drove across the riverbed and gradually lost sight of the little clump of trees hiding the face of Qianfodong, the Mogao caves.

Autumn is almost here—the leaves are beginning to change colour. The caves in Dunhuang sometimes do odd things—a sudden window frames a breathtakingly beautiful view; or, as this morning, I passed along a gallery to bid farewell to the caves. At the corner was an opening, and through it I saw a tree—first of all just a tree, with green leaves, and then a small part of it was yellow—autumn leaves—and beyond the tree the sky. It sounds so ordinary when described like this, yet it quite shook me this morning.

13

The Start of the Return Journey via Yumen

We are journeying back. I am sitting in a hotel room in Yumen, drinking cup after cup of jasmine tea. I feel so thirsty. After the slightly brackish water at Dunhuang, it's so pleasant to have 'sweet water' again. I indulged in another orgy of bathing today—a steaming hot bath, after many days of lukewarm catlicks. I never feel really clean until I have washed behind my ears and cleaned my toenails. We had some European food for dinner—tastes awful after Chinese cooking, and I felt so strange handling a fork and knife after so many weeks with a bowl and chopsticks. We saw a radio in the room and I was ecstatic at the thought of some news at last—perhaps the BBC. We battled with it for an hour, and all we got were whirring sounds, or else Chinese and Vietnamese programmes—a fleeting snatch of an Indian film song, which rapidly vanished, and to my great sorrow never returned. So we decided to abandon the radio and write letters instead. But somehow, I couldn't. I feel tired now and maybe I shall sleep. Two Chinese boys are playing ping-pong in the hall outside, and the steady knick-knock of the ball keeps me awake.

Yumen is an oilfield, discovered about twenty years ago, and set up in the last two years. We decided to come here for a day on our way to Jiu Quan because Dominique wanted to make a 'story' about the Old Silk Road having now become the 'New Oil Road'. The oil from both Yumen and another source in Xinjiang goes to the refinery at Lanzhou. I tried telling Dominique that historically her comparison is invalid because the Silk Road functioned altogether differently—but for a journalist what matters is that it is a 'catchy story'!

I don't like this hotel. It smells of colonialism and bad taste. Architecturally, it is badly designed. For the rest, it has central heating and all mod cons. It is inartistically furnished because obviously some poor   chap with a wholly Chinese background was trying desperately to bring in things that would make the foreign experts—Russian and East European—and foreign friends feel at home. The hotel is built for these two categories of people. We belong to the second, of course. The large cumbersome-looking arm-chairs, upholstered in a big-patterned textile with lace antimacassars and the flowered plastic tablecloths on the dinner table—somehow give me whiffs of the Leningradskaya again.

When we arrived we bumped into a very sour-faced Russian woman, quite terrifying—and another two who stared down at us from an upstairs window. I was reminded immediately of colonial wives in the time of the British Raj. That is why, I suppose, I smelt something of the colonial attitude. This may be a wholly unfair judgement. Perhaps they have social contacts with the Chinese—perhaps the relationship is different. Most of the experts are here for three or sometimes more years. Why can't they live in houses alongside the Chinese—why must they huddle together in a hotel? The country is strange, the culture is different—that is understandable. It is difficult for a Mrs Podsvinov coming from a small-town Russian back-ground to hobnob with the Chinese from the start. But if they are here as friends, and they are genuinely respected by the Chinese, as one is told that they are, there should be no special attempts to house them differently. Possibly this is just Chinese courtesy and politeness again... Ah, the ping-pong has stopped. Now I can sleep.

I feel quite shaken up with the last 30 kilometres of our journey: jolting along a rough track, through streams and ditches and up mounds. The poor Land Rover really rattled like a tin can. But it was an enticing land-scape. Desert around us with variegated sands—green, red, yellow in streaks—and mountains, purple, blue, blue-black, violet, red, pink, yellow, changing colour in the changing light, all dappled with the shadows of the isolated clouds moving across the sun in a clear sky. There are fields in some parts and the rest is covered with a yellow-green scrub, interspersed with curious rock formations set in layered earth. Sometimes, it looks like the moon landscape. I wish I had taken the trouble to read at least the elements of geology with reference to China before coming. To pass through such country and not know how it came about is a real shortcoming. There were moments when it was even more fantasy-ridden than a colour film on a sci-fi dreamland.

The little village on the top of the red sandstone cliff evoked endless stories. Empty desert for miles and then the daemonic sprawl of the oilfields; it looked so powerful and menacing under a storm cloud, in the dark evening light, with its silver tanks shining like monstrous eyes. As we came closer, it became quiet and more like a town—or a town where something is happening. It has the magic of an oil town, with the drills and jets and cranes and tanks and the dark pools of oily surface. If this can be called magic? There were crowds of people playing baseball in every inch of free space. They play baseball everywhere—it seems to have become the national game. I walked down the street later. Men and women in groups together and movement all over—and watermelon peels in large heaps. Many of the faces are familiar from a type one meets in northernmost India and these, I am told, are the Uyghur minorities. The women are quite lovely. We lunched at Yumen Xian, a small halting place, where the road turns off for Yumen from the main road going to Dunhuang. There were groups of people with baggage all over the place, waiting to catch a bus and move on. I noticed the inns and restaurants had signs over the door in Chinese and also in Arabic. The Arabic signs usually read 'Musulman Serai'. It is surprising that the Muslims still maintain their exclusive eating places, probably serving halal meat and no pork, and pork is important to Chinese cuisine. Their women wear black veils over their heads, but the veil is thrown back, revealing their faces—and just as well as they are impressively good looking!

The countryside is studded with what seem to be lookout towers built of mud set in encircling walls—vestiges of the conditions existing ten years ago. It is impossible to believe that as recently as that all this area was bandit-ridden and highly unsafe. That the road on which we travelled did not exist. But more than that, it would have been almost unthinkable for four women to make this journey unless heavily escorted by an armed guard. These are all borderlands and frontiers of earlier times with a scatter of garrison settlements, some of which developed into centres of exchange in the Central Asian trade. The aridity is partly of modern times and resulted from changes in the ecology produced by mining in the region, and the extensive deforestation wherever there were the occasional forests.

Still En Route—Jiu Quan (As Su Zhou Was Then Known)

I am lying on a bed under a thick quilt, waiting for the plane to leave for Lanzhou. Never waited like this for a plane before. We were due to leave at 6.30 a.m., but the weather at Lanzhou is bad, so we've spent two hours waiting. I wonder if we will go today. It's freezing cold outside, hence we are all under quilts.

It was equally cold yesterday morning at Yumen. I was wearing two layers of woollens and still shivering. Eventually when we drove out over the oilfield, I had to wear the driver's padded coat before I was comfortable. It was another early morning—how I hated getting up at 6 a.m., because for a change we had spring mattresses that were really quite luxurious. We had the usual 'brief introduction' lasting an hour on facts and figures regarding the oilfield, some of which I should include here.

Elevation: 2,400 to 2,600 metres. Ground surface covered with gravel similar to parts of the Gobi Desert. The weather is dry, with light rain and snow. The sun and winds are strong. Temperatures range in the year from 40° C to -25° C. The town grew as the oilfield developed, and it is planned as an oil town, well laid out and remarkably clean. It is called the Lao Chi Miao Oilfield after the temple of the same name that became the nucleus of the oilfield. The first structure was started in 1936. Originally the people living there panned gold from the Oil River, a fast-flowing river that rushes down a long gorge with dark fissures. The oil was first discovered by a geologist, but even in Tang times, invaders used flaming oil sticks, drawing oil from the river water to attack their enemies. Crude oil was also used to lubricate the axles of wagons. We were given endless facts about the drilling of various categories of oil.

In 1947, an American geological group prospected for oil in Gansu and Qinghai and drew up plans for buying the oilfield. But when the Communist government came to power, they had to abandon their plans. Interestingly, at that time foreign gasoline was being sold in China at a cheaper price than Chinese oil. With the development plans, considerable emphasis was laid on oil. In the past few years innumerable Soviet experts have visited the oilfield and one wonders how the American experts feel about that.

The population of the town is 70,000. There are 2,000 women workers out of a total of 6,000 women. The authorities realize that there is a grave lack of women and are concerned about this matter. The ratio is something like twelve men to one woman! I didn't notice any especial disparity—in fact the men and women going down the roads struck me as being quite at ease with each other. Not that such a thing is evident, or, as Dominique says, the men, if there aren't enough women, look sad and don't work! These symptoms were not noticeable. There was a marked preponderance of men. But we also saw women workers all over, by the drills and in the refinery, all in blue suits, or overalls with their hair plaited in long plaits and tied with bright pink ribbons.

I was surprised to hear that only 800 of the workers belong to the National Minorites, since these regions have many national minorities—but preponderantly the Uyghurs. The women of Yumen are strikingly good- looking! They say there is a particular town in Xinjiang where every woman is a beauty. I could believe that of many places around here. I asked if they have separate services for the minorities, as for instance, separate canteens for the many Muslim minorities who don't eat pork, and was told that that was so. It is the policy of the government not to disallow religious practices and customs, but I feel that if some of these practices are not absolutely essential, and if certain other things are being swept aside, surely separate canteens should also be disallowed. Muslims need not be required to eat pork, but there could be a single canteen for everyone. This type of segregation seems to aggravate the separation. It is comparable I suppose to the segregation of non-vegetarian from vegetarian in India.

I enjoyed the 'trip' around the oilfield. The mountains are impressive in their complete barrenness—more than that, the red of the earth and the rocks is unusual. And in between the curves and the folds of the rocks, there rise up the tall derricks of the drills. Near the derricks are pools of black crude oil, shining like patches of tar against the red earth. The sky was covered with thick clouds, and the distant mountains enveloped in mist. But there was no smoky, foggy atmosphere of an unhealthy town, probably because everything was well-spaced. But there was the smell of oil around one.

14

Retracing Our Steps at Zheng Zhou

I can still hear the sound of the kettledrums and the cymbals ringing in my ears—the sound of battle. We went to a Henan opera this evening—the story of a Song princess, an epic heroine who leads the army into battle. The best opera I've seen in China until now, to my level of understanding. The well-known Henan actress Ma Qing Fang played the Song princess. Her performance—her singing, her miming, and all her movements—was really quite spectacular. Henan opera seems to have more miming, but perhaps I have this impression simply because it seemed to be such a good group.

The costumes were evidently the result of careful study and well-designed. No colour or form seemed out of place. The décor was as usual limited to four chairs indicating a court scene, a curtained stand for a bed, and a table if need be. The narrative is built up entirely with the help of music and dialogue. Eye movements are expressive as in Indian dancing, and hand movements equally symbolic, and in both, Ma Qing Fang was most accomplished. I noticed that she used her lips and mouth with the same range of expressions. There was something pristine about her movements, each movement was well defined without being jagged or jumbled. And the eye movements were most expressive, despite the heavy make-up with pink around the eyes, gradually shading off, strong black eyebrows which turn up a little and into the hairline, and a faint white line down the nose, all of which brightens eye movements. In the earlier scenes, she is the submissive wife. She looked the part—*Dream of the Red Chamber* by Cao Xueqin come alive—and gradually she asserts herself, until in the last scene, when she goes into battle with the banner above her, she is an altogether different person. It's amazing (or maybe it isn't) how even the uninitiated can distinguish between a good performance and an average one. We went backstage later to congratulate her. She was obviously pleased, because the news of the Indians coming to the opera had spread all over the theatre. She was quite unaffected and very informal.

The orchestra intrigues me. Three drums of different sizes, an army of cymbals of varying size and thickness. They are used for producing the clashing sound at the beginning and end of each scene. Two erhus, beautifully carved, and particularly their necks; the pipa, a kind of lute, a lovely-looking instrument, pear-shaped and with four strings, played like a guitar; a multitude of clappers, also used at the beginning and end of each scene; and a reed pipe. In addition to this, there was a cello and a violin, both played in the European way. This is a new addition, which I personally think unnecessary, particularly as the erhus can be tuned to a low or a high pitch, with the difference of an octave.

The theatre is a new building, somewhat bare inside. Beneath a large balcony were rows of upholstered seats. The patterning is all in the stonework and cement. No painting or murals, in comparison with some other theatres we have been in and just as well perhaps. There would now always be the danger of finding picture after picture of rosy-cheeked young men and women hanging onto sheaves of wheat, or holding aloft a spanner against a background of chimneys and funnels, in conformity with some kinds of Socialist Realism art. The floor of the theatre is uncarpeted, with not even a rough mat, possibly because the audience spits with great gusto right through the performance, and spitting onto the floor is quite the order of things, although the authorities prefer the use of the spittoons that are placed at regular distances. I was a bit put off in the beginning by the woman behind me, who kept leaning forward, clearing her throat noisily and shooting out a gobbet of spittle. I was scared it would land on the back of my neck by mistake. But I soon got used to it, and by the end was hardly conscious of it. And, thankfully, it did not land on the back of my neck.

Another change from the theatres I am used to, was that there was no question of the better-dressed people in front and the ragged ones in the back. Since everybody dresses in the same way, there is little differentiation. In the theatre people could sit anywhere. Conversation during a performance is not 'shooed' at, as in Europe. Fortunately, most of it carries on in hardly audible whispers. There is a real sense of audience participation.

I did notice that the costumes, or some of them, are similar to those worn by the royal figures in European playing cards. These were Song costumes. I wonder if there is any connection.

The rest of the day was spent in nosing around the town. Zheng Zhou, which I had thought was another small place with excavations and that alone, turns out to have a population of 400,000, and is now the capital city of Henan province. Again, the city is very Indian in feeling, the new town with its masses of shops, all with open fronts and long counters, so that walking down a street or driving slowly one can see exactly what each shop is selling, the large islands at the crossroads, with posters, the newly tarred roads running through the main streets (but they are clean, partly because animals are not allowed to wander along these roads); and the old town with gravel streets, low houses and shop fronts, lots of little children playing all over, pigs and dogs wandering lazily across the roads and being hooted at all the time, and clucking hens that look with such contempt when the car misses them by inches as they scurry off the road. Children running behind the car in a cloud of yellow dust, shouting, 'Sulian pengyou' (Soviet friends!). We were obviously foreigners and obviously most of the foreigners here are Russians. The station wagon in which we went around was quite charming. It was like being in a Sultan's harem, cream-coloured curtains on all the windows, a 'ceiling' of padded black cotton, with designs, and a fringe with silk cords hanging at the sides—doubtless the Chinese equivalent of the surrey with the fringe on top. We were three women, Mingo, Anil, and I, and we had an escort of six men, members of the Cultural Association and local archaeologists and local 'friends'.

The hotel we stayed at boasted of central heating and all mod cons. I liked the outside, grey stone and red brick, the central part in grey, having Chinese modulations, quite neatly worked in. It was still not impressive architecturally, but better than some of the others. Inside however, there was the same heavy, block-like furniture, and so self-consciously un-Chinese, not anything in fact. It is distressing as they must be spending vast sums on these hotels and guest houses. But this is a malady sweeping through Asia. So many of our new buildings are quite unattractive. It will take another few decades before we work out an aesthetic that is pleasing and carries traces of a cultural identity. Saw a few Russians in this place, probably they work in the new textile mills which are part of the development of Zheng Zhou. It is amazing how no place is left out—even Louyang is to have tractor factories.

We started chasing relics by visiting an excavation of a Shang city wall. A small excavation, but well labelled. Defences of ancient cities have a touch of similarity. I picked up three Shang shards from the surface, and was allowed to add these to my little collection of Chinese potsherds! The entire area around seems to be bursting with remains, given what surfaces, but there aren't enough trained archaeologists to excavate it.

We were then taken to the workshop of the Zheng Zhou archaeological group, where we saw the results of a really thrilling dig, the sort of thing that makes my mouth water, the sort of site whose excavation I would like to be included in. It's like Tutankhamun and Egypt all over again. In a Henan village, the tomb of a nobleman dating back to the Warring States period (475–221 BC) was excavated. We arrived at the workshop where a number of local craftsmen who work in wood, were busy carving wooden models of cups, figures, pots, and a monster-figure. In the next room, we saw glass tanks, basins, and pots of various sizes, full of formalin and various chemicals, in which were soaked the wooden remains from the tomb. The tomb contained a wooden coffin, around which were spaces containing objects in wood and bronze, everything from cooking utensils, musical instruments, mirrors, and a chariot, and whatever may be of use in the next world. The bronze objects, though very fine specimens, were much the same as have been found in other tombs, but the wooden remains, all in dark wood, with alternating red and black lacquer in the designs, were unique. Unfortunately, I couldn't take any photographs as they haven't published a report yet.

We then saw the Shang exhibits, 'finds', over the last few years. Excavated, they say, which in fact again means found whilst digging for the construction of new buildings and roads. I had some problems with their chronology but we agreed to disagree. The objects, now exposed to the light and air of the twentieth century, couldn't have been better displayed, and that is of the utmost importance. In the workshop I saw a little girl squatting on the ground playing with round pebbles, in exactly the same way as we play with them in Punjab. If we had had more time, I would have squatted beside her and played!

Before the opera we dined with our six hosts: much 'campé-ing' in red wine, many toasts, and more unusual food, monkey mushrooms, and apple slices in hot caramel. To our pleasantest surprise, we were given a set of charming chopsticks—with the heroes and heroines of the Classics depicted on them although rather minimized. Incidentally, they match the beautiful rulers we bought at Yumen, also with pictures of characters from the *Dream of the Red Chamber* and the *Dream of the West Chamber*.

15

On the Train to Nanjing

In the train this morning from Zheng Zhou to Nanjing, I felt so sleepy that I could have just gone on sleeping. I was writing till late last night after we returned from the opera and we had to get up again at 5 a.m. to catch the 7 a.m. train. And it was such a comfortable bed, with a big thick spring mattress, and a cool night, with the full moon. I've decided that I simply must write a record of daily doings every night, even if hurriedly, and in half an hour, even if just the bare record. I would need far more time if I am to meditate on all I see, and I don't have the time in this infernal rush. So, like the ox I shall gobble greedily now and digest it at my ease when I return to London. Then, if I have the time, which I may not have, I shall write about the journey.

The journey to Nanjing is through dull, flat country, endlessly flat. Acres and acres of fields. The sun is shining in a clear sky. We seem to have left behind the areas of rain and are once more in the dry belt. It is hot and very dusty, layers of dust on everything. This is a different train to the others: it has no small compartments, just a long carriage with a series of berths and an open passage to one side. It's fairly crowded, as it goes on to Shanghai. So we've been the object of great curiosity. People keep passing up and down, and this morning there was much speculation as to which part of the world we were from. The local facial type seems to have changed: darker skin, and more rounded faces and features. Perhaps I see them like this after the very marked Mongolian features of many of the people of Gansu.

The peasant women on this train are elegant-looking. Their hair is often taken back and pulled into a small bun at the back of the head, so that their faces stand out clearly. They are dressed in white, black or blue peasant jackets with high collars, loose black trousers, wrapped around under a 'putti' in black or grey from below the knees to the ankles, and then the tiny feet in pointed shoes. I see that the shins are thus bandaged, and I presume it is intended to show off the feet to greater effect. But I still can't appreciate the beauty of bound feet, because each time I see such a one I am reminded of the cruelty of it. They walk with such dignity too. None of the sloppy attitudes of the city-bred woman, who has her hair cut short and hanging, who wears a blouse and ordinary slacks, and just hasn't the same bearing as the peasant woman, though as compared to other city dwellers elsewhere, she is quite elegant.

How true it is that elegance is more than just in the dress. It is the same with the peasant men, in their loose trousers, black jackets buttoned down the front, with a white jacket underneath, and sometimes a sash around the waist. The faces look rather rugged and handsome. The features of the city-bred person seem to get modified and merge into a common mould. Of course, I still can't get over the beauty of Chinese children. It isn't just the round face and the small narrow eyes that open wide in curiosity, but the entire personality of the child that is so attractive. Chinese children seem not to hang on to their mothers. They seem to be more outgoing, but this may be my imagination. It is common enough to see the father carrying the child in the villages, and I wonder if this dual proximity of both parents isn't better for the development of the child's personality.

There was a funny little conversation here a moment ago. A woman complained to the officer in charge of the train that the man in the berth opposite her was sleeping only in his shirt and underpants, and so would he please ask the man to put on his trousers. To which the officer replied that perhaps the man was feeling hot, and after all, he wasn't indecently dressed, but he passed on her message. The other men listening to this conversation commented, 'How feudal!'

I suppose I should be very conscientious and industrious, and utilize the time in the train to update my daily activities and meditate over and digest the archaeological relics and the factories. But I just don't feel like exerting myself. If only I could sleep in a train, then at least I could catch up on sleep. I spent the whole morning reading and found it most relaxing. I was reading *The Brothers Karamazov* and it was just what I needed. I started it almost as soon as we moved out of the station and was completely immersed in it. The more I read of Dostoevsky, the more 'sympathique' I find him. Is he the great humanist? Or have I been born after what should have been my generation? This is all rather trite. Most of the time, my own commonplace reactions infuriate me, not because I want to be different, but because I appear to be incapable of seeing beyond the obvious, and so often I don't even see the obvious.

I remember reading *The Idiot* ten months ago, I was so carried away by the central figure that the others seemed inconsequential beside him. But *The Brothers Karamazov* is different, more complete from that perspective. This is no doubt because my own awareness of people has become sharper over the past year. I must reread *Crime and Punishment* that I read a long time back. How do the Chinese react to the tragic pessimism of Dostoevsky? They would appreciate his sensitivity, but they might reject the tragic personality and the orthodox philosophy. Contemporary Chinese writers are no doubt acquainted with the Soviet literary scene. Do they delve further into the past? Do they read Pushkin and Tolstoy? Does the imprint of Soviet culture include the stamp of Russian literature? I don't see much evidence of that. The Chinese literary tradition in its own right is equally powerful. From what I have observed so far, the Soviet imprint seems to be limited to technical knowledge and the interior decoration of hotels for foreigners. Somehow I can't quite visualize a Sino-Byzantine marriage. It's a bit nightmarish, but then why not? Many strange unions have occurred, wilfully or by force. The Indo-British union couldn't have been more strange, or the Spanish-Mexican, which did eventually produce a Diego Rivera. Here comes another platitude—a culture cannot be judged by isolated examples.

Talking about elegance, this train seems to be more elegant than the others that we have travelled in. I believe that I am now sitting in what must be a renovated version of the old glamorous Shanghai Express, that became a household word because of the film of the same name, made I think in the 1930s, and starring Marlene Dietrich and Anna May Wong—also household names, all in a story wrapped around lost loves and immanent murders. It was set in what was always referred to as 'the inscrutable East' with equally inscrutable fellow passengers. Alas, the luscious blondes, pistol shots and screams, secret agents and spies don't seem to surface any more! Instead the three of us are sitting in a very comfortable compartment on an ample, soft berth, drinking lemonade—no, not green tea—and commenting on the multitude of ducks in the fields which we see as we whizz past. The train is full of 'Soviet friends' who are largely technicians, some of whom have been pacing up and down the length of the corridor, a couple of women from East Germany, and us, among foreigners and, of course, the many Chinese passengers.

There is no mistaking the fact that the train is going to Shanghai. The entire train has a more luxurious and westernized look. I walked past one carriage that had a carpeted corridor and very comfortable looking chairs. The restaurant car too was smarter. Each table had more than just the usual beer and sweet red wine bottles, for here there was brandy and vodka as well. A couple at the table next to us were striking because they were smartly dressed—she in well-cut slacks and a colourful blouse. Apart from the 'foreign friends' there were a few young Chinese at another table seemingly quite sophisticated judging by their dress and their order of a European meal. Perhaps they are overseas Chinese. One of the men wore brown trousers with a black shirt and a brown jersey with black and grey leather shoes. There were no blue suits. This is one noticeable thing about Nanjing and I presume Shanghai. The women gave the impression of being better groomed than those in Beijing. I thought perhaps this was comparable to Bombay and Delhi where the commercial city of colonial times is smarter than the official capital and its history of many centuries. Perhaps it is my imagination but I feel greater warmth emanating from the people we met in Beijing as compared to these who seem much more reserved.

I get the feeling that I have now entered an area where one has to be smartly turned out and may even be whistled at! The city feels more European. I am glad we went to the north-west first and to areas that are relatively remote. The journey yesterday was tiring and long. We crossed the Yangtze River by ferry since there is as yet no bridge, and the train had to be split into three sections since the ferry could not accommodate the entire length of the train. It was a strange sensation to switch from the rhythm of the train to the gentle rocking of the ferry. It was dark and I couldn't see much except for the silhouette of a fast-moving junk passing by.

16

Arrival in Nanjing

Nanjing station was impressive in its cleanliness and fresh paint and in the orderliness of movement. The platform was crowded and the usual rushing up and down noisily was more evident as compared to other stations. We soon discovered why. Across the platform was a students' special train going to Beijing. The academic term was soon to begin and these were students from the Shanghai area and further south returning to their senior high school or college. The boys and girls looked as if they were going on a mid-term picnic except that their many bags and bundles gave them away. Their books were strung together in string bags and bundles, and boxes of various sizes were being adroitly dragged along the platform floor. I was impressed that an entire train had been organized to carry the students. There was music being played over the speakers in the station and it wasn't Peking opera as was often the case elsewhere, but European dance music—waltzes and foxtrots again.

We drove through deserted streets to the hotel—a modern building with furnishings that were Eurasian but far more pleasing in style as compared to the other hotels we have been to. There was something about the atmosphere of the place that suggested that it was part of the sophisticated Orient undergoing Westernization or rather being Europeanized. The hotel staff were dressed in white coats and trousers and were offering glasses of green tea at the required moment. The well-scrubbed bath had a tin of Vim placed conspicuously nearby. My first guess was right—it had been an international club before Liberation.

I went down for breakfast this morning and sat at a table with a spotless white tablecloth, had coffee with cream, toast with butter and jam— where generally butter was omitted in most hotels—delicious cold ham and fresh fruit. The waiter brought us glasses of milk that we hastily rejected to his surprise. He obviously assumed that as Indians we would be vegetarians and milk drinkers. The Chinese, of course, seldom take milk. One hardly sees a cow for miles on end, and a glass of milk would be excessive. I sat and waited for the waiter to break into pidgin English, and sure enough at the next round he asked us if we would like some eggs. I may be familiar with such a situation from colonial days, nevertheless it gets me down and I recognize that this is entirely a sign of my discomfort with the colonial past.

I was made aware last night of my enjoyment of big modern cities. I felt at ease driving down broad, smooth streets lined with trees. The luxury of a hot bath, of a soft spring mattress with freshly laundered sheets still crisp from washing—these are said to be the good things of life. I suppose I could claim one redeeming feature that the hard-wooden beds of Maijishan and the thick somewhat damp bedcovers under which we slept didn't prevent me from enjoying every bit of it there.

Spent the day at the impressive museum, the first of more than one. Once a building from the palace complex it now houses objects from the past. It is a large, spacious, airy building with a lovely yellow-tiled roof surrounded by well laid-out gardens. A Ming period building has now been converted into a number of galleries. Low white walls with an upper section that was glazed brought in the natural light which also reflected off a white ceiling. The floor of dark polished cement offset the light from the whiteness of the walls and ceiling. Altogether it provided a neutral comfortable background to what was displayed, the kind of background that is seldom given to displays in museums. Objects are exhibited in glass cases with plenty of space between them. There is none of the crowded claustrophobic feeling of the galleries of the British Museum. There is only one museum I have been to where the luxury of display was appropriate. This was the National Museum in Athens that I visited last year, where there was one gallery of a reasonable size, painted a very pale blue and there was just one object placed in this gallery—the bronze figure of the discus thrower. The impact of seeing it displayed in this simple but nevertheless dramatic way was unforgettable.

The collection in this museum is rich and varied, from recent prehistoric finds to some of the Anyang culture, strikingly beautiful objects from Han and Tang tombs, with smaller galleries devoted to porcelain, cloisonné, costumes, furniture, musical instruments, and a charming collection of clocks. Other rooms had displays of maps and rubbings. I spent much of my time making notes on a comparison of museum exhibits with what we have seen at the two sites. So my focus was on painting and sculpture, with a little less time for other objects. I am beginning to think that the Chinese may surpass the rest of the world in setting up historical museums, so consistent are they in exhibiting whatever is found of the past. But, alas, no catalogues—not even for the displays that go back to pre-Liberation times. Some of the objects may be recent finds but much of them are from older collections. There seems to be a hesitation in publishing catalogues that visitors can take home. This is very frustrating.

We drove around the old city with its suburbs where there had once been gracious living in elegant houses. Green-tiled roofs over red-brick houses embedded in gardens with willow-lined streams. In some ways these are clichés of Chinese architecture and landscaping, but when seen as a kind of museum piece they can be very pleasing. Mingo mentioned that these were the homes of bureaucrats in the old days and 'bureaucrat' is a wide-meaning term in China. I would have liked to have visited them in their heyday. Now they are used as offices. There is an undertone of sarcasm about Nanjing as it was a capital under Chiang Kai-shek, but one has to concede that it carries the aesthetics of cities of that period.

17

The One and Only Shanghai

So this is the fabulous Shanghai, a name popularly associated with Hollywood films and pulp fiction, and with a not-so-complimentary meaning as an idiom in contemporary times! But what was perceived as the ambience of Shanghai in old times is a different ambience now. I suppose it would be somewhat like going to Chicago. Cities are like persons who when they are given a bad reputation become intriguing. It is absurd to think of them in those terms but that is often how they are thought of. From my window on the tenth floor of the hotel I overlook the rooftops of nearby buildings and the tall buildings in the distance. I wonder what is happening beneath these roofs. It is now, as we are told, a new city. It has been cleanly scrubbed but remains Europeanized. This latter has left its mark as it does on all Asian cities where it has had a strong presence.

There seems to be a systematic organization in the way in which the city and its vicinity functions. It isn't just in the different appearances of city and village. The village houses are whitewashed and have black roofs unlike the mud and thatch of the north-west villages. The fields are carefully laid out in orderly rectangles. The attitude of the people seems to be different. They treat the need to be efficient as inborn. Is it just the result of many more years of having to work this way, or is it the result of the control of colonial interests and practices in the coastal cities? I can understand Shanghai from my familiarity with Bombay and Delhi and my experience of London. The major difference, viewing it admittedly at a superficial level, is that the signboards are in Chinese as is the spoken language. These are just first impressions and I have hardly walked in the city to know it better. I may recant everything I have written so far.

We were told that in Shanghai people were used to seeing foreigners and no one would take notice of us. By the time we got to the car we had collected the usual crowd all trying to get a proper look at us and find out who we were. What added to the interest was the Asian Film Festival currently in Shanghai. Anil and I would have looked like very bedraggled film stars. But one person caught on that we were from India or thereabouts and immediately started humming 'Awaara Hoon' with others joining in, so I joined in as well.

'Cathay Hotels' was woven into the bath mat, so it must have been run by a colonial entrepreneur earlier and was probably part of a chain of hotels—rather like the Imperial Hotels of India before they were bought by Indian entrepreneurs who established their own chain. Except that in China it was the government that had taken them over. The fittings in the bathroom are all English fittings made by 'Standard'. The furnishings are really quite elegant: cream-coloured walls and ceiling, and upholstery, blue bedcovers with white embroidery, and dark mahogany furniture. Smart uniformed lift boys, a steward in the dining room and an exchange bureau on the ground floor, as well as a neon-lit shop selling trinkets intended for tourists. I seem to be developing a mania for hotels and hotel rooms but there is so much history in all this I cannot help but notice the very different ambience in these towns from what we experienced earlier.

I rang the bell for breakfast this morning and a waiter appeared predictably dressed in white coat and trousers with highly polished black shoes. He spoke pidgin English as I knew he would and brought breakfast on a trolley as I also knew he would. When we checked in last night, I suspected that there would be a garage for cars in the space below and that there would be a small Chinese-style garden, and when I looked out this morning, there they were. But there was one big change. What woke me up this morning was hooting cars and the sound of trams going down the street. These were sounds I had not heard in the last few weeks. And then there were the loudspeakers blaring forth music of a martial kind and numbers to help in keeping track of the physical exercises all Chinese are expected to do in the morning and which all radio stations broadcast at the same time around 7.30 a.m. I am puzzled why we did not hear this in the other places where we stayed.

We drove around the city in the afternoon accompanied by a young woman who was our guide. She was smartly dressed and had her hair done up in a complicated style. She was employed in the government-run tourist office. So we were shown a part of the city that was a slum and then taken to the other side where the slum was being torn down and new housing was going up, and were duly told this was happening all over the country. This she need not have said as we had seen some of the country and had drawn our own conclusions about the change. But she went on and on about the difference between pre- and post-Liberation in a rather vacuous manner. It was like listening to a parrot repeating a badly taught routine lesson.

I thought they should train them better because what has been done to Shanghai post-Liberation is impressive in terms of cleaning up the city and also clearing it to some extent of unwanted characters. The constant reiteration of this makes one a little wary, but then I suppose they think that the point has to be made with little attempt to assess the person they are talking to. This was the reaction of people I spoke to and I was willing to take their word for it, but, of course, one is aware of people simply saying what is required. And would they be frank with a stranger? The best of us hesitate to tell our woes to strangers. Shanghai was always spoken of as a tough nut to crack and they seem to have done a fair amount of cracking, judging from what one sees.

I am getting tired of being taken around all the time except when we are alone with Mingo. We understand each other without even saying anything and I make it a point not to ask her awkward questions that she may not wish to answer. So I keep it at the level of information and some comments and try and read her reactions. Telling jokes can be helpful in creating an informal ambience. I do ask her about what she enjoys and what she overlooks. When the mood suits us we talk about our families and our earlier past. Mingo is the only child of a couple, both of whom work in government offices. School was relatively easy but college was hard as she wanted to be an interpreter and this needed special training in English that was not easy to come by. By becoming a good interpreter she hoped that she would be taken with a delegation to somewhere outside China and would be able to see the world. We did our best to describe our various worlds to her, but I dread to think of the confusion that we may have created in her mind about the world outside.

Our guide pointed out the landmarks—such as the Palace of Culture. This set me off on a critique. Do the Chinese have to imitate the Soviets in everything? Associating culture with a palace it seems to me is most inappropriate as a post-revolution label. It also seemed to me a bit of a contradiction to be constantly applauding the past that they are supposedly averse to, namely feudal and bourgeois forms of cultural articulation. The context has to be explained with much sensitivity to prevent it from becoming a cliché. What is displayed inside the Palace of Culture is supposedly working-class culture but, in fact, is a pale imitation of bourgeois culture. The working-class culture is more visible in the villages we went to, and the streets of the cities as in the temples to Confucius—of which, of course, few are functioning. The Daoist temples have been virtually closed down. Soviet-style architecture has invaded Shanghai with the Sino-Soviet Friendship Building, a sprawling structure with the same banal architecture as the Soviet buildings in Moscow, comparable also to the Palace of Culture in Warsaw. As if the French and the English with their colonial stamp had not done enough damage to Shanghai, it has had to host this as well.

The old racecourse where horse and dog races were also once held has now been converted into a sports stadium. The open area, now named People's Square, seems like a cliché. Broad streets with large shop fronts with inviting window displays suggest that some remnants of the old polity still remain or are deliberately being kept alive to attract the Overseas Chinese. Communist China is very conscious of the usefulness of this category, much more so than we are of our Indians who are living abroad. But there is, of course, a difference. Overseas Chinese have been settled as traders and craftsmen in neighbouring countries for a few generations and are willing to take on a range of occupations even if specializing in some. The settlements of Indians as commercial entrepreneurs or as middle-class professionals have shifted from the earlier centres to the ones that have emerged as potentially important in the period after World War II. Indians are now beginning to migrate in larger numbers to what was previously the colonial country. What seems new is the small numbers from the Indian middle class trained in professions such as medicine, engineering, and such like who are beginning to settle in countries outside India, the concentration being in Britain. They tend to go where there is some familiarity with the host society, as there is vaguely with things British, and where jobs are available. In earlier periods, they were more adventurous and went looking for jobs in many more places. A comparative study of the Indian and Chinese who go abroad and the kind of connections they build might be a worthwhile exercise.

Then we went shopping. We looked at some of the textiles such as the remarkably beautiful brocades, but I couldn't see myself in a brocade coat, so we moved on to a small shop tucked away in between the big stores that had rubbings. This kept me engaged for a couple of hours since the rubbings were of excellent quality made in the old Chinese way that is entirely different from the rubbings I had seen in some churches in England, since ink-dabbers on rice paper give the rubbings a special texture. The owner being a learned man caught our attention with his narration of the historical context of each. Many children walked in and poked around and asked questions, all of which were patiently answered. Gradually the attention shifted to the two foreign women who were obviously not Russian and they began asking questions, and poor Mingo had to be all attention in translating the questions and the answers. They were not content with just looking at us. The questions led to much rowdiness and excitement and they were then gently asked to move to another shop.

In the evening Anil and Mingo went to the local opera but I wanted to wander around the city. So Mingo asked for a guide. The guide began by suggesting that we go to the People's Amusement House—what had been the red-light district as well as the haunt of gangsters, dope pedlars, and criminals of various kinds. It had now been cleaned up and offered what was called 'clean' entertainment. I decided to give it a try, so we entered a large four-storeyed building with a courtyard in the middle, paying an entrance ticket of 20 cents—virtually nothing. The courtyard had a stage for performers of every kind from acrobats to opera singers. I was amazed at the variety of programmes available—five kinds of opera, theatres with drama, puppet shows, a hall for music, exhibition halls showing mainly paintings in a Chinese Socialist Realism style, a recreation room with facil-ities for games such as ping-pong and carom both of which are remarkably popular, a reading room that had newspapers, journals and some books, and the occasional snack bar, as well as an open-air cinema just outside the building. It was not an air-conditioned, soft-cushioned place. The seats were hard and wooden, the snack bars didn't have many machines and gadgets. There were people serving hot noodles and the like. Nevertheless the place exists and all it costs for a visit is 20 cents. It functions every day of the year yet it was crowded on an ordinary day when we went. It seemed to be an attractive place for amateur or even experimental theatrical groups and for young playwrights wanting an audience—or for just an evening's outing.

One of the magicians was a woman in a white coat with a black bow tie. There were other women in pink blouses and black skirts, probably doing odd jobs. They look so much better in the Chinese-style dress with the slit skirt yet they wear European skirts and blouses. The men, presumably also doing jobs around the place, wore loose baggy trousers but had colourful orange and brown shirts. We sat in at a concert of Chinese music in the music hall. They played what was explained to me as traditional Chinese music on traditional instruments. I recognized the erhu, and drums of various shapes and sizes, flutes, as also stringed instruments, cymbals, clappers, tambourines, and something like a xylophone.

The puppets were performing Peking opera and obviously a well-known one as it was a full house and there was some humming along with the formal singing. The string puppets were so dextrously manipulated that they performed complicated movements, while attired in exquisite costumes. I wanted to go backstage and handle the puppets but that was not possible. My problem was with the stage and box for the puppets draped in heavy satin with gilt designs that stood out—somehow very un-Chinese. The backdrop was painted in oils in a European naturalist style, quite out of keeping with the opera. Is the definition of opulence defined by the amount of gilt woven into designs? The cinema was a disappointment as they were showing a rather pedestrian Russian film. The dubbing was strange as the actors were obviously Russian but the dialogue was in Chinese. This works if the people look similar and speak related languages but it does seem a bit bizarre when they look entirely different and the language is unexpected. The other highly popular attraction was the distorting mirrors near the entrance, and when one moved in front of them they produced ridiculous distortions, inevitably causing much laughter.

Leaving the People's Amusement House, we drove to the famous 'bund', the embankment along the river on the banks of which the city has been built. It was a lovely evening with every possibility that the moon would soon shine on the water. The benches were occupied by young couples sitting and holding hands and gazing solemnly and moon-eyed at the water. There is no bridge across the river so a system of ferryboats is active, connecting various parts of the city on both banks. Motorboats of various sizes are the faster ferries. There are beautiful large country craft with three dark sails and these are used largely for bringing in cargo from the ships docked at the head of the estuary and too big to come down the distance from the sea to Shanghai. Further down were moored some sampans, the famous flat-bottomed country boats that appear in every picture of Shanghai. These are used largely to transport cargo and sometimes take passengers upstream to the villages on the riverbanks. Further up the river are the homes of the families plying them.

The riverfront in the city is edged with small formal gardens and palm trees. Vendors wander around selling hot dumplings sprinkled with soy sauce. The cooking and serving is on the hoof as it were, in the two large baskets attached to a pole and slung over the vendor's shoulder. Some were selling hot roasted freshly cracked nuts. Each vendor had a little red pennant with Chinese characters in white—the proof of registration with the government. I remembered exactly such vendors from my childhood in North India, so it seems that carrying goods in baskets slung on a pole across the shoulders is normal in many parts of the world.

Meanwhile, I was trying my best to explain to the woman accompanying me that I wanted to visit the old city. She kept insisting that it had all changed after Liberation. Eventually, after much insistence on my part, she said to me, 'I know where to take you. I am sure you would like to see the native quarter.' I was stunned into silence and at first couldn't understand that it should be called as such in 'Liberated' Shanghai. But then I realized that this was the obvious term used in colonial times and has probably continued when using the English language. I asked her if it was called that in Chinese and she seemed to think not. I presume it is used for tourists but surely someone must have pointed out that it was an anachronism.

We set off and first drove down a broad smooth street that prior to 1949 had been the divider. It was explained to me that on the left was the international settlement with its electricity of 220 voltage and on the right was the French concession with 110 volts. I wondered whether this was just a piece of casual information or whether it was symbolic of something that was lost on me. We then turned into the 'native quarter' with its cobbled streets so narrow that a single lane was just about possible. Groups of people were chatting around open-fruit stalls and the noodle-maker was spinning out his last noodles for the day and a tailor was ironing the clothes that he had stitched, a few people were playing carom outside a shop window. People at windows or leaning over small balconies were chatting with others similarly placed. The houses were small but looked impressive with their ageing facades giving them what one might almost call an architectural grace. Some of the first floors seem to lean over and extend a little beyond the ground floor. Some have glazed in their lower floor. In other sections of the streets the profile changes and the effect is quite stunning in a narrow winding street.

We wandered in and out for a while and then landed up on what is called the Tibet Road, for no known reason, and this becomes more incredulous when one is told that it was once home to prostitutes and pickpockets! The former have been sent to reformatory schools that are said to have been remarkably successful in rehabilitating them. The claim is that there are none left in this area now. One wonders.

The Shanghai Museum is housed in the building of what used to be the Race Club and it actually makes a rather fine museum with large airy, well-lit rooms overlooking an open space in the centre of the city. I felt quite nostalgic for the Poona Race Club that has similar buildings in the same colonial style. The photographs of the thoroughbreds had all been removed and replaced with reproductions of Chinese painting. Fortunately, the room with the reproductions was separate from the room that had the originals. The display in this museum was impressive. The stone axes of the prehistoric gallery were mounted on wood to show how they could have been used, the bronze mirrors stood upright, the large bells were suspended on frames. It houses an impressive collection of Neolithic artefacts collected and organized in the early twentieth century as well as an excellent collection of Zhou bronzes. The bronzes were of greater interest to me when they were aesthetically pleasing, but some of the forms seemed alien to my sense of aesthetics. We had a long conversation with the director, a very knowledgeable woman.

Shanghai women are smartly dressed, and despite the regulation blue, they manage to get around it, and dress in cool colours, and in Chinese style. The women working in the museum, for instance, wore the simple Chinese dress with a small waistcoat just to give it that extra finish. Their shoes were not the mission-school type shoes that one sees in other places. Their hair is better cut. Generally, people here show some concern for the way they dress. This may be due to its having been more cosmopolitan than Beijing in the past. It is perfectly understandable that in asserting an equal status the appearance of people should be more uniform than is usual but even the desire for uniformity, can nevertheless, make some concession to a touch of colour and style.

An artist, who was also a member of the Cultural Association, came to visit us carrying a rolled-up collection of paintings. The bundle had a representative selection of the work of modern artists in Shanghai. There had recently been a rather vocal controversy over the continuation of the traditional style versus the use of oils. He unrolled the bundle of paintings and there were some in traditional style and some modern. A few of the former were strikingly beautiful or perhaps this was my taste. So I asked how old the artists were on an average especially the one whose work I was particularly impressed by—Ling Fan Mian. He had apparently died the previous year at the age of seventy plus. The others were all well over sixty and only one was thirty-seven. I had hoped to see the work of young artists, and to see what they were painting in oils, a medium so different from the earlier ones.

None of the paintings were for sale. He told us that sale was no longer important in China because artists were now employed and not dependent on the sale of their work. He was teaching at the Arts Academy in Shanghai and unfortunately it was closed, else we would have visited it and spoken with others as well. To become a member of the association, an artist has to exhibit his work of the past few years and a preliminary judgement is made by a panel of painters. An exhibition of this work was then put up and people invited to see it and make comments. Thereafter, there was a final judgement and these comments were also considered. The criteria of quality are drawn from traditional practice and forms, but it wasn't clear as to what happens if an artist choses to experiment. I thought of India and what would be the nature of opinions if this procedure were to be applied.

The next evening was dedicated to going to the opera—Shanghai opera is different apparently from Beijing opera. I, however, could not follow the niceties of the differences. We went to see what Mingo called a tragicomedy but which was in fact largely comedy and farce. Set in the Yuan period, the story involved a woman who for a length of time was pretending to be a man, and the narrative concerned the problems that she met with. There was, therefore, far more dialogue than in the other operas we had seen and a complicated story not always easy to follow. However, the miming was quite superb. The costumes were well designed. The musicians sat in the orchestra pit with their beautifully carved instruments, the long, slender necks of the stringed erhu and the lacquered, dragon-headed stand for the gong. The singing I could neither understand nor appreciate greatly so I treated it as a narrative with Mingo whispering the story as we went along.

The theatre was large and in classical style with balconies built, we were told, some time ago when presumably even European operas could be staged. The seats were fairly bare and upholstered in green and red. Since it was sparsely furnished the expense in maintaining the theatre was less. The audience was better dressed than in other places, so they were not all in the regulation blue suits. Some of the dresses were quite colourful and certainly better cut than the regulation dress. The rule of no spitting and no talking during a performance was strictly observed. The intervals saw the arrival of vendors of packets of nuts and ice creams, but the empty containers were carefully put away in their allotted places. The tickets were absurdly cheap so that the performance was available to many. This is in some ways symbolic of much in China.

We went to the local market to shop for small ceramic bowls and such like to take back as gifts. What was on sale was diverse and some of it immensely attractive. But it became difficult to shop because everywhere we went there were curious locals who followed us into the tiny shops and it was difficult to see things or move around. That's when I began to lose patience even though the people were orderly and didn't push and shove. What comments were being made about us I could not understand and Mingo diplomatically did not translate as she focused on our attempts to shop. This was in the old part of the city, the area with cobbled streets and therefore largely pedestrian. Rows of small shops produced the most pungent smells of spices and delicacies, but every now and then there was an open WC that produced an unpleasant odour. Little seemed to have been done about the latter. We were followed by a number of children obviously returning from school with their books in bags slung over their shoulders. It had been raining and I inadvertently stepped into a puddle and came out with an 'oops'. This became a game. Every few minutes a child would cry out 'oops' and then they would all laugh. I hate to think of what 'oops' may have meant in Chinese.

The area was full of laughter and seeming light-heartedness. An old woman in a shop was selling fruit and dried meat. She had other things all arranged in a row of porcelain jars with the most magnificent blue glazes, recognizably from an older period, and therefore precious, but somehow everyone just took them in their stride and nothing was made of their age. The most colourful toys lit up the dark corners of another small shop. Pottery with brown to red-brick glazes of various kinds took my breath away. They seem to have seen another Indian movie, *The Rani of Jhansi*, because a group of people asked Mingo whether I was the leading lady from that film! One never knows whom one may be identified with.

The Handicrafts Research Centre was a place where what was being produced was new to us and, therefore, of much interest. I was pleased that some attention was being given to non-machine crafts as these are often ignored and tend to die out. The director, a shy, retiring man, showed us around. Each craftsman was expected to initially teach a couple of apprentices so that the techniques and the crafts would continue. The work was of a superior kind. The lanterns made of paper and cloth were among the most beautiful that I have seen. The cloth golden dragon was worth taking home except that it was not for sale. Some modern designs were attempted such as patterns with what was now common to the entire Communist world— the peace dove, but these were not so successful, perhaps because the theme was still too alien to the traditional craftsman.

And there was training in calligraphy. This interested me greatly since it was Chinese calligraphy that had first drawn me to looking at Chinese art. Some were carved on small pieces of ivory used for stamping, but much of it was the more common using of the black ink brush on white rice paper.

Polishing of ivory was done with diamond and jade dust. Most impressive were the ink engravings on white porcelain that I had not seen before. A group of craftsmen were working on a large vase commissioned by the Muslim community of Shanghai who were sending it as a gift to Gamel Abdel Nasser in Egypt. The most striking feature of all these crafts was the delicacy required and the accuracy of the fine points that were made for a start.

Later in the evening we were in the dining room and noticed someone seated alone but seemingly wanting to join our conversation. So we introduced ourselves and invited him to join us, which he seemed happy to do. It turned out to be Pat Hannan, a specialist in Chinese literature who taught at the School of Oriental and African Studies, but we had never met although we were both in the same institution. We were happy to meet him not simply because he was so friendly, but also because our many questions could now be more easily answered. He could explain some of the nuances to Mingo in greater detail than I could, and in any case he spoke Chinese well.

Shanghai at night is so silent. I opened my windows and looked out over the city. There were lights in the windows of many buildings, some tall and some low. The roads are deserted, except for the one running alongside the hotel where a person was walking along whistling what sounded to me like a tune from a pop song. Was he Chinese or was he a visitor?

Pat and I took a walk along the riverfront and then took a tram ride in that part of the city just to see more of the place. It was a lovely change to be travelling like everyone else rather than in a fancy car. The tram was crowded and for a time I had to stand. I was amused to see that none of the Chinese men got up and offered me a seat as would have happened in London. Perhaps they were too surprised to see a foreigner in their midst or else did not care. We went to an area that was once the underworld of Shanghai, the area associated with all the illegalities—drugs, fake money, and murders. Now, of course, it has been cleaned up. We soon collected a crowd of children who tailed us shouting comments and were stunned into silence when Pat replied to them in Chinese.

We walked rather aimlessly until we came to the famous Canton Road, well known for its curio shops and art dealers. Walking into one seemingly small shop full of porcelain and glass we were then ushered into another room and yet another until we realized that there were a series of rooms, each stuffed with porcelain, ceramic, and glass in various shapes and sizes, and in many colours. It was almost like a kaleidoscopic dream. There was everything from the predictable and boring laughing Buddha statues to those of the goddess of compassion, Guan Yin, mixed up with porcelain models of landscape gardens and other scenes. It was not a single shop but a conglomeration of many. Each had an elderly Chinese gentleman who bowed and asked in broken English what he could show us. When we casually said that we were just looking around, our statement was greeted with an openly contemptuous look. Clearly, they had recent memories of Western visitors to Shanghai who bought much of their merchandise.

Then suddenly I turned into a smaller shop that had a heap of small jade objects in the centre of a showcase. My heart soared and I started looking carefully at them with Pat whispering all the time that I should not buy anything as there were many fakes. Not that I had the money to buy anything really valuable. The owner was a true salesman with stories about each object that became more and more intriguing—the history of the piece, some anecdote connected with it, and who had previously shown an interest and why. I finally succumbed and bought a small inexpensive little piece. But the place was incredible, and it was exciting to be handling a pendant from Han times to a vase of the Ming period, and not caring whether they were genuinely old or modern fakes. His assistant had as much ready 'puff' on each piece as the owner and was obviously well trained.

It was a great evening with the abacus. Each time I asked for the price of an object the beads on the abacus shot hither and thither and a price was mentioned. I was fascinated by the use of a pre-modern system of counting and had thought when I first saw it in action in Xi'an that it was used only in the more distant areas. But here we were in sophisticated Shanghai and it was being used regularly here too.

We took a pedicab back to the hotel and passed through the old town to the new. The latter had all the paraphernalia of new urban places— posters, advertisements of soaps, hair oils, cooking fat, and some rather discreet posters advertising various ways of rejuvenating the body. The same semi-Europeanized faces with toothy smiles all in bright colours were plastered in a few public places. At first the ads puzzled me but then I realized that some of the economy of the city was still tied into businesses that were half-private and half-state. There are still remnants of the British business houses although fast disappearing. It was only too evident that the revolution had not cleared away the bits and pieces that surround the demarcated Europeanized urban areas. Shanghai was significantly different from the other cities we had been in such as Xi'an or for that matter even Beijing.

The boats on the river that once carried contraband are now used to bring cargo from the large ships that cannot come upstream to the warehouses on the river. Most of the packages had an official stamp—a red star and a number. Transporting the cargo were men pulling carts. The streets were cobbled and crossing them was no great chore and the pedicabs gave us passage and the occasional car, driving slowly anyway, would pull up and let us cross.

Had another fantastic meal. A fish soup, one I have never had before, which had fish balls as light as meringues, and the spice in the chicken was more an aroma than a taste. All through dinner there was a programme of European dance music—mainly rhumbas, waltzes, and foxtrots—but no one danced. This is apparently a regular Wednesday programme. I wish someone would introduce some jazz to the Chinese as I suspect they would take to it. Dixieland would be appropriate as the music of the American underdog, but the preference seems to be for rather out-of-date Tin Pan Alley type of music. Rock n' roll is not difficult to imagine with teenagers in T-shirts. As we got up after dinner to walk to the door, they switched to something that is called 'Hindi-Chini bhai-bhai' but it is difficult to make out what it is. Actually Hindi film songs would be a hit and should be made more available. Easily the most popular Hindi song in China is 'Awaara Hoon'.

18
A Weekend Break in Hangchow

Our next port of call was Hangchow (as Hangzhou was then known). This, we were told, was a brief vacation for us, a break from the labour that we had put in during the previous weeks. The hotel was an upgrade with a soft mattress and a hot bath. My room had a small balcony that looked over the vast West Lake of Hangzhou. I could see the islands that dot the lake in the distance. The landscape immediately all around is flat with meticulously measured rice fields, water channels, windmills, and whitewashed houses with the usual black roofs. A clearly prosperous area, assisted no doubt by being a centre of commerce and tourism, such as it is. It is a charming old town and I noticed with pleasure that the houses resemble those of the old town in Shanghai—the upper storey jutting out a little over the lower one and the small balconies with finely worked balcony rails. The streets were full of light and life. Apparently as a place of scenic beauty and much visited, Hangzhou goes back to the Tang period. A tree-lined avenue extends to the lake with a link to a long causeway. Surrounding the lake are low hills, perhaps the only ones in the area.

After dinner we went to see a modern Chinese film based on a novel by the much-admired Lu Xun featuring one of the better-known actresses. The story relates the suffering of a peasant woman in the society of forty years ago and ends in tragedy. I went armed with a couple of hankies as I can never control my tears when I see a sad film. I was expecting melodrama to be laid on with a trowel but it was surprisingly restrained. The colour was poor and there were technical flaws. Nevertheless, nothing was rammed down our throats and there were no pietistic maxims. With a better director it could have been a worthwhile film. I had expected that Chinese films would have some of the sensitivity that is apparent in Japanese films but the cultural perceptions are obviously different.

The day at the museum was needlessly tiring. It was a holiday, therefore, many came to the museum and we were as much of an exhibit as the objects on display. I often carried a light folding tripod stool for sitting every now and again to take notes on particular objects, and at which point a dozen or so people would surround me, and without much noise just watch me writing in my notebook, and looking at my face for an indication of what I was doing. They were, of course, most interested each time I did a sketch of an object to illustrate my notes and this would make me even more uneasy. Some hardly audible comments would be murmured and I would wonder what was being said. But I didn't have the heart to complain to anyone since their curiosity was well intentioned.

In the evening we went into town to look at the crafts—fancy scissors, fans, baskets, small stone carvings—all of which are the specialities of the place. We walked into a basket-making factory and I did not like the working conditions that appeared to be somewhat primitive, presumably because there were only about forty workers and this may still have been treated as a cottage industry. I was intrigued by the complicated techniques that they all seem to handle with absolute ease. As with making pottery, this was another instance of human ingenuity in creating techniques that convert a practical object into a thing of beauty. The transformation of a stem of bamboo into an intricately woven basket is almost magic. Here there was nothing but bamboo and they all sat on small trestles or locally designed little chairs, cutting, scraping, and weaving their amazing designs, with children wandering in and out clutching rice bowls and chopsticks. It did seem to me to be a small waste of human labour when mechanical jobs like cutting strips could perhaps have been done by a machine. But obviously they knew better. What was striking was that there was ample space between each craftsman and I thought then, as I have often thought, that the Chinese perhaps have a sense of space that disallows them from overcrowding their working locations.

It had rained all morning so when it stopped after lunch we were taken to the lake for a short boat ride to the other end. I asked if I could take one of the small boats and just casually row around the edge of the lake, but was told politely that, as a guest, this would not be permitted. So we all clambered onto a larger boat. The lake itself was quite dreamlike with the surrounding hilltops distant and partially hidden in mist. At times I had the feeling that we were moving into a Song landscape. Those painters merely painted what they saw and the juxtaposition of space with forms was not entirely imaginary. It was the classical formula for landscapes—the branches of a willow trailing over still water with distant mountains hiding in the mist—that immediately evoked an afternoon such as ours. I am not surprised that many artists apparently spend long years at Hangzhou. Every hill and mist produces a view that inspires a painting or a poem. How is this moment to be captured?

We stopped at some of the islands in the lake, and one was particularly lovely with a Song period garden complete with small bridges and rock decorations over a lily pond—so subtle and evocative. I thought to myself that it would be such an experience to travel back in time to that age. The names that were given to these places had evoked phrases from Chinese poetry, called as they were, 'Autumn Moon on the Calm Lake', 'Orioles Singing in the Willows', 'Pagoda of Six Harmonies', 'Place of the Smoke-like Evening Clouds'. If only we could travel back in time—but provided we could choose where we wanted to be and with whom! Or maybe it is best that the past remains a part of one's imagination as the reality could be rather disappointing.

Talking about travelling, not back in time but certainly into another space, we wandered into the lounge of the hotel and saw a mid-August copy of *l'Humanite*, the paper of the French Communist Party, which Dominique and I fell upon hungrily. This was news of the other world of which we had had none almost from the time we left it. The front page reported troubles in Syria and complications in Middle Eastern politics, and a full-page report of the furore in Britain over the remarks of Lord Altrincham (later John Grigg) on the royal family, clearly not complimentary. This included the story of an Italian monarchist who had challenged Lord Altrincham to a duel for daring to make these remarks about British royalty. So much fuss about something so trivial. It had the feel of the absurd. We also dug out a copy of the *Daily Worker*, but unfortunately it was dated 23 July. So I am back at wanting to know what is happening in the world but seem not to be able to get any information.

One of the things about travelling in China these days is that one is constantly bumping into delegations of all kinds. Staying in the hotel are

212 • ROMILA THAPAR

film delegations that have come for an Asian film festival but it is clearly not a very large gathering. They are all state guests and are taken to the same places. We met the Japanese and the Lebanese more often than the others. Another Indian delegation included Kaka Kalelkar and Rameshwari Nehru who had been to Japan for an anti-H bomb conference, and who were attending a meeting on Asian consolidation. These circuits have now become an activity of the new Asia, the Asia of newly independent nations.

The next morning, we visited a monastery nearby, built in the early centuries AD, with a temple that was very much in worship and collected large numbers of people, especially on Sundays. Legend has it that this was also a monastery where an Indian monk spent many years translating the Buddhist texts. The location was quite dramatically set near a village of black and white houses. The temple reminded me of a baroque church—a large building with the required number of doors and with niches holding gilt images all lit by red or blue lights, and a plain floor looking up at a heavily decorated ceiling with squares covered in floral designs. The fragrance of burning joss sticks was so thick that it was almost opaque. The largest image was placed in the centre flanked by a smaller image on each side. Elderly women in black trousers and blue jackets, their hair securely knotted at the back, moved from shrine to shrine, kneeling before each, murmuring a prayer and planting burning joss sticks into bronze vessels half-filled with sand placed beside each image. Now and again a shaven-headed monk in a long black robe would walk past the main altar unsmilingly. As it was raining there were open umbrellas all over, cheerful umbrellas made of a central stick of bamboo with coloured parchment of blue, yellow, green, red, forming the cover.

Our arrival in the temple was again met with curiosity on the part of others and much discussion about our nationality. To our great annoyance many thought we were visitors from the Soviet Union. I almost started singing 'Awaara Hoon', to make the point that we were Indian, but that would not perhaps have been appropriate in the precincts of a temple. I was puzzled because this time we were wearing saris and not our slacks and Chinese jackets. We were obviously not Russians so presumably we were taken to be a national minority from the USSR. Clearly there are not enough sari-clad Indian visitors for the local people to make the right connection.

The monastery had an evocative name: the Peak that Flew from Afar. This was because the Indian monk when he saw the peak maintained that it was the very same peak that was in the vicinity of the monastery in India from where he had come, therefore the legend grew that the peak had flown from India. The grottoes facing the monastery have caves and overhangs with Song period sculptures carved into the rock. Parts of this are now covered with moss and vegetation and this adds to the beauty of the sculpture giving it a touch of gentleness as well. At one place there is a low relief of a scene depicting Xuan Zang bringing back bundles of sutras from India.

This episode is almost foundational to the traditional Chinese understanding of India. Xuan Zang is virtually a cult figure among some Chinese. Now, of course, with both cultures experiencing modernization this will change. It does rather make Chinese Buddhism beholden to teachings from India, a thought better perhaps kept to oneself. One can't help but think of the many occasions when there has been persecution of Chinese Buddhists, such as the one in the ninth century AD. There is a strong historical perspective to the establishing of Buddhism in China. We in India pay little attention to those that in the past have come to India seeking knowledge, or for that matter Indians that have gone out to explore the known world for various reasons.

Leading into the entrance was a magnificent bronze drum. I struck it gently with my fingers and it produced a remarkably resonant sound lasting for over a minute. I could feel the vibrations on the drum for longer. A row of arhants sat on each side of the drum, well-modelled but much gilded over. The distinctiveness of each face suggested that they may have been known monks. The Pearl Fountain is so named because when one stamps on the ground at the edge of the fountain, the water throws up bubbles that look like pearls. The Jade Fountain is so called since the floor surrounding it has a floor that looks like jade, although it isn't so. This fountain (as also many others) has large black carp and gold fish, the two seem always to go together. We watched them being fed with small pieces of pumpkin. I don't particularly like fish with their big glassy, unblinking eyes, their large, open mouths, and their blood-filled gills that open when they breathe. I have never wanted to get to know them. Perhaps if I was to spend a long time with fish I might get to like them. And what this means in terms of a Freudian analysis doesn't bother me!

Last evening was a misty autumn evening with an occasional drizzle. The twilight comes so suddenly. A little earlier I was in the park with Mingo and enjoying the autumn just beginning to change the colour of the leaves. We walked slowly picking up the leaves almost turning red and yellow. In another month the trees will be bare, all but the willows. When the snow comes even the water chestnuts will be without their round, spongy leaves covered in frog sperm. The weathered rocks with their cavities and hollows, looking like the sculpture of Henry Moore, are scattered in the garden, giving it the feel almost of a prehistoric site.

19

A Summation in Beijing

We were returning to Beijing and this was our last train journey taking a day and a night. It was uneventful. The train was comfortable and clean. A corridor ran alongside the cabins with facilities at each end of what we in India would call a bogie. I sat up at night watching once again the complicated procedure of crossing the Yangtze River by ferry. But my anxiety peaked when I suddenly found myself locked inside the toilet by mistake. The toilets are locked at every station where the train stops to prevent passers-by on the platform from using them. In this case the person in charge did not check to see whether the toilet was being used. I practically fell out of the window when drawing the attention of the policeman on the platform, followed by my best efforts to mime my being locked in. Finally, he understood, came onto the train, tried the handle, and then went to find the steward who had the key. Fortunately the toilets on this train were as clean as were the compartments.

The landscape was again flat. We travelled through rice fields on either side with occasional small waterways full of water chestnuts that were being harvested. Where the water was deeper and there were narrow canals, transportation was by boats. These were small, shallow-bottom boats with a tiny thatched room in the middle. Gradually the rice fields gave way to more fields with maize, millet, and sorghum—and we knew we were back in the north. Back also to the mud-built village houses and this time there were a few people flying kites. In terms of the Indian calendar this was not the time of year for flying kites but obviously the Chinese calendar differs. Suddenly, the train loudspeaker came alive, playing Bach's Fourth Brandenburg Concerto. This gave me quite a jolt—the thought of Bach being played on the Shanghai-Beijing train. Anything can happen. Mingo said it was a broadcast from the Central People's Station in Beijing. One section of this station broadcasts only music and a mixture of classical and popular music from various parts of the world. It is a way of familiarizing people with varieties of music. She mentioned that the Song and Dance Experimental Group put on the opera *La Traviata* in the original and it was so popular that it continued to be performed for three months. If Peking opera was to be performed at Covent Garden or Italian opera at one of the cultural centres in Delhi, I doubt that it would have a run of more than three nights.

It got me wondering. Are the Chinese so open that they are willing to listen to Bach or is it being imposed on them as part of their general education? What does the regime get out of making them familiar with Bach? Is it just showing off to the occasional Western visitor—an attitude that seems to hover over some other activities? When will we, touched by colonialism, drop the need for such showing off? Or, do the Chinese have a natural curiosity to a greater degree than many others from this continent? Do we in India, for instance, lack the curiosity to explore the unknown? Would we play Bach over a loudspeaker on a train? Or is it that we have such a well-evolved system of musical forms, both classical and popular, that these suffice our curiosity and leave us uninterested in exploring to any depth other forms of music, or any other artistic expression for that matter?

It is a bit like the other question that puzzles me and more so since coming here. Chinese Buddhists visited India and more so in the latter part of the first millennium AD, and most left an account of what they had experienced. Some are brief statements, some are lengthier accounts such as that of Faxian, and one is a detailed itinerary, that of Xuan Zang, with many incisive reflections on what he saw and heard. Equally many Indians visited Central Asia and China as Buddhist missionaries and teachers or else as merchants. Some settled in these places and played an important role in Chinese thought and religion through their teachings. But none has left an account of this experience. It wasn't lethargy since their teaching was rigorous. There seems to have been an unconcern with commenting on actual experience in the belief that either none in India would be interested, or else that such experiences should remain a part of one's own being and go no further.

We were back at the hotel Xin Qiao and it felt a bit like a government dormitory after the gracious service of the Shanghai hotel. Beijing is a little more uncertain in comparison. It hasn't the smoothness of Shanghai. The town is full of foreigners and each day a new delegation arrives and one hears another new language being spoken. This time it is for the October anniversary celebrating the revolution. The Indian embassy is in a whirl with President Radhakrishnan having arrived as a state guest, and everyone is rushing around in circles. Work gets done at a slower pace here than in Shanghai and I found myself getting irritated more than once at the slowness and had to check myself from saying so. A young Indian diplomat on his first posting was holding forth in the hotel lounge on China, and commenting on how much the women work, and the confidence with which they do so, and that the Chinese are not the opium-eaters that some Indians think they are. We really need to be more knowledgeable about our eastern neighbour.

Comments in the form of easy-reading generalizations about China are pouring forth everywhere these days. I am also questioning myself as to the value of my reactions to being in China. One can at most be a witness and write what one sees. I have been here for over three months and am only just beginning to feel that perhaps I have a minimal glimpse of what is going on. Not knowing the language is a great disadvantage. My attempt is only to describe what I have seen just to remind myself of my visit. I still haven't got used to being described as someone who comes from the West. It gives me a bit of a jolt each time!

As I was thinking these thoughts, a woman with a child came and sat at the next table. I made friends with the child and then tried out my hopeless Chinese on the mother. We did get to speak a little and she seemed to understand me. I thought this was actually my meeting with China when I was trying to communicate not through Mingo but by myself. It introduces a different feel to being here. Returning to Beijing, I did not go about searching for tea shops as I did in the first week that we were here, because I know now that they don't exist in the manner in which I had imagined them to. In short, now that I am acquainted more with China and have made contact with even just a few Chinese persons I feel a little more confident in my observations—I am beginning to find the context.

In the evening, Mingo and I took a rickety bus that crawled to the central market. It was around 8 p.m. and the stalls were folding up for the night, the boards being put up and the roofs dusted. We went into a music shop. It was a curious little shop, somewhat grubby, but full of records—78s mostly—and a few of what looked like home-made radios. I picked up a small clutch of records of instrumental music that I selected after listening to them. It did not seem strange to me that I wanted to hear 'The Moon over Guan Mountain' or other such compositions. Picking up the packet of records we walked on. Passing a grocery store we asked for apples preserved in syrup and these were given to us in a beautiful green-glazed pot. That is one of the joys of China that eatables come in such exquisitely glazed bowls and pots.

I wanted to go somewhere where there would be lots of people so we walked to the crossroads with steps on one side. So I suggested sitting on the steps and eating our apples. Mingo explained that this was really not done so I teased her and said she could always say that the foreign barbarian had insisted on doing so. The Beijing world walked past and stared discreetly, and I occasionally heard the word 'Indu' so they had at least guessed where I was from. It was a clear starry night and the searchlights were making patterns in the sky—rehearsals for the celebratory day. We strolled back through the now darkened hutongs with their infrequent street lights and the houses showing only their bare almost inhospitable white walls. But beyond the walls and behind the door one sometimes caught a glimpse of light and the sound of laughter or of the radio. Life goes on beyond the walls but seems not to spill on to the street. Do the 'experts' on China, those who write books on China, get to cross the threshold and enter behind these walls and know the life within? I could not do so and therefore felt that I knew so little.

On returning to Beijing I had planned on giving priority to two things: one was to return for more and longer visits to the museums now that I had visited some of the sites that were the locations of the objects, and the second was to get a chance to discuss my ideas with some of the scholars to whom I had been given introductions from Sinologists at the School of Oriental and African Studies in London. The first was easily done and I got to spend many days studying a range of objects with much note-taking as I went around. The second proved to be extremely difficult. There were two historians whom I wanted to talk with, Professor Xiang Da and Professor

Chang both in the History Department of Beijing University. I mentioned that I had been asked to see them by historians of China at London University. Back came the answer that they were too busy to see me.

I began to wonder why. Surely courtesy demands that if someone has travelled many thousands of miles and comes with an introduction from people one knows professionally then one does make an effort at least to manage a brief meeting. The Chinese are not lacking in courtesy. Clearly there were other reasons. One had heard about the 'rectification campaigns' that were currently going on in many offices, where people working in the office would gather, and in a kind of self-analysis session speak of where they had made mistakes and were then told what they had to do to rectify them. I began to see analogies with the Catholic confessional! Perhaps this made them reluctant to meet foreigners lest some of the issues inadvertently got talked about, or even that such meetings were perhaps frowned upon, or that given the time these meetings took they really did not have the spare time to meet anyone. Or was it the intention of our hosts that we exhaust ourselves with sight-seeing and have no time to meet our counterpart professionals? This would not happen elsewhere whether in India or Europe.

I have repeatedly been requesting meetings with young people, university students and researchers, and young intellectuals, and all I have got by way of a reply is a polite smile. It makes me so frustrated and even angry that this should be happening in a country where I want to meet people and talk to them about how they visualize the structure of their society, because we are doing the same in India, albeit in a different way, and because there might be parallels. I want to talk about what university means to them and what they hope to obtain from a university education. I also want to discuss the kinds of history that they learn and teach, and how they envisage the future research in historical subjects, not to mention the kinds of intellectual problems they are likely to face. I am interested in the experience of others because I believe that one learns from comparative studies. I can't go out and find them as I don't speak Chinese. I am beginning to tire of being shepherded all the time and being treated with kid gloves as a foreign guest, although I do realize that this has made it far easier for me to do what I had come here for in terms of working at the two sites. But I get no further than polite responses when I make these requests.

And while I was ranting about not getting to meet historians and archaeologists, there appeared the one exception. This was Professor Xia Nai from the Institute of Archaeology, who graciously gave me an appointment, and we discussed at great length the more important aspects of what I had seen and my comments on these. I also learnt much from him as to what their priorities of research were and how they were trying to meet them. I was anxious to discuss their excavation of the recently discovered Neolithic site of Banpo, particularly as it was not the result of salvage archaeology but had been properly excavated. This made a welcome change from the earlier discussions that I had had with others on using archaeological material. He provided me with a set of photographs and was quite keen that I should write an article on the excavation and publish it in a European journal, so that archaeologists would become familiar with the work in China, and with important sites such as this one. When I told him that I would publish it in *Discovery,* the editor of which had specifically asked me to consider such an article, he seemed delighted. The lengthy conversation with Xia Nai across areas of the early past gave me hope that I would have a chance for the same with the historians at the university. A couple of days later, when speaking with an acquaintance from the Indian embassy, I was told that this long conversation with Xia Nai was an exception as he was well connected and regarded as special—whatever that may mean—by the government. The implication being that unlike other academics he did not have to conform to the rules, whatever they were.

I was still left with not being able to talk history with professional historians. My frustration left me depressed and inevitably led me to look afresh at all the people we had met and to reassessing conversations. Living constantly in hotels was also getting me down. I could see that I was gearing up to moving towards the end of the visit and therefore said to myself that I should not give way to negativity. Anil was also beginning to feel that her positive vibes were running low. We sat down for dinner in the dining room and at the table next to ours sat the British swimming team delightfully inebriated and raucous after their success in the day's events. Just as Anil and I were saying that this was the last straw, in walked Pat. He was examining historical documents kept in a small institution in Beijing and was staying at the hotel. So we cheered up and decided to go into town after dinner. We thought of taking a boat and rowing on the North Lake but when we got to the boathouse at 8.27, they informed us that it closes at 8.30. We thought of seeing a film but not a single cinema house in the vicinity was showing a Chinese film. All the films were Soviet films and we thought that would be too depressing. By then it was 9 or just after, so we sought a place where we might get a drink. We went to the heart of the city to the bazaar with the well-known Peace Café where we thought there might be some nightlife, but it had already closed for the evening.

We wandered around the bazaar but the shops were closed. We came to a long hall that had billiard tables and ping-pong tables and a small handful of people playing but rather wistfully. We even went to the old city area, the famous Liulichang Street, but it was quiet with just the occasional sound of Peking opera behind the closed doors of people's homes. So much for Beijing's nightlife. Obviously it was not approved of or did not exist. It was such a contrast to a central bazaar in an Indian city that even later in the night would have had something of a buzz.

This was followed by a full day at the university. I did finally get to meet the people I had wanted to but it was all rather frustrating. Pat and I set out together as he wanted to meet a couple of specialists in literature at the university as well. But there was an objection to his accompanying me. I was told that I had already been provided with an interpreter and his presence was unnecessary—in so many words. This certainly put me in a hostile mood. Pat was later told that because he was a foreign guest he could not just wander into the university but would have to go via the association that was hosting him—even though there was no association hosting him in Beijing and he was there on his own.

Both Professors Chang and Ji had agreed to see me. I was met by a student and taken to the history faculty and the office of the dean. Professor Chang joined us and we sat for almost an hour making small talk. I found this exhausting and kept trying to raise topics of professional interest but these would be politely brushed aside. The smiles were a permanent fixture and accompanied the polite conversation about virtually nothing of much interest.

I introduced the subject of the Romanization of the Chinese script on which he was an authority and he answered in the briefest possible way that it involved three stages—the popularization of Mandarin Chinese, the working out of basic characters in a simplified form, and the actual translit-eration of the ideograms, all of which would take an immense amount of time but it had to come. The answer was literally just that. When I started asking questions about how this would be done and how it would affect lit-eracy, social norms, the transmission of knowledge, and how that might change in the process, we smilingly moved again to some aspect of our travels in China. I began to wonder whether my questions were being resented or thought to be too elementary, or whether there was a disincli-nation to answer them. I had the same experience when I asked some ques-tions about Chinese historiography. Yet they seemed quite content to go on sipping green tea and talking about nothing in particular.

I was then taken to see Professor Ji, the professor of Sanskrit and Pali. He had studied for ten years in Germany and had been a student of Ernst Waldschmidt. We had met when we first arrived in Beijing at the small dinner for us and on that occasion had spoken about ancient texts. This time surprisingly he did not say much about his own work but did ask about my thesis remembering our last conversation. I asked him about his stu-dents of whom he hardly had any. It was the same story with books. There were few in the library. I told myself this was better than none. In the best of Indian universities there would be hardly any books on the Chinese lan-guage of past times. There are four Indians here teaching Hindi and Urdu and they have about eighty students. This seemed a large number. I met two of the girls who had studied Hindi and they spoke a Hindi that sounded reasonable. They intended to work as interpreters and translators and this suggested something of a flow between India and China if so many are aspiring to jobs in this field. It was never clear to me whether Professor Ji was teaching Sanskrit to any of his students.

After this I went to the university library and browsed through the cat-alogue. The section on books in English was large. The archaeology section had books by Mortimer Wheeler and Gordon Childe and a few others. Indian archaeology had John Marshall on Mohenjo-daro and on Taxila. There wasn't much on any early history, Indian or otherwise. European his-tory had a few standard books by Herbert Fisher, Edward Hall, William Muir etc.; all rather out-of-date textbooks. Economics had Karl Marx, Maurice Dobb, Adam Smith, Lionel Robbins, and Arthur Cecil Pigou. There was a surprising absence of more recent studies from a Marxist perspective that I had assumed would be there. A long list under psychology included Alfred Adler and Sigmund Freud. And so it went on. I did ask if a lot more had been translated into Chinese but my question remained unanswered. I found it strange that there was so little on Marxism given that that is crucial to the ideology of the governing Party. So, I am now wondering whether it is the works of Mao Zedong and Zhou Enlai and other Chinese Marxists that are preferably read rather than the original texts of Marx, Engels, and the early thinkers. It would be good to know how many of the original texts had been translated into Chinese, and how good were the translations. Were there commentaries in Chinese that were used as shortcuts to reading the actual books?

The campus itself is very attractive with its nucleus in the old pre-Liberation university. I have now got used to measuring time in terms of pre-Liberation and post-Liberation. The old buildings in traditional style are surrounded by gardens, by willow-lined walks, and even a small lake nearby, a landscape that puts Cambridge into the shade. The modern extension, however, is aesthetically not so striking. Reminiscent of extensions to Indian universities, it consists of a series of barrack-like grey buildings, some in stone and some in concrete, with flat roofs. This was because there was a rush to put up new buildings since 8,000 students had to be urgently accommodated, it being a residential university. They admit the dormitories are overcrowded. However, the architecture could have been easier on the eye.

I went to one of the girls' dormitories. The rooms are small and bare walled with four bunks to each room and two small writing tables. At one level, I suppose, this is real dedication to learning. The rooms in Miranda House are luxurious compared to these. But predictably it was said that there is a special dormitory for foreign students, better furnished than the ones for Chinese students, and foreign students also eat in their own special canteen. This did annoy me, and I could not decide whether this was just the Chinese sense of hospitality or whether it was segregation with the intention of warding off criticism. Yet we are all aware this is not necessary. It is the early years of the revolution, the changes are still to come and it is expected that everyone should be subjected to the same conditions. It is like the hotels where Chinese food is served on the ground floor but Western cuisine is available on the topmost floor with its superior furnishings.

I was told there were six Indian students at the university so I asked if I could meet them but was told that none were around. I asked if there were common rooms for students and they mentioned two clubs. So I suggested visiting one of them, but again it was lunchtime so the clubs were closed. I thought to myself that surely that was precisely the time when a club should be open. I asked if I could have a chat with some of the English-speaking students. There was rapid consultation among those with us and I was informed that such a meeting would be arranged in a couple of days. I cursed under my breath but explained with great patience that I was not interested in a formal meeting with speeches and such like, but just a casual chat. Yes, I was told, this could be done, but not now as it was lunchtime and we had to return.

I don't think they want to necessarily hide things from those visiting, but they require permission for every move. It seemed that Beijing was much more conscious of this than the other places we had been to, and Shanghai least of all. I find all this somewhat irritating because it really gets one nowhere even when one is not imputing motives to anyone. It is doubt-less a hangover from the heavy bureaucratic system from which China has suffered over centuries, combined with the seeming continuation of the same system despite the revolution or even sometimes fuelled by the bureaucracy of the Party. This does seem to happen when a single party has overwhelming control.

I pondered the question of the treatment of foreigners and told myself that if the Chinese are over-courteous towards foreigners that should not irritate me. Instead, I should try and explain why this is so. After all, or so we have been told, it has been normal in this culture to regard all foreigners as 'barbarians' and Europeans as 'foreign devils'. The former would presum-ably have included Indians, or did the fact that Indians came from the western heaven of the land of the Buddha, preclude us? This is predictable in all early cultures and would be parallel to Indians referring to aliens as Mleccha. Did the good Brahmana at the court of Harshavardhana treat Xuan Zang as a Mleccha as he was supposed to do technically? This idea may no longer be current but the traces of such ideas take ages to fade out. Is the emphasis on heavy courtesy actually a message of exclusion or is it because the Chinese are still innately suspicious of foreigners? The peasants in places that we have visited have been curious but affectionate and willing to talk, as have the people in the streets that we walked in, but the mandarins remain distanced. They observe the formalities and leave it at that.

We have not been invited to a single Chinese home, not even for a cup of green tea, and whatever occasional entertaining there has been, it has always been in a restaurant. Could this be because it is thought that homes are not well-furnished and this would suggest a lesser standard of living than what is projected? Now that I am coming across the intellectual world the feasibility of straightforward conversations seem problematic. Here the contrast with India is enormous. We talk quite openly about whatever may be bothering us, or about the problems we may be having with ineffective governance, but not so here. The intellectual world everywhere is complicated but that it seems to be un-get-at-able here is scary, especially for someone who is trying to understand how it ticks.

We drove back from the university in silence. We drove through broad, tree-lined avenues, newly built with monstrously large buildings on each side—office buildings inspired by Soviet architecture. There was literally only one building that I did not think was an eyesore and this was a recently completed hospital for children. At one point I sneezed. The person accompanying me immediately rolled up the windows and asked if I was cold. I said that I was not and sank deeper into a gloomier silence.

The late afternoon, however, was very pleasant. We were taken to see the secretary-general of the Dramatists' Association and we talked at length on the history and evolution of the Chinese opera. The conversation then moved to the modern theatre in China. This led to a discussion on how a contemporary theme could be treated in a traditional form. This is a universal problem so we all had much to say on it, extending the discussion to defining folk art. It was more provocative than any discussion I had had in the morning but here too I felt there were subconscious brakes in what was being said, or possibly since we were unfamiliar with the subject, there was no point in going into greater detail.

The delightful Miss Wu, whom I have come to like so much, took us to the export shop and I trailed around it with joy as it had a selection of cheap rings, the kind one can buy in twos or threes and wear to match an extravagant mood. Miss Wu has the utmost patience when she is with indecisive shoppers and covers our hesitations with charming, although sometimes somewhat devastating, comments, and above all seems to be genuinely affectionate. We came home to a small packet of mail for each of us, and that was a delight after many days of no mail.

In the evening we went to the theatre. This time they were presenting a modern play and another set in the Ming period. The building itself was attractive and designed by an East German architect. The first play was about psychological problems among a group of actors, one of whom finally dies. The occasional cliché that we recognized even without the translation of the text did not seriously disturb a quite sensitive play. The second play was based on a well-known story of the Ming period and was presented in historical costume. The stage was set in a remarkably sophisticated manner. It was like a brightly coloured Ming painting placed in a brocade mount, but nothing was exaggerated or overdone. It was theatre setting of a high standard.

The following evening we were invited for supper by two of the officials involved in our visit to Beijing. It was such a delicious meal that I can hardly describe it. We went to a tiny little restaurant in a dark hutong, a backstreet of Beijing. We were served Yunan cuisine with tea eggs, chicken in ginger, fish in a salty sauce, shrimps on rice scraping, fine eel slices that tasted like soft bacon, duck morsels cooked in spinach with an alternating flavour of duck and spinach, rice noodles in a lamb soup, all served with a mild white Shaoshing wine served in a spouted jug made of fine glass. We sat at a small round table on wooden seats. There were wooden sculpted Buddhas and bodhisattvas in each corner that made the room even smaller than it was. On the wall to the side was a much-varnished, yellowish painting of ships in a harbour, reminiscent of a European style—probably a poor quality original or a copy. The varnish was so dark one could hardly make out the figures. Over the door was a picture of Mao in the regular blue suit. The door led to another room with a fireplace on one side and tables on the other at which a few people were eating. They called it a family restaurant and it had an air of informality. We toasted all manner of things since the wine was so mild. This mildness puzzled me but I understood the reason for it when one of our hosts said he had to go early to a meeting the next morning and it was likely to take the whole day. It was on the tip of my tongue to ask him whether this was another rectification meeting, but I refrained.

The fury of the rectification campaign seems to have abated somewhat as compared to when we first arrived in Beijing. The posters are still up— bright, bold cartoons and statements in black on green, pink, and purple paper stuck everywhere. The pictures show the Rightists as snakes being crushed. The posters at Lanzhou had been much more graphic and the Rightists had been presented in all sorts of ugly and contorted ways and as a real menace. They reminded me of the anti-Japanese posters that the British put up all over India during the years of World War II depicting the Japanese in despicable ways. These are the origins of what usually mutates into hate campaigns of a worse kind. Somehow these posters and cartoons seem out of context given the aspirations of the revolution. Have the aspirations changed?

To be called a Rightist has now become a convenient term of abuse, applied to anyone almost without specific meaning. Any controversy in any field can lead to a person being dubbed a Rightist and therefore condemned without going into the details of what was being objected to. The Chinese may not have intended it to go this way, but there it is. Or that is how it appears to be to those of us who are onlookers. There is a parallel here to McCarthyism in the US, where being called a Leftist or a Commie was the height of abuse. If the aspirations of a revolution are directed towards a better society for all, can it not be achieved in a less belligerent way? Does there always have to be a scapegoat? And doesn't the insistence on a scapegoat introduce the threat of fascism into revolutionary change? This is now beginning to sound like the conversations that we have in the refectory of Birkbeck College in London University!

Earlier in the evening we had looked in at the home of an official of the Indian embassy who was hosting a party. A strange conversation ensued that evening with a couple of people visiting from India who said that they couldn't possibly live in China because of the presence of underfed and overworked Chinese. Such a statement coming from people who live in India was very odd indeed. Another gentleman said he had been told that Chinese intellectuals resent the present system because writers and artists don't know where they stand vis-à-vis the government, and they have to accept Party directives that keep changing. I saw the validity of that argument in the context of sessions of self-analyses and rectification. He went on to say that no textbooks had been written since Liberation. So I corrected him and said that I had seen the new textbooks written on history and archaeology, and that government-sponsored textbook writing could reflect either an attempt to improve the quality of such books, or to hammer home the ideology of those in power. In the latter case the result is more often a distorted history unless great caution is exercised.

We worked at the Library of the Institute of Archaeology, going through their publications on recent work on Maijishan and Dunhuang. The publications were an attempt to give up-to-date reports, even if brief, on the work that was being done of recording casual finds, and at greater length of excavations. The latter were few but the reports were detailed. The publications were well-produced and accessible. Our days at the institute were most useful as we did manage to have conversations with younger scholars who were also working there and I slowly began to get a sense of how they were approaching disciplines such as ancient history and archaeology. There was an interesting mixture of using conventional Marxist phraseology in describing various cultures as also some slight awareness of a couple of the other theories that were current in the world of historical writing. There was a tendency to repeat the information they had read in prescribed books in Chinese without perhaps fully grasping the implications of what was written. What was missing was the discussion about the theories of interpretation irrespective of whether they were Marxist or not. Gordon Childe was known, although less from reading his books as from being told what was in them, which is what I surmised from a few comments about his ideas.

One thing that I miss very much is not having access to newspapers other than those in Chinese published in China. I am told that if one really searches for them there are last week's papers in some tucked-away place. But I no longer wish to go newspaper hunting. I picked one up from the British Legation office and the most exciting news was the release of Charlie Chaplin's latest movie, *A King in New York*. But reading about it did initially conjure up an image of a somewhat disconnected world.

I can hear a donkey braying outside and can't think quite what he is doing in Beijing. The hotel is slowly getting crowded with the celebrations coming up soon. Each hour brings more bewildered people standing by their suitcases or making for the lifts. The lifts in this hotel are of German manufacture, probably East German. I miss the predictable Waygood-Otis that one has used in other places. The dining rooms are at each end of the hotel, one for Chinese food and one for European. I can't see the usefulness of such segregation.

The city is now preparing for the anniversary of the revolution. Wooden stands and floats are being constructed and painted bright red. Buildings are being decorated with large globular red lanterns hanging at the entrance. Red lanterns are considered auspicious. Banners of varied colours are beginning to be strung up in open spaces and loudspeakers have been fixed to lamp posts. Now and again they are tested with snippets of music. This afternoon when we passed the Forbidden City they were rehearsing the Dragon dance in the forecourt. The masks were most impressive as was also a squadron of women marching down the main road. The city is clearly entering a festive mood.

The Forbidden City continues to intrigue me and I could just settle down in one place and give vent to visions of what it may have been like in its time. The comparison is obviously with Fatehpur Sikri and I can't decide which is the more elegant. I don't know what attracts me most—the yellow and green roofs, the white carved marble balustrades and railings, the paved courtyards embraced by expansive red walls, or the magnificent halls. Why don't the Chinese use some of this aesthetic in their contemporary buildings instead of the altogether unattractive lengths of barrack-like structures that are located all over? Obviously the Ministry of Transport in 1957 cannot look like a Ming palace, but there are elements that can be used creatively to furnish a pleasing building. Being functional does not mean lacking an aesthetic. But, of course, there is also the problem of what one chooses from the past. The frequency of Ajanta-type arches and Sanchi gateways introduced into Indian government architecture or kiosks looking like Mughal dome-lets is a case in point.

We were invited for tea at the home of a member of the Indian embassy after a day at the museum. The plan was to go rowing on the Pei Hai Lake after that so I was in slacks and a sloppy joe. We entered the sitting room with its brocade-upholstered sofa and chairs, and a clutter of small and large Indian objects. Tea was served from a leaky silver teapot that poured all over the tray and finally poured into fine eggshell china teacups. Accompanying the tea were tiny mouthful-sized eats. Our host explained that he was rather bored after three years in Beijing with little to do except attend exhibitions and receptions of various kinds, mostly in connection with the new societies emerging in Eastern Europe and such like. I am always puzzled when people living in an entirely different culture complain of being bored. Surely there are new things to observe and think about and perhaps even learn about. I sympathized with his complaint that outsiders are never invited home so there is little scope for friendships of any kind. Friendships would, in any case, be something uncertain given the watchful eyes of the regime. He added, however, that he had invited some Chinese home, such as Lao She, adding that she was the well-known novelist who wrote *Rickshaw Boy*, in case we did not know! But no more about how the evening went or what was talked about, not even as answers to our questions.

He said that we had not seen the essential China since we were in a kind of 'foreign guests cocoon' and I informed him that we were well aware of this and did try to catch a glimpse of Chinese reality wherever we could. The example he then gave us was that we had not seen the beggars, because they do not beg from foreigners but only from the Chinese. But surely we would have seen them doing that even if they were not begging from us? And yet earlier we had been told that the Chinese government was totalitarian because they had forcibly rounded up all the beggars and sent them off to various factories to work. That may well be. But I have seen no beggars. On one passing occasion a small child came up to me and asked for money.

We were then shown a film about contemporary life in China called *Profound Friendship and Love*. The story was about two biochemists who are working in the same laboratory and on the same bacteria. Predictably there is a controversy about the methods that each uses in analysing the material, and they fall apart. Later there is a highly melodramatic event that throws them together again. I kept thinking how it was just like a movie of the Bombay Talkies. The location was in a Westernized part of Shanghai, different from the rest of China, and the photography was quite professional. There were no glitches. I was amused by the way in which references to Pavlov kept popping up even in the scene where a young man is proposing to the woman he is in love with. Love was expressed by holding hands since kissing was not allowed. We were told that the Chinese are very conservative in these matters. I had expected more sophistication in the handling of the theme. The message it seems, was that adopting a new method was sufficient in solving scientific problems. This was naïve if not unscientific in itself. But one could gather that it was an attempt to legitimize new methods since these were being adopted in various ways.

Communism has so far surfaced in huge territorial systems—Russia turning into the Soviet Union, and China—but what shape would it take if it came to far smaller and more developed countries, such as France or Sweden? Will the 'basic contradictions' be eased out? In countries such as Russia, China, India, and those of Eastern Europe there is an emphasis on certain aspects of life while there is a lack of recognition of others. Socialism in such countries can get somewhat hijacked by the jubilation over building to accommodate new ventures and technological development. In countries that are already more developed the challenge would be of a different kind. Not that I deplore the construction work that is going on but it can tend to take precedence over other kinds of required change. Because of the special nature of the period it is the age of scientists and engineers in China. They are the new heroes and have the power required to make the country economically strong, converting the other professions into stepchildren. The question is whether this change is at the expense of not enough attention being given to what we are now calling the social sciences and to new forms in literature and art, and not just in terms of what is written but more as an encouragement to ask multiple questions about the changes wanted and why? The 'why' and the 'how' questions, it seems to me, are fundamental.

The creative arts get to be tabulated and there is talk about infallible systems for writing and painting and composing. Are these effective? Socialist Realism should not mean writing according to a recipe. It means the expression of a social consciousness that may pertain to the totality of a society or to a segment thereof, and if it is the latter then it should not be confused with the totality. Paradise scenes of the Song period may not be as literal as a contemporary painting showing a group of miners and labelled 'The Proletariat', nevertheless there is a consciousness albeit of a limited kind. The consciousness is something quite personal and cannot be legislated.

So far so good in China. Lu Xun is a hero, Lao She is the leading novelist, Gou Moruo knows what he is about as minister for education since he himself is what they refer to as 'a man of culture'. I have no doubt that as long as they are respected, the Party line on these matters will remain elastic. They cannot afford to antagonize the leading writers and artists. Qi Bai Shi was venerated when alive and when he died ten days ago was given a state funeral. We don't know what may happen in another ten years when another rank of writers will come to the fore who have perhaps not been so close to the initial Communist movement as to forgive it its trespasses. They will demand intellectual freedom that exists elsewhere in varying degrees of free expression. Will they be required to conform to the single accepted technique and produce a book as directed or will they be allowed to gradually evolve their own form of Socialist Realism or quite something else? Obviously the problem is not so acute for scientists and engineers unless a Chinese Lysenko surfaces, and I can't see that happening in a hurry. But it is a real problem for creative artists and writers as well as for academics. Will they stand firm? These problems surface not just where Leftist regimes are in power but equally with Rightist regimes built to support a particular ideological structure.

I get the feeling that the last three months of rectification campaigns and self-analyses have been a period of crisis, although they do not speak about it. The change to a Communist government cannot be easy, therefore some upset is to be expected. The Communist Party it would appear has been relatively restrained and has not tightened the reins too much, although we have had only the barest acquaintance with what is going on. Perhaps the Ministry of Culture will realize that works of art cannot be produced to political and government order. There is a different criterion for them.

We drove to the Ming tombs and had a picnic lunch that the hotel had packed for us—a Russian taste with chunks of brown bread, lots of salami and gherkins; and with Chinese thoughtfulness there were two toothpicks in each packet. The tombs are a series of spectacular monuments set in an open plain with blue and purple mountains in the distance. The approach is through an avenue lined with marble animals and human figures—lions, elephants, camels, horses, mythical beasts, generals, and statesmen. In the centre, we moved from hall to pavilion and what a juxtaposition of colours. The roofs were again of yellow and green tiles supported by red pillars and decorated with the finesse of Ming style. Initially, I was not so taken with the monuments but as I saw more of them, they seemed to fit in with the surroundings. There was one particularly beautiful tomb offset by the mellow green of pine trees and broad-leaved chestnuts against the red wall. The surrounding gardens were well kept and full of autumn flowers, the stone pathways sprayed with fallen autumn leaves, and then there was a view of the shrine itself, rising out of a cluster of trees on the hill behind.

Standing on the terrace of the tomb, I was struck again by the subtlety of earlier Chinese architecture. It has, of course, the same precision and orderliness that classical architecture has the world over. It is lucid, get-at-able, and comprehensible in its obvious qualities of careful planning; building follows building in a well-defined order; symmetrical placing is important, yet not in a lifeless, routine way but through the compulsion of producing a place that has meaning. Despite its being grandiose at times, and overwhelming at others, it chooses to ignore the pomposity that sometimes mars the Roman buildings or the plethora of decoration that covers later period buildings in India. The classical always carries the essence of subtlety. Nevertheless, this architecture brings a feeling of being aloof even when it seems to be at ease with the landscape around it. Perhaps it is to be seen in fragments, drop by drop, and not visualized as a monolithic whole.

We drove back through the outer fringe of Beijing. The blocks and barracks of the new buildings in the suburbs began to look a trifle offensive. We returned in the early twilight, a particularly beautiful light in autumn that comes quite soon in these latitudes. The city was on the move with people returning home. Office workers cycling it seemed by the hundreds occupying a major part of the road; many were walking along the pavements. It must have been a small city in earlier days with its narrow lanes and little shops. Now one sees expansion all around and a suffusion of people in blue jackets and on the whole cheerful faces. Slowly a dust haze gathered over the city and the air became a little chilly. I was reminded of early winter evenings in Delhi.

More clashing cymbals and clappers and Chinese tones at yet another regional opera that we went to. This was from Hebei and seemed somewhat similar to Peking opera. The story goes back to pre-modern times and tells of a princess who falls in love with a flute-playing shepherd and is imprisoned for doing so by her father, the king. This is almost a stereotype in herding societies where the hero is a shepherd, as with our Heer-Ranjha in the Punjab, except that Ranjha was unsuccessful. Here the hero brings the sea to a boil with three magical objects, thus threatening the kingdom, so the king releases his daughter and lets her marry the shepherd. The story was clearly a suitable one! The theatre was a hall with quite comfortable wooden seats and a bare floor. The man sitting next to me had three packets of dried melon seeds and right through the performance I could hear the cracking of the seeds. Apparently this was the customary thing to do in the old Chinese theatres along with drinking green tea. The three cronies sitting behind us made comments throughout the performance, just about audible, some of them quite amusing and in broken English so obviously intended for us. So we chatted with them in the interval. Audience reaction was more fulsome than in other performances I noticed.

Spent an afternoon with Mingo and joined by Pat as we walked along the oldest commercial street in the oldest part of the city. The street was so narrow that two pedicabs could barely get through. The shop windows are gaily and fully decorated, in fact stuffed to capacity with almost everything one could think of. Rows of silk shops, brocade shops, shops selling padded clothing now that winter is approaching, shoes by the hundred from three-inch shoes for erstwhile bound feet to large sizes for men. A delicatessen shop had dried litchis and salami of various kinds. Shops with musical instruments where lots of erhus rubbed necks with fiddles, rows of horns jostling among the Japanese banjos—the tashitoshikoto that I used to play as a child in Rawalpindi.

We stumbled into another shop where we fell over reproductions, posters, and calligraphic displays and where I could have happily spent many hours. But I did spend time in selecting some superb pieces of calligraphy in black ink on rice paper. These were the loveliest gifts for friends and so easy to carry, apart from the sheer joy of just looking at them. I did lay them out in my hotel room for the remaining few days, and eventually decided that I would not give them away. There were many laundry shops with their large steam irons and where one was being used, the other was put on to 'roast' with this going on turn by turn and not requiring electricity. There was a tailor's shop, chaotic with sewing machines and half-sewn clothes hanging everywhere, and every now and again, an old face with a white two-strand beard and spectacles balanced on the nose would appear from behind the clothes, peer at us and disappear.

Open fruit stalls with orange and red persimmons on the side of the road. People squatted in open spaces with a variety of things spread out on a sheet in front of them—from Ming coins to polished walnuts. The latter came from aristocratic families of olden days when elderly men sat on easy chairs and spent hours in thought, accompanied by rubbing two walnuts together and in the process polished them. What a wonderful pastime. Another stall had a small collection of comic books. When I asked if I could buy two of them I was told they were not for sale. It was in effect a lending library and I could borrow a couple and return them next week. The subjects ranged from old legends and stories about the Great Wall to biographies of those who were now regarded as icons of work, especially labour—the equivalent of the Russian Stakhanovite.

We also stumbled into an old apothecary's shop selling traditional medicines with its strong, sharp smell of spices and herbs. There was a long counter following the lines of an oval room behind which stood white-coated men putting sticks and herbs into various packets. Behind them the wall was lined with small drawers about 6 inches by 6 inches in size from which they kept pulling out things. I recognized some of the ingredients as being the same that we use such as malatthi, ajwain, hing. There were sliced dried mushrooms of various kinds. Behind the corner at one end sat the doctor, old, partially bald, with a beard and strikingly bright eyes, whom I insisted on consulting. So I went with Mingo and asked him what I should do about the pimples that I get on my face. He looked at me good-humouredly, smiled and told me why people get pimples, and then pre-scribed some pills. Unfortunately there was such a long queue at the prescription counter that we decided not to wait around and carried on.

Further along we came across a covered passageway and I suggested that we go in. A large man appeared from a side door and beamed at me so

I asked him what the place was. He replied that it was an old inn dating back to the Qing period and asked if I would like to see it. Of course, I would, I replied, to some consternation on the part of Mingo and Pat. So we walked from the entrance into the courtyard surrounded by rooms, each numbered and with windows shaded by wooden trellis work all painted the same red colour as the pillars of the courtyard. There was a tap in one corner, a huge tap like the sort we have in Indian gardens and near it was a large vat of clear water. To one side of it was a cubbyhole with a big stove on which was placed the large steamer with rice bowls.

Up a few steps was another courtyard with the same room arrangement. I went into one room, a small sparsely furnished room with bare walls. The bed was a trestle-bed like the ones we had in Maijishan. The place had a distinctively Chinese air to it, or was I imagining it; as I also imagined that if I had come fifty years earlier it would have been an experience—but maybe not. In the early 1900s, I would have stayed at such a place with its pots of flowers in the courtyard and the chatty innkeeper who talked all the time while we wandered about. We came to the third courtyard where they were sifting coal under an oak-like tree that had a pumpkin creeper going around and up it. I could smell the lavatory in the vicinity and that rather put a full stop to my imagining staying there fifty years ago. We asked how much it would cost to stay and the amount quoted was ridiculously little. Modern hotels everywhere in the world lack this charm even if they are more comfortable. The innkeeper invited us to take tea with him but we wandered on.

At the end of the road, Pat stopped before an open door and said, 'So this is where it is.' It was a restaurant where he had been brought for dinner two nights ago but having been driven here in a pedicab he could not recall its whereabouts. It was a famous Beijing restaurant run by Chinese Muslims. Presumably these were Muslims that had come from Xinjiang and may even have been descendants of the Uyghurs. I suggested going in and having a cup of tea but Mingo said they would only serve a meal. So I walked up to the man at the door and asked if we could have a cup of tea which he refused vigorously. I pleaded with him and explained that we were very tired as we had walked the length of the street all afternoon, and that we had heard so much about the restaurant and just wanted to spend a few minutes inside. He paused and then stood aside and waved us in.

It was well worthwhile. It was an open courtyard now being washed and gotten ready for the evening. It had wooden cubicles all around it, the pillars and trellis-work being painted red and a beautiful tiled roof. Outside the kitchen was a line of pewter pots. A cook was chopping up a large hunk of meat and next to him was another chopping onions. It seemed that there were going to be burrah kababs for dinner. We sat at tables whose colour of natural wood matched the surroundings. We noticed a central heating radiator in one corner. Beijing is only too familiar with the cold winds from Mongolia that blow in during winter. We sipped jasmine-scented tea from small cups—rather different from the green tea with the faintest of fragrance served in large mugs elsewhere. We sat there chatting for a long while.

We've just returned from a state reception hosted by Zhou Enlai to welcome all the foreign delegates and guests for the National Day. It was a huge affair with many thousand people. We were driven in a large, comfortable car through streets lined with large numbers of Chinese just standing to get a glimpse of the cars. I kept thinking that they must be resenting the fact that they only get to cycle or to ride in buses and trams, while the cars are all for 'foreign guests' and the top brass of the Communist Party. The Peking Hotel, where the reception was hosted, was the Leningradskya all over again— garish floral designs and much use of gilt. Various delegations were introduced and applauded. Indians were welcomed and thanked for their support of China. The speech then went on to mention that the targets of the Five-Year Plans had been exceeded at which there was the expected loud applause and now China was moving even further forward.

I stood there hanging onto a glass of red wine and helping myself to a dish with small eats mainly tasting of a rather delicious quince. We were introduced to the actress who had taken the lead in the presentation of Kalidasa's *Shakuntala* in Chinese, and she was warmly embraced by Mrs Rajan Nehru, the wife of the Indian Ambassador. Everyone was bubbling over with affection. I had a brief conversation with Xia Nai who gave the impression of being a little uncomfortable in these surroundings. Joan Robinson, the economist, fresh from Cambridge, murmured some interesting asides on the Chinese Five-Year Plan that seemed to differ somewhat from what had been announced. And then there were the two boring young Indian lawyers who had attended the Moscow Youth Festival—their first outing outside India. They were determined to tell us that they had had such a good time in Moscow and we could guess what that meant.

What did give me much pleasure was the chance to chat very briefly with the actress Du Jin-fang of the Peking opera. She is a petite, very elegant, and quite exquisite person, obviously sophisticated, who was dressed in white satin offset with minimal embroidery on the jacket, and ample lipstick on a face framed with shining black hair. She has noticeably beautiful hands with finely manicured red nails and a ring with a single small diamond. Her not so small feet were in gold sandals. She has a soft, gentle voice and moves with a rare grace. Our brief conversation was about women who sang in the tradition of classical music in India. She is the pupil of the great actor Mei Lanfang whom I had hoped that we might see in a performance before leaving China. Soon after this there was a farewell toast that we all drank and promptly tumbled out of the Peking Hotel and into our posh cars and back to our own hotels.

I had invited one of Cedric Dover's friends from the Academia Sinica to lunch. He was the second one among those whom I had invited. Unlike the first one, the second accepted and arrived. He was easy to talk with, interested as he was in many aspects of the world around him apart from his own specialization. I complained about the endless rectification meetings. He was good-humoured about this and agreed that too much time was being spent on these and therefore work suffered. He explained what happened at these meetings. For example, if a person suggested that the social and economic aspects of a subject should be treated separately from other basic aspects, then his ideas would be discussed at one of these meetings, but they could be dismissed as anti-progressive. If so, his methodology would be said to be Rightist.

I mentioned that a discussion on methodology would be a routine matter in all courses in European universities, carried out as part of teaching, and would not demand a special rectification meeting focusing on the teacher. He did mention that measures taken against the methodology of the person thus being rectified were not severe. He would usually be given a brushing-down and told to mend his thinking apparatus. By severe, I suppose one has to think in terms of Russian severity where people could be imprisoned for life for such offences. It is only when a person is proved to be a Rightist in more than one aspect of his thinking that he is in for tough brainwashing or punishment. That might explain why a couple of the others whom I wanted to meet were not available. But the person I was speaking with seemed to speak fairly freely.

We talked at greater length about the emerging of the social sciences. The change came after World War II. But the big problem, he said, was a lack of the required books and the fall in the number of academics who could read English as the advanced language of their research. It has now become compulsory for anyone doing research to know at least one European language and most have a reading knowledge of English or Russian. This, he said, was the only way that they can keep up with advances in various fields. An area that was demanding much attention now was the question of how national minorities fit into the overall social and political structure and this involves their working out a new relationship with the state, a relationship that would ensure the equal status of all.

There is a bottleneck in the middle schools as there are not enough such schools since universal education has been enforced only recently. Many specialists on school education are being consulted to find the best way of making school education meaningful. He spoke of the problems both social and psychological that people had in making this transition from a traditional to a modern society and the resulting individual maladjustment. The theories of Freud are being discussed although the solution is often thought to lie in the change to a socialist society where some of the earlier obstacles can be and are being swept aside.

I was sorry that the scholars I wanted to meet were not available either because everyone was busy with the National Day or they were individually busy with the analyses and rectification that they were being put through. I was particularly sorry not to have met and talked with various historians whom I had been anxious to meet. But one evening I was told that Professor Zhang and his wife, who was a scholar of Classical Chinese, would be coming to meet us. I was delighted. But my eagerness was spoilt by the rooted presence of a couple of China enthusiasts from Britain who joked endlessly and pointlessly about certain French scholars of Chinese studies, and then went into a long harangue on the English and French working class. I tried desperately to bring the conversation around to our Chinese guests but each time I was buffeted off course by the obsession with the European working class. Had I been on my own this would never have happened.

My irritation with this must have been expressed without my noticing it because Professor Zhang quietly announced that they were taking us to his mother's house as he and his wife lived rather far away on campus. I couldn't believe my luck. The house was home to a middle-class family. It was not built in traditional style around a courtyard but stood as a three-storeyed building in the midst of others. The furnishings were as expected. The living room had a sofa and two ample and comfortably padded arm-chairs, around a circular table with a lace doily beneath a glass top. A tall stool in the corner held a vase of flowers. A small table next to an easy chair had a radio and had three smaller tables fitting into it. Family photographs were everywhere and filled every space as well they could with eleven siblings and appropriate progeny. The meal was enormous and served by a woman who seemed to be a maid. A large refrigerator stood on one side of the dining room and I noticed a number of electric gadgets that spoke of a comfortable life. Judging by the number of people that were peeping at us through a side door, I assumed they were members of the extended family. The ambience was very much that of a comfortable middle-class home in a metropolis in India.

Professor Zhang's mother was over eighty years old, but still physically strong and a staunch Buddhist. She was vegetarian but this did not stop her from allowing meat dishes to be served at dinner. She maintained a small private shrine in another part of the house. She had the air of a matriarch as do some widowed middle-class women in India. The family it seems was largely of professional people who would have had a comfortable living before the revolution and to a slightly lesser extent were continuing to do so. Professor Zhang's wife knew English well so the conversation went from subject to subject. Through her I managed to ask some of the questions about Chinese history and the study of the Classics that had been bothering me. Her answers to my questions about historical interpretations were somewhat hesitant and she explained that this was because she was not a historian. I was pleased that there was awareness of what was involved in being a historian. As a Classicist, she was concerned that there was a little less attention given to the Chinese Classics in the new curriculum. My couple of hesitant attempts to comment on politics were hastily brushed aside. Many of my private observations were being indirectly confirmed.

The next day was 2 October. Mahatma Gandhi's birth anniversary was being celebrated in the Indian embassy, so we went along. There were speeches of no consequence on the Father of the Nation. One had the impression that the routine was the usual annual activity without much effort at change, as is so often the case with such functions. However, later over tea Joan Robinson was asked to speak informally on the Chinese economy and she was both educative and entertaining. Being a professor of economics from Cambridge University she was held in awe but nevertheless was asked endless questions. She answered with great good humour and, as was required, at a basic level of economic understanding. She kept it all to common sense explanations especially when speaking about agricultural cooperatives that are not all that easy to organize.

The National Day was observed with immense enthusiasm and good cheer. The huge morning parade went on for more than three hours, far too long in many ways. Why have huge military parades become so central to celebrating national days? Some of the parade underlines a military statement that seems unnecessary on the occasion. Much of the parade, like ours, was a predictable series of spectacles but of a reasonably high order. However, there were differences. There was a mammoth procession of workers from various factories which went on for over an hour. Following this were pageants of the arts and demonstrations of culture. National minorities, as they are called, were performing their folk dances in their own costumes and waving paper and cloth dragons and various other mythical animals. This was a familiar item. There was a tremendous juxtaposition of a variety of colours.

Then came contingent after contingent of athletes associated with a wide range of sports. The sides of the huge square were filled with masses of schoolchildren arranged in ranks waving huge colourful paper flowers beneath equally huge portraits of earlier 'great men' that were referred to as the 'ancestors' and concluding with Sun Yat-sen and Mao Zedong. Mao stood on the balcony of the Gate of Heavenly Peace and waved to the crowds. We stood in the special enclosure for foreign guests. We had set out quite early driving through half-empty streets with a few clusters of people who looked at the car and us, and turned away. Were they resentful of these foreigners who drove by in luxurious cars? I myself felt unhappy about being a pampered guest in a situation where so many still lived with degrees of poverty. The enthusiasm of the crowds was electric and seemed to scoop up all those who were there, experiencing it no doubt as fun and games. But an unkind thought did cross my mind as it often does on such occasions elsewhere as well: there is a thin line dividing mass enthusiasm from mass hysteria.

At the place where we were stationed the arrangements for car parks, refreshments, and toilets were excellent. I could only marvel at how much attention had gone into the details. The discipline of those associated with handling the crowds was also impressive. We drove back to the hotel after the show was over and the streets were still half-empty since many had gone to the major streets where the processions were due to pass through.

By the evening I decided that I had had enough of special treatment and wanted to mingle with the crowds. So I took off my sari and got into my slacks and peasant jacket and asked Pat if he would like to join me. We worked our way through dense crowds and finally after more than half an hour got to the square to see the fireworks. These were a little disappointing as they were like the ones in Paris on 14 July. I was expecting to see golden dragons and red phoenixes falling out of the sky especially as I heard so much about the Chinese genius with fireworks. Many groups were dancing in the square with their own small bands of music and we kept getting caught into having to dance before we were allowed to go. Then there was an insistence that we sing. This was a problem since Pat was Australian and could only sing 'Waltzing Matilda' which I barely knew, and he had no idea of any Indian songs. So we tried 'Waltzing Matilda' and then I broke into 'Awaara Hoon'. This was an instant hit with many people joining in.

What amazed me was that in this huge square with much dancing and singing there did not seem to be any obvious unpleasantness. I remember that three years previously, when we were holidaying in Avignon in southern France, celebrating 14 July, I had a terrible time as an obvious foreigner being pushed around. But Pat who understood colloquial Chinese said that all the comments were either complimentary or were questions arising out of curiosity. A group of young soldiers joined in and were teased by the girls but took it very well.

The loudspeakers were blaring out an assortment of music. I could recognize some Cossack songs, a part of the Katachurian violin concerto (that I happened to like very much), Viennese waltzes, a Bengali folk song that seemed a little out of place, all interspersed with snatches of Peking opera. We wandered around for a couple of hours going from group to group after which we took the main road to the centre of the city. Buildings were decorated with banners, flags, red lanterns, and large posters of Chinese characters written up in black and white. We walked into a large and rather grubby looking restaurant with fat waiters dressed in white aprons and caps, yelling orders down to the kitchen. We sat at a wooden trestle table and ordered some local wine with our dumplings. People kept coming in, wolfing down bowls of hot food, and leaving in the midst of tremendous bustle, excitement, and movement. There were army men with their young women, and university students, and a fair number of grand-mothers holding babies and small children, and couples.

We sat there and looked and listened sipping our cheap wine—hardly two shillings for a half-litre bottle. I suppose it was just a cut better than what one would get in an Indian city if one asked for tharrah, country liquor. Wine is incredibly cheap in China and generally of a high alcoholic percentage and yet one hardly sees drunks in the streets, as we could have where the crowds were really thick—rather like New Year's Eve elsewhere— and presumably people had been drinking. Is all the hard-drinking done at home so that drunks don't wander around on the streets, or have the Chinese authorities achieved the impossible of making liquor available and yet keeping drunkenness more or less at bay?

We were sorry to leave this most interesting restaurant when it closed at midnight. We tried to get a bus but nothing was available so we had to walk it and a fiercely long walk it was too. I didn't want to take a pedicab. We passed the square where we had been earlier and it was beginning to thin out. At the other end there was a tram just starting up so we raced to it and caught it with just a moment to spare and received the applause of those already seated in it. We arrived at our hotel with a driveway filled with luxury cars—Chevrolets, Buicks, Russian Taksicars, and Czech Škodas, all lined up row upon row, their chromium glistening in the sharp light of the half-moon. The 'foreign guests' were having an early night. All of them had not been dancing in the streets!

I can't believe that in a few days I shall be flying out of China and on my way home. This extraordinary journey is coming to an end just when I am beginning to feel that I am getting some inkling of the place. In a reverse procedure it was towards the end of our stay that we drove fifty miles to Choukotien (as Zhoukoudian was then known) the site where the Peking Man—Sinanthropus Pekinisus—was found. Such prehistoric sites have a similarity of landscape and natural formations. I could have been at the site of Le Moustier or of Cro-Magnon. Doubtless to the expert they are quite distinctive. As with many prehistoric sites in China there is always something contemporary in the vicinity. Here there was a modern limestone quarry at the foot of the hillock that housed the cave where the Peking Man was found, and a small museum as well. As it happened I was reading a few short articles on prehistoric China by contemporary Chinese archaeologists. Most articles ended with a statement as to how right Friedrich Engels was. This was post-Liberation.

The evening was both pleasant and fruitful. I had invited the Curator of the Palace Museum for dinner under the assumption that he was a historian of ancient China and had my battery of questions ready. He answered the questions as best he could and revealed that he was a specialist in natural history! This I had not been told. But somehow we soon got onto talking about silk and we were immersed in the history and development of silk-weaving in Sichuan. From there we spoke about the tonal system in the Chinese language. He soon had me chanting what I remembered of Shastriji in Pune having taught me of chanting a hymn from the *Rigveda*. There was nothing comparable in the two systems. I can't think of what the people at the next table thought I was reciting. But his incisive mind and wide reading enabled him to speak on a range of subjects, and yet with modesty that prevented him from sounding conceited or boastful.

What amazed me was that he was informed yesterday that I wanted to discuss a few topics with him today so he was phoned as soon as we got back, and he came right away. I felt deeply embarrassed by his being summoned in this manner—another example of how governments and bureaucracies in our countries show so little respect for academics. I am not surprised that some of them say they are too busy to meet 'foreign guests'. I would probably feel the same way. I should have been the one going to his office to meet him. And then I thought that perhaps coming out to dine with us may have been a change for him. Who knows?

Much later in the evening, Mingo and I went to see a lovely Hebei puppet performance. They were stick puppets rather like the Javanese but of a much simpler design. They are made of sandpaper, cardboard or celluloid, and dressed in cloth or paper. The shadow is coloured by a strong light and then reflected on the screen in the midst of a fanciful décor. The stories are taken from the Chinese classics, epics, folk tales, fables, and fairy stories and are therefore familiar to the audience. Some were taken from the travels of Xuan Zang, and I have discovered that the Chinese audiences treat his work rather like the way we treat the *Mahabharata*—the well of stories. The theatre was a small, intimate hall in the heart of the Ren Min bazaar. The approach was extremely complicated via back alleys, market lanes, and past some Ming buildings in brick and red-coloured wood. It was obviously the haunt of puppet lovers. The puppeteers handled their puppets to perfection and were quite ready to teach me when I went backstage to see the puppets.

I have had hardly any sleep these last five nights. The night before last I was up till 2 a.m. talking to Pat and Anil. It was sad and somewhat shattering after our time and work in China to now come to terms with what is another aspect of what is happening. I had phoned a few people I had met in Beijing to say goodbye. One of them told me that there was something in the paper about Professor Xiang Da that would be of interest to me, since I had wanted to meet him to discuss Dunhuang. So I got the paper and asked Pat to read the relevant portion. It was an article by another historian explaining why Xiang Da had been accused of being a 'Rightist'.

I knew by now that to be accused of being a 'Rightist' is the end. What really shocked me were the charges that were brought against him in view of what one hears about Chinese Communism being liberal and adopting the middle way. He was charged with not accepting the interpretation of history as authorized by the government; and he is said to have remarked that a hundred flowers were not blooming in the field of historical thought in China today, as is claimed, but only five, and that these were not sufficient since they all said much the same thing; and he had criticized another historian who had written a new preface to his book on the history of Buddhist thought in China, where this historian had confessed that by applying Marxist thought to his study he had found many errors in his own work, and which he had, therefore, corrected—but this statement was only made in the preface, since the main text of the second edition of the book had remained unchanged.

The implication of this was that the rectification undergone by the historian was superficial. The ideology of the government cannot be questioned or criticized. And the next step is that the government itself cannot be criticized. But this is the behaviour of autocratic and dictatorial governments. In Chinese history, Qin Shi Huang was the emperor who burnt books and killed scholars who had views different from his. Some supposedly advanced modern regimes did revert to those practices as in the fascist governments of Italy and Germany. They attacked the intellectuals they disapproved of by calling them Leftists and arrested them for criticizing the government.

I can now understand why some of these historians did not wish to see me or had no time to see me—perhaps they were busy trying to defend themselves against similar accusations. According to the newspaper report, Xiang Da was condemned about a month ago. I was unaware of this and, of course, no one mentioned it when I asked to see him and some others. When the more outspoken people are accused of having the wrong views then naturally the less outspoken ones, who don't have a strong spine, fall in line. I couldn't find out whether there has been a follow-up of the rectification campaign by exploring the complexities of Chinese society from either Marxist or from other perspectives. Perhaps there was but I wouldn't know as this was not discussed. Other literary persons are also under attack including Ding Ling, the novelist, who remains a much-respected writer.

Dictatorships, whether of the Left or the Right, require ideologies to legitimize their power, and those that question these ideologies tend to be silenced or removed. Dictatorships are unhappy when their ideologies are freely debated. In this regard we are in currently a better position in India as there is developing a range of worthwhile studies of Indian history across the spectrum of theory that are beginning to trigger intensive debates. We do not have to conform to any official ideology. Fortunately, so far at least, we are not a dictatorship, whether of a person or a party.

This aspect of the current campaign in China is disturbing as it implicitly will not allow a hundred flowers to bloom. It is the systematic building up of a movement based on hate, and this is another requirement of dictatorship. The campaign against certain persons for the way in which they think is accompanied by stirring up hate against them. Posters, inevitably rather nasty, are put up everywhere attempting to justify what is being done. For some, this kind of populism would take away from the seriousness of the argument. It becomes a tool in the hands of those who claim to be defining what the correct practice and the right ideology are. In the course of conversation, the occasional person has said that it is necessary to prevent a Hungary happening in China. So far there have been no tanks and no bloodshed. But will it stop at this? Was it not the same in the USSR, where the early days looked good but eventually the thirties did come?

I am fearful of what may happen in the coming future. Seen as a totality it is possible to appreciate the attitude of the government in seeking to improve conditions and wanting support and loyalty to do so, but are the methods adopted invariably above question? What is thought to be above question also becomes debatable. Need one be so averse to facing criticism? It only leads to silence all around, a silence that muffles discontent. People are too intimidated to speak and when that happens then the dictatorship becomes absolute. The fundamental purpose of a socialist society is then lost. Admittedly, rooted attitudes can be an obstacle to social change but how these are to be tackled has to be thought of with some sensitivity. These are all impossibly difficult questions to solve and cannot be solved without careful thought. It is important that mistakes be corrected as soon as they are recognized so that they are not allowed to fester. Perhaps I am being too pessimistic but I do feel it will be such a terrible shame if dictatorship prevails, since much of the rest of what is happening in China in terms of actively building a better society seems so worthwhile. Political criticism is more unaccountable when it is crushed.

Being in Beijing brings one up-to-date with contemporary China. It becomes more apparent here than it is in the places where we have been working, perhaps because it is politically imminent in the capital. The change in those distant areas is less burdened with political icons and theories and there seems to be more of leeway for flexibility and negotiation. I could be wrong in making this assessment but that is what I think.

There was a banquet at the Indian embassy to celebrate President Radhakrishnan's official visit to China. It was not as dreary as I had feared. There was a galaxy of important people—half the names of whom did not register with me. But then there they were—the greats—Mao Zedong, Zhou Enlai, Zhu De, the lot, who I did not know would be there. We were seated at a table located to the side of the podium so I had a chance to observe them for quite some time. Mao looks exactly like his photographs, big and round, but I noticed that he has an impassive facial expression—strong but unreadable. Zhou Enlai has a far more open expression and his face registers changes.

I could barely contain my excitement as we were taken to the platform where they stood with the Indian Ambassador R. K. Nehru, and, turn by turn, we shook hands with them. Was I really shaking hands with Mao or was I imagining all this? It was like shaking hands with history! But his face remained quite impassive with what I suppose I had imagined was the barest hint of a smile. I can understand people like him finding it a chore to be standing there and shaking hands with dozens of people and thinking of it as meaningless. Zhou had obviously been reminded that we were the ones who had been working at Dunhuang. He gave us a broad smile, an interested look, and enquired if we had had a successful visit in studying what we had set out to study. I could happily have discussed the caves of Dunhuang with him. I remember being told that he was a good friend of Joseph Needham and had closely followed Needham's ideas and discussion in the study of science and civilization in China.

We returned to our table and I sat there looking at them and thinking about the difference between the two men. One has had an extraordinary political effect and has become iconic both for his supporters and those in conflict with him, whereas the other seems to have a more humanistic range of concerns and was certainly the one I found more 'sympathique'. Mao is undoubtedly extremely popular as everywhere we went, we were constantly told that Mao would bring in a better society and that people were looking forward to the future with him encapsulating governance. The song about him is symptomatic: 'Out of the east comes the sun and out of the east comes Mao Tsedong'—sung by many and almost invariably when anyone is asked to sing. This worries me. So much adulation inevitably brings its own reversal to a smaller or a larger degree. More than that the promise that is held out is so enormous that it gets converted into a magic potion. It diverts attention from that which has to be done in a humanly possible way.

Mao today is iconic in many parts of the world, not only as an enigma in politics hinging on the question whether he will be able to build a new kind of socialist society, but even beyond that as an icon of opening up perceptions to new ways of thinking. Is this for real or is it the romanticizing of an icon? Many questions went through my mind as I sat there observing him. Was this the man who gave priority to the peasantry and converted it into a proletariat in order to bring about a revolution? Was this the hero who led the long march that virtually ushered in the Chinese revolution? He did not argue for a return to a past utopia, to reviving a golden age, because his vision in his writings was of an ideal society of the future. I wondered how exactly he visualized it and how different was his vision from that of so many other revolutionaries the world over. I wondered whether he would succeed and, if so, then to what extent and in what manner? Endless questions, so difficult to find answers.

Dinner was served in a vast dining hall and we all sat at small tables each for about half a dozen people. We had the Reuters correspondent at our table, unmistakeably an English person in speech and manner, he has been in China for eighteen months, and is writing two books on China virtually simultaneously. He knows no Chinese so is entirely dependent on interpreters, but he travels and each time quickly returns to his hotel in Beijing and describes what he has observed. Predictably he is regarded outside China as a 'China expert'. It does seem rather easy to become that. He spoke about the discontent among the younger Chinese, especially among those who were not training to be scientists or engineers but wanted to study a subject in one of the humanities. For this the scope was limited and the articulation restricted. According to him, there has also been criticism of the Communist Party. It first invited a critical view of its policy but followed it up by calling the critics 'Rightists' and condemning them. Nevertheless, some that did criticize the Party are now well-established in the system. He mentioned that all citizens have to register with the police.

I thought to myself quietly, that obviously a hundred flowers were not blooming, as indeed one did not expect them to. There has clearly been much turmoil over the rectification campaigns but I really don't know enough to judge the veracity of these views of our fellow guest. I would like to talk with younger Chinese about these issues but alas I don't know the language. This assessment that he gave us was based on information through interpreters. I wonder if he had first investigated his interpreters, as indeed one has to do if one is dependent on them. Were they reflecting their own views? Were they reporting back all that was discussed to the government? Presumably the government would have been informed as to whom he had interviewed and probably more so those who had dissented from the official line.

But the lighter side of the evening was the catching up on Indian news from the two air force officers that were part of the President's entourage and who were seated at our table. We discovered many common friends as Indians often do when they meet outside India. And then there is always someone whose father knows my father and so on. We chatted as if we had known each other for years. One of them gallantly agreed to carry back to Delhi all the records of music that I had collected, and especially the set of Peking opera with Mei Lan Fang singing the lead role in *The Drunken Beauty*; and the few objects that would not travel easily such as my erhu which I was beginning to play without producing the most awful screeches.

The speeches at the banquet were fortunately short and as expected quite cliché-ridden. Radhakrishan spoke about the coexistence of Confucianism, Daoism, and Buddhism at a particular point in Chinese history, and compared it with the current coexistence of socialism, rationalism, and humanism in China: in sum, a fairly innocuous speech. We all rose and drank a gambei to his words in a mixture of grape and apple juice, since Indian embassies do not serve alcohol. The strong lights of the photographers' spotlights faded as we sat down to our chopsticks and bowls. It was all very formal and after we finished eating an Indian film, *Kabuliwala*, was shown with dialogue in Bengali. Mao and Zhou had, by then, left. When the film ended the banquet was over and we all departed almost in order of rank.

Spent the next day at the Institute of Archaeology again and had long conversations with the director and a couple of others on their proposed study of the two sites that we had worked at. Dunhuang was particularly important and they were setting up a major research centre near the site. I recall the director having been very diffident when we had first met him on our arrival. But now he was most forthcoming and provided us with details of the proposed work. I wondered why there had been such a marked change in his attitude towards us. Either, they were all going through meetings two months ago and felt harassed and were preoccupied with other things and these had by now been sorted out, or they had figured out that we were not just having a jaunt in China but had put in some serious work at the two sites. He too spoke in English today whereas previously he had stuck to Chinese and conversed through an interpreter. He mentioned that they had plans to excavate the tomb of Qin Shi Huang, the first emperor of China, and that they were expecting it to be as spectacular as the tomb of Tutankhamun.

The following afternoon one of the officials linked to the Archaeological Department, with whom we had been unable to discuss our plans before we started out on our journey, was in the hotel dining room with some friends. He came up to us and chatted cheerfully in excellent English and enquired about our visits to the Buddhist cave sites. He suggested that we meet for dinner to discuss the work we had done. I almost fell through the chair. On one of our first evenings in Beijing he had presided over the small brief reception that had been given to welcome us, when he spoke entirely through an interpreter claiming that he knew no English, and was extremely formal, if not distant. I could only explain this mystery by his having been under stress at that time if he was undergoing rectification.

It was also then that I asked to see the director of the Institute of National Minorities to whom I had an introduction from a friend in London. I was informed that he was too busy and did not have the time to see anyone these days. I don't believe that he would have been so impolite so I have assumed that he too is on the mat. Again I wished that I knew Chinese and could perhaps follow a little more precisely as to what was going on instead of making guesses. In the given circumstances of a lack of communication one can only guess the direction of politics in China at this time, and I could be mistaken in how I am interpreting conversations and activities.

We got talking casually over breakfast with a British journalist who said he had visited China fairly frequently and claimed to know it well enough. I raised the questions that I had been asking, of not getting to meet people. He had his own version of what was going on in China and the 'meetings'. His explanation was the stock one—that in the context of society one has to consider the totality of the good achieved before passing judgement on a system. The contradiction lies in who has freedom—the many or the privileged few? Freedom in the abstract is non-existent.

This was a view I was familiar with. I thought he oversimplified the Chinese situation by saying that the Rightists want abstract freedom, as in America and England, and for him that was asking for what did not exist even in America and Europe for most people. He had suffered under this fantasy of abstract freedom in America through his experience of McCarthyism. But I was arguing that a distinction has to be made between those wanting the kinds of freedoms that supposedly existed in other parts of the world irrespective of local conditions, and those who were more focused on having the right to criticize the party in power and the freedom of expression and speech—hence the possibility of the hundred flowers blooming and the schools of thought contending. How does one draw up a balance sheet of the present system? We are told that so much has been gained in other spheres of life, that one must set aside for the moment the right to freedom of thought and speech. The obvious danger is that once set aside it might remain forever absent.

Absolute and complete freedom for each individual is unrealistic since freedom has always been a matter of degree, and then too dependent on so many other factors. The atmosphere here appears to be healthier and perhaps more optimistic than what it was in Russia, judging from the histories of the early years of the Russian revolution. For the present, I might perhaps give China the benefit of the doubt but I am anxious about the future. Either the Soviet pattern will be replicated or China will have to solve the contradiction in a better way than in other socialist countries. The recent discussions on the Twentieth Congress of the Communist Party in the Soviet Union and Khrushchev's statements are still fresh in my mind. I am impressed by what we saw as the improvements in daily life for many, and one hopes that such improvements do actually extend to the many, an assessment that we could not make. He was confident that the Soviet imprint on Chinese culture would wear off once the economic dependence for 'experts' ends. He agreed with me that Chinese children were quite exceptionally beautiful and relaxed. This he explained was because they all wear slit-knickers up to a certain age, so the stress that comes from toilet training is absent! I have heard the same theory about children elsewhere, that if they live in a society that does not require the very young to even wear knickers, then they are without tensions!

Then we had another evening of opera, this time the Shaoxing opera performed by a group from Nanking. I have become quite an addict of Shaoxing opera that I have been hearing in many places and especially on the trains. This story concerned the last Yuan emperor and was almost like a Greek tragedy ending with many suicides and a murder. There was curiously less singing and more dialogue and drama in this evening's performance. The all-woman cast brought it off amazingly well. The libretto was flashed up to a panel on one side of the stage presumably to enable the Beijing people to follow the spoken and sung words. By way of an aside, when the character wished to convey an intense emotional disturbance, he or she did not say 'my heart is breaking' or is 'beating faster'. Instead the person said, 'my intestines are breaking bit by bit', perhaps a more meaningful description. I was reminded of the reference to the liver in some Indian poetry rather than the heart, when love is being described. The applause was loud and clear and some enthusiasts went down the aisle and up to the front of the stage. The theatre was a simple hall in the middle of the market.

We tumbled out onto the cobbled paving of the market amidst a crowd of people presumably shopping. We were stared at, smiled at, and then comments were passed. The road had its rows of pedicabs waiting for customers.

It was a joy to watch one rather elegant-looking, middle-aged man climb stylishly into a pedicab and flick open his equally elegant fan to go with his assumed sophistication, as the vehicle moved. Opera going seems to be a popular pastime among the locals as the theatres are always full. Children come from an early age presumably because parents cannot leave them in the care of unknown people, and it is incredible how quiet the children are, almost as if to the manner born.

The next day was Sunday so we drove out to see the Buddhist temple from the Yuan period, although heavily restored in 1932. There had however been an attempt to conform to the original forms and colours. So the roof tiles were glazed yellow and green. The ceiling was covered with a floral design in green and cream and was held up by wooden beams varnished in a rich red-brown. The gilt images enveloped in red banners and the saffron-coloured hangings were embroidered with pale blue flowers. Scattered across the hall were white banners with Chinese characters in black and these, I was told, were quotes from the Buddhist texts. A brilliant scarlet-coloured drum was placed near the main shrine and there was a large bronze bell in one corner. There was a general impression of a mellow richness. I asked if I could attend one of the ceremonies with the monks but was told that lay people were not permitted to do so.

On our return to Beijing, the sunset gave way to a gathering storm that had been gently brewing all day. Eventually torrential rain poured all night accompanied as usual by frequent thunder and streaks of lightning. This was surely for us an appropriate farewell to Beijing. Woke up in the morning with the storm having abated somewhat but the skies were not clear. As the Chinese would say I felt that my intestines were breaking bit by bit at the sadness of leaving China. I said my last farewell to the quiet nobility of the Forbidden City. I have affection now for the brick paving of the vast, silent courtyards, and the yellow-tiled roofs shining even in the dull sunlight. And the museum and the endless crowds surrounding an object, and then noticing a foreigner and immediately arguing about her nationality, and on being told she was Indian some would start softly humming 'Awaara Hoon'. The pine trees hugged the outer wall and stone shapes lay at random out-Mooreing the stone forms in the sculpture of Henry Moore.

We lunched at the Indian embassy to say goodbye to Mrs Rajan Nehru who had been so supportive and helpful during our visit. It became a women's do as there was a delegation of women visiting including Lady Rama Rau, Pushpa Mehta, and Ila Chaudhury. Some of the women of the embassy maintained that Chinese women were forbidden to sleep with their husbands so as to avoid more children being born. There was a small altercation between Lady Rama Rau and Rajan Nehru on this matter, where the former believed the story and the latter doubted it and tried to explain the problem in its social context.

After lunch I went off to the Summer Palace. I could understand the unpopularity of the Dowager Empress because of the fortune that was spent on building it, but it is a spectacularly impressive building. It spreads along a low hill with the main palace rising up in the midst of tiers of lesser buildings. An artificial lake has islands covered with pavilions. We rowed to one of the islands and on our return a minor storm blew up so we were commandeered and brought back. I missed out on rowing to the Camel-Hump Bridge and the Bridge of Seventeen Holes, and so on. Finally we walked through the manicured gardens with their abstract rock shapes and into the palace. Since it is autumn, the leaves of the well-trimmed bushes are turning yellow-red. It is all a little overwhelming—the enviable luxury, the excellent taste, the subtleties of good living, and the immense power she wielded. And she led a full life if anyone ever did. I was reminded of the powerful Queen Didda of Kashmir, but her palace has not survived. Did either of them ever give a thought to the poverty that lay like a halo around them, or to the lives and condition of the many women—visible and invisible—they depended upon? Or was their time entirely spent in balancing the ill effects of court intrigues among the many factions at the court?

The evening was passed in a broad exchange of presents between those who had worked with us and ourselves. I had been looking forward to the weight of our gifts for them being taken off my baggage to make it lighter, but with the return gifts it was equally heavy.

20

All Good Things Come to an End in Canton

We flew to Canton (as Guangzhou was then known) and were to exit via Kowloon to Hong Kong. All around us in Canton was the China that has been made familiar through the writings and sketches of Chinese life that come from travellers to China. Rice fields stretch for miles broken only by small irrigation channels. The rice farmer in his fields stands knee-deep in water, wearing a conical straw hat to shield him from the sun. The bright yellow–green of the fields is a contrast to the dull blue-brown of the low hills in the distance. Here and there terraced fields seem to climb up a slight elevation.

There is no doubting that we are back in the tropics. We arrived in Canton in the afternoon and it was steaming hot—a contrast to the cool of October in Beijing. I was uncomfortable in the damp, humid heat that reminded me of Calcutta and Bombay. We were back in the landscape of low trees with thick, broad leaves and groves of bananas. Canton is even more like Bombay than Shanghai because it lacks the high sophistication of the latter. It hasn't been completely cleaned up like Shanghai. There are still large areas along the river where people live on boats all anchored to a pier jutting out from the riverbank. Other parts of the city, where transportation is on the many streams, the houses are built of wood and are placed on tall stilts looking like museum reconstructions of the early historic Lake Dwellers that we learnt about in school.

The Pearl River is full of life—certainly the busiest river that I have ever seen. Last night, from the hotel window overlooking the river, I saw boats going past. There was a medley of them in various shapes and sizes—sampans with beautiful, shell-shaped sails, and junks with long, flat, wooden cabins, and small rowing boats with long oars where the boatman stands to row so that the boat travels at a terrific speed, and river steamers with their piercing whistles, and tugs with low-sounding horns. If I had had my way I would have opted to travel by junk to Hong Kong down the Pearl Estuary and across the Macao Strait. We passed a village on the banks of the river and I saw a large fishing net hoisted to two poles that is lowered by a pulley into the water, and when drawn up again hopefully has a catch of fish. Villages here seem to be clusters of stone-built houses located in the midst of paddy fields.

Canton, I thought, was the most colourful town among the ones I have visited in China. Buildings along the streets have verandas supported by pillars. These carry signs/statements in Chinese ideograms painted in black or red. The verandas are almost continuous, so they provide a covered sidewalk for pedestrians. Perhaps this also accounts for a brighter window display. The façade of the town has the appearance of being westernized but on a closer look it is quite Chinese. One has only to turn down one of the very narrow lanes that run at right angles to the main road and that have booths on each side to find oneself in a different world with varied attractions. I was sorry we are not staying longer in Canton.

We had bid a sorrowful farewell to our lovely dear friend Mingo in Beijing. I shall miss her very much as we did tramp around places together on many evenings and it was a pleasure to see China through her eyes. Being in her company was a learning experience. She knew a great deal about China and where she did not know she would rush to find out. But more than that it was just so lovely to observe her reactions to what one said and to get an instinctive understanding of what one was enquiring into. Considering that she was virtually self-taught when young, struggling with learning English in order to become an interpreter, I was constantly amazed at how much she knew. What I most loved about her was that she was game to break every minor rule and quite ready to try and meet even our more difficult demands, provided they were not impossibly demanding.

Dominique had left us after Dunhuang and had done a story on the oil refineries in the Yumen area, after which she had returned to Paris. What I most enjoyed about being with her was her photographer's eye in observing aspects of what we saw that would have passed me by. Anil was fun and her forty plus years seldom came in the way. She was as ready to explore as I was and to consider explanations of many kinds for what we observed. There was a strong pan-Asian feeling in how she looked at China that was most attractive and sometimes even provocative. And the two of us were constantly making connections and comparisons. Some of these would often amuse Mingo.

We now are with another interpreter. She was very nervous yesterday and never smiled and translated everything like a machine in a voice that had no modulation. But this morning we teased her a bit and finally got a smile out of her. Now she is smiling and speaking at a comprehensible pace. She is obviously quite young and must be extremely anxious to do things properly.

We spent the day yesterday at the museum. The local artefacts from South China that are on display here do carry some differences with what we had been seeing earlier and this was of interest. Not surprisingly a few have traces of similarities with objects from further south, from what was once a kind of Chinese sphere of influence. Last night we were taken to a Cantonese opera, 'Worshipping the Moon', a pleasant story about the vicissitudes of two lovers. The music and singing were in a way smoother than the Peking opera but somehow it did not sound completely authentic to me. But who am I to judge having heard only a few operas?

The evening was concluded with a dinner of local Cantonese cuisine. It was yet another dinner worth remembering with an amazing delicacy in the taste and the aroma of what we were being served. I was explaining to our hosts that we had eaten such fabulous meals the like of which we had not even imagined. And how true this was going to turn out to be. The soup came and I took one spoonful and it was heavenly—a taste that I could not even have imagined. And with every spoonful I asked what the ingredients were, and each time I asked, the conversation was changed. When my insistence became a little unbearable, I was warned that I would perhaps be troubled if I was told. I still insisted. So our host drew out the sieve that separated the soup from the ingredients and I could swear I saw a small, snake-like thing curled at the bottom. It could, of course, have been a small eel, but whatever it was the sight of it unnerved me. My face must have become ashen as our hostess quickly passed me another dish and hastily spoke of something else. I was afraid that I might puke on the premises. I have never again in my life asked about the ingredients in a soup.

❀

Back in the bigger world or approaching it slowly we had to remember all that we had not bothered with in the last three months. We had to keep an eye on our baggage, and remember to tip people. No one would have dared to steal anything from our bags in China but now we were coming closer to societies where such things were common. We have also got used to arrangements being made for us, of being met everywhere, and being taken to places we wanted to see. We had had no worries about arranging for hotels, transport, food, and such like.

We relaxed a little on our final day and took a gentle walk in the neighbourhood. The grand finale came in the evening with a banquet. As with all farewell banquets we were both in Canton but already travelling to Hong Kong. We were in an uncertain space of neither here nor there. Our hosts insisted on a farewell dinner and, after making the required polite noises, Anil and I agreed. I was still stunned by last night's experience, but after drinking a toast in moutai, a refined grain alcohol, I felt I could cope. The dinner was spectacular—not only in the number of courses, about which our interpreter had warned us, so we went easy on each, but also in the affection of our hosts that was expressed in the final gambei to the enduring friendship between India and China.

EPILOGUE

All this happened almost a lifetime ago. Both China and India have changed unrecognizably, moving from impressive degrees of democracy to periods of dictatorship—incipient and actual; and from endorsing an expansive positive nationalism that includes all, to a narrow negative nationalism that excludes all but one. Implicit in this was the alteration in patterns of living and the clash of ideologies that can come with change. How we looked at the world then and how we look at it now are immensely different. And I, too, have changed over the last sixty years! Yet on reading this text again, a couple of years ago, I experienced inevitably the revival of a memory of a memorable segment of my past.

For me the visit to China was the discovery of another world—the world created initially by a study of the Chinese past, handling objects from that past, and thinking about the ideas that conditioned that past and brought it to life in my mind. I was face to face with something that I could not have imagined but for my small forays into what was until then an almost exotic world. I was jolted on the first occasion when I was referred to as an honoured guest from the West, even if this was geographically absolutely correct. And then later I realized that there was even a hint of respect attached to this statement, as the West was, at least for Chinese Buddhists, the place where the Buddha lived and preached. But here again I am speaking of some time ago.

I thought of the people from the Indian subcontinent who had come to China in previous centuries, and who had settled in China and preached and taught in local monasteries, or lived in the cities as merchants conducting a lucrative trade. If only they had written their memoirs or even accounts of what they had experienced! Then the thought crossed my mind that perhaps among the Khatri merchants trading in Central Asia as many were, one among them might have been my remote ancestor from the Punjab, who in an utterly miniscule way may have contributed to the making of some of the cultural patterns that I was getting to know through the visit! What were their reactions when they came face to face with the Chinese patterns of life? One wishes one knew.

It was also the time when Chinese Buddhists visited India and fortunately, they left accounts of their visits. We read them largely as descriptions of what they saw as indeed that is what they are. But it might be worth reading these texts from a Chinese perspective to see how they understood the culture of what they regarded as the revered Western region. A more perceptive understanding might make us aware of how the one viewed the other. Those were perhaps the halcyon centuries, which if they ever return, would do so in another form.

Yet, however much I may have changed, or however differently China and India looked at the world then from how they look at it now, there are some imperatives that continue, embedded as they are in our respective histories and in the lives of contemporary Indians and Chinese. I recall moving around in Beijing on brief visits in later times and talking with a variety of Chinese people when I could feel the potential of a worthwhile continuing dialogue on the issues that had been so central to my first visit. And dialogue is always a clarifying experience, one way or another. My generation, nurtured on the larger vision of a resurgent Asia, still believes that dialogue is regenerative. We live in the hope that we won't all be silently mangled in the unimaginable future of a world of regressive ambitions.

Historians attempt to discover and explain the past in the hope that the interpretations they provide can illumine the past but also assist in a better understanding of the present. Neither the past nor the present can be used to predict the future since the future is not predetermined nor is it accidental. But where there is clarity in comprehending what went before it becomes possible to suggest some tenable prospects for the future. These suggestions would require nuanced sensitive perceptions in clarifying the boulders, crevices, and smoother surfaces of the present. Such perceptions often ensure a future worth waiting for.

A SELECTIVE CHRONOLOGY OF THE HISTORICAL EVENTS INCLUDING DYNASTIES

BC	China	India
c. 1600–1046	Shang	
1146–771	Zhou	
770–476	Spring and Autumn Period	
475–221	Warring States Period	
	Confucius 551–479	Buddha 544–486
		Mauryas
		Ashoka 268–232
221–207	Qin / Ch'in	

AD	China	India
206–9 AD	Former Han	Shakas
25–220	Later Han	Kushans
220–265	Three Kingdoms	
265–316	Western Jin	
317–420	Eastern Jin	
304–439	Sixteen Kingdoms	
396–581	Northern Dynasties/Wei	Guptas 320–550
		Faxian in India c.400–410
589–618	Sui	
618–907	Tang	
		Xuan Zang in India 630–44
755	An Lushan Rebellion	
907–960	Five Dynasties	
960–1279	Song	
960–1127	Northern Song	
1127–1279	Southern Song	Delhi Sultanate 1192–1526
1271–1368	Yuan/Mongol	
1368–1644	Ming	
		Mughals 1526–1857
1644–1911	Qing/Manchu	
1912–1949	Republic	Independence, 1947
1949–	People's Republic	

INDEX